THE MEDIEVAL
LATIN AND ROMANCE
LYRIC

THE MEDIEVAL LATIN AND ROMANCE LYRIC TO A.D. 1300

by

F. BRITTAIN
LITT.D.

Fellow of Jesus College, Cambridge
University Lecturer in Medieval Latin

CAMBRIDGE
AT THE UNIVERSITY PRESS

1951

KRAUS REPRINT CO.
New York
1969

PUBLISHED BY
THE SYNDICS OF THE CAMBRIDGE UNIVERSITY PRESS

London Office: Bentley House, N.W. 1
American Branch: New York

Agents for Canada, India, and Pakistan: Macmillan

L.C. Catalog Card Number 51-13702.

First Edition   1937
Second Edition   1951

First printed in Great Britain by the University Press, Cambridge
Reprinted by offset-litho by Bradford & Dickens

First published 1937
Reprinted by permission of the Cambridge University Press
KRAUS REPRINT CO.
A U.S. Division of Kraus-Thomson Organization Limited

Printed in U.S.A.

To
L. N. BATTERSBY
and
in memory of
W. L. KNOX

NOTE TO SECOND EDITION

THE continuing difficulties in book production prevent me from enlarging this work and compel me to make as few alterations as possible. I have therefore limited myself to re-writing (in the light of Dom André Wilmart's researches) the part dealing with *Dulcis Jesu memoria* on pages 13 and 14, to re-wording some references to the Goliards on page 16, and to banishing Philippe de Grève from pages 18 and 167–70, where he had usurped the place of Philip the Chancellor.

F. B.

1950

PREFACE TO FIRST EDITION

THIS book attempts a survey of the main features of the Medieval Latin and Romance lyric down to the year 1300. In it I have first discussed the origin and development of the lyrical verse of each language in turn, and then, in order that the Latin and Romance lyric may be studied as an organic whole at different stages of its evolution, I have presented selected lyrics as far as possible in chronological order, irrespective of language, and have prefixed a brief commentary to each author or poem. When poems—the selections from the *Carmina Burana*, for instance—cannot be exactly dated, they have been deliberately scattered among those in other languages, within the possible limits. I believe that this is the first book in which poems representative of Medieval Latin and all the principal Romance languages can be studied side by side.

In order to avoid the confusion which often arises when a reader consults an index or is referred from one part of a book to another, I have refrained from numbering the poems. All references are therefore to pages. In the texts, except where I have stated otherwise, I have followed the reading of the editions from which I have drawn. I have also followed their spelling, except that I have throughout printed consonant *u* as *v* and consonant *i* as *j*, and have standardized the spelling of Latin texts (but no others) as far as possible. I have not always kept to the punctuation of the originals.

My chief sources are acknowledged in the Bibliography, but I will mention here my particular indebtedness to the works of M. Joseph Anglade, Mr Aubrey Bell, M. Alfred Jeanroy, Sr J. J. Nunes, and Dr F. J. E. Raby.

F. B.

First Court
Jesus College
Cambridge

CONTENTS

[x]

CONTENTS

CONTENTS

ACKNOWLEDGMENTS

I beg to thank the following publishers for permission to include extracts from the works stated:

E. de Boccard, Paris—J. Audiau, *La pastourelle dans la poésie occitane.*

G. D. W. Callwey, Munich—M. Manitius, *Die Gedichte des Archipoeta.*

Cambridge University Press—K. Breul, *The Cambridge Songs*;
A. S. Walpole and A. J. Mason, *Early Latin Hymns.*

Honoré Champion, Paris—P. Meyer, *Recueil d'anciens textes*;
G. Raynaud, *Recueil de motets français.*

Delagrave, Paris—J. Audiau and R. Lavaud, *Nouvelle anthologie des troubadours.*

Drei Masken Verlag, Berlin—P. Lehmann, *Parodistische Texte.*

N. G. Elwert, Marburg—K. Bartsch and E. Koschwitz, *Chrestomathie provençale.*

Raffaello Giusti, Leghorn—O. T. Tozzetti and F. C. Pellegrini, *Antologia della poesia italiana.*

Ulrico Hoepli, Milan—V. Crescini, *Manuale per l' avviamento agli studi provenzali.*

Institut d'Estudis Catalans, Barcelona—*Anuari* 1907.

S. Lapi, Rome—E. Monaci, *Crestomazia italiana dei primi secoli.*

Max Niemeyer, Halle—C. Appel, *Die Lieder Bertrans von Born.*

Oxford University Press—A. J. Butler, *The Forerunners of Dante*;
E. Moore and P. Toynbee, *Le opere di Dante Alighieri.*

Piloty und Loehle, Munich—F. Beck, *Dantes Vita Nova.*

O. R. Reisland, Leipzig—C. Appel, *Provenzalische Chrestomathie*;
G. M. Dreves, C. Blume and H. M. Bannister, *Analecta Hymnica Medii Aevi.*

Julius Springer, Berlin—K. Bartsch, *Altfranzösische Romanzen und Pastourellen*; K. Bartsch and L. Wiese, *Chrestomathie de l'ancien français.*

Weidmann, Berlin—K. Strecker, *Die Cambridger Lieder* and *Die Gedichte Walters von Chatillon*; *Poetae Latini Aevi Carolini*; *Zeitschrift für deutsches Altertum.*

Also the following scholars for similar permission:

M. René Lavaud—*Nouvelle anthologie des troubadours* and *Les poésies d'Arnaut Daniel.*

Herr Max Manitius—*Die Gedichte des Archipoeta.*

Signor Ercole Rivalta—*Le rime di Guido Cavalcanti.*

M. Mario Roques—*Classiques français du moyen âge,* viz. J. Anglade, *Les poésies de Peire Vidal*; J. Bédier, *Les chansons de Colin Muset*; A. Jeanroy, *Les Chansons de Guillaume IX* and *Les chansons de Jaufré Rudel*; A. Jeanroy and A. Långfors, *Chansons satiriques et bachiques du treizième siècle*; A. Wallensköld, *Les chansons de Conon de Béthune.*

Société des anciens textes français—G. Huet, *Chansons de Gace Brulé*; A. Wallensköld, *Les chansons de Thibaut de Champagne.*

Herr Karl Strecker—*Die Cambridger Lieder* and *Die Gedichte Walters von Chatillon.*

I wrote to Senhor J. J. Nunes for permission to include texts from his *Cantigas d'amigo* and *Cantigas d'amor,* but my letters were returned with an intimation that he was dead. I have since made unsuccessful efforts to trace the owners of the copyright, and apologize to them for any infringement.

THE MEDIEVAL LATIN AND ROMANCE LYRIC

TO A.D. 1300

I

EARLY LATIN VERSE, like modern European verse in general, was built on an accentual basis, and took no notice of the length or shortness of syllables. About 240 B.C., however, the principles of Greek versification were introduced, and artistic Latin verse from that time onward was written on the Greek quantitative principle. So great was the prestige of Greek culture and literature, that native verse in the old accentual or Saturnian metre was thenceforth considered unworthy of the attention of cultured writers. Throughout the classical period, all great Latin poets accepted the quantitative system as the only permissible one; and the accentual system passed to the limbo of the camp, the market-place, and the tavern.

The classical period of Latin literature came to an end about the middle of the second century after Christ, and with the death of Marcus Aurelius in A.D. 180 the Roman Empire itself began to decline. As it declined, Christianity, a hitherto despised religion, began to grow in power. Slowly but steadily it increased its strength, even though for many years to come it remained a proscribed religion.

Although the Christian Church was to be the medium through which Latin was "to pass itself off as a living language when it had been dead for centuries", it was at first a Greek-speaking body. Even at Rome, its liturgy was celebrated in Greek until about the middle of the third century. It was in Africa—the chief home of Latin literature during the third, fourth, and fifth centuries—that Christian Latin literature first arose, and that it produced its first writer of note in Tertullian, who flourished round about the year 200. Like nearly all the Latin Fathers for three centuries to come, he was educated in the pagan public schools, and the practical rhetorical training which he received there is evident in his writings as in those of so many of his successors.

During the third century, the Christian Church grew fast, but was still on the defensive. Hence, this century is, in Christian Latin literature, pre-eminently the Age of the Apologists. Faced with the necessity of defending the Christian faith, the Apologists had at first no time for verse-writing, but confined themselves to prose. Not until the middle of the third century at the earliest did the Latin Church produce its first verse-writer, in the person of Commodian, and it is by no means certain that he lived before the fourth century. His poems, of no value as literature, are nevertheless important linguistically, for in them are to be seen the beginnings of a return to the Old Latin system of versification and the introduction of a new principle which was in course of time to change the face of Latin verse.

As the classical period of Latin had progressed, the gulf between popular Latin and literary Latin had widened. Classical Latin verse, with its foreign basis, had obtained no deep hold on the people, and cannot have been fully appreciated except by the cultured few. The accentual system, on the other hand, though ignored in strictly literary circles, had never lost its hold on the masses; and Christianity, with its popular appeal and popular membership, brought it to the surface again.

As early as the second century A.D., the principle on which Classical Latin verse had its foundations began to break down, for the language itself was undergoing revolutionary changes. Long vowels and short vowels were tending more and more to be pronounced alike, and poets began to hesitate about the length of syllables. During the third century, their difficulties increased. By the end of the fourth century, the distinction between long and short vowels had probably disappeared entirely from unstressed syllables in ordinary speech, though it perhaps survived for another century or more in stressed syllables.

This breakdown is very evident in the works of Commodian. He aimed at writing his *Carmen apologeticum* in dactyls; but, of the 1066 lines in the poem, only 26 are quantitatively correct. On the whole, he observes quantitative distinctions in stressed

syllables, but neglects them in unstressed syllables. He tries to
end his lines with a spondee preceded by a dactyl, but his endings,
when correct at all, are correct on the accentual principle only.
Further, he introduces a principle which Latin verse had never
known—the principle of rhyme. In pre-classical and classical
writers, rhyme had been rare. Even where it appears, it is generally
accidental, though in a few instances it is introduced for emphasis
or rhetorical effect. Commodian's rhyme is but a rudimentary one
in *e* and *ae*, but is evidently introduced deliberately as an ornament of style. His verse, therefore, sets the stage for two of the
characteristic features of Medieval Latin verse—accent and rhyme.

Christianity entered a new phase of its history in the year 313,
when Constantine's Edict of Milan gave it freedom of worship
throughout the Empire. Its writers now began to take the offensive
against paganism and also against the heresies—the greatest of
them being Arianism—which soon began to divide Christendom
against itself. The Church began to organize itself thoroughly.
In public worship, extemporization gradually gave way to a fixed,
written liturgy; and, before the end of the century, Latin hymnody
had settled down to fixed verse forms.

The earliest Christian Latin hymns were, like the Hebrew
Psalter which inspired them and the Greek hymns of which some
of them were translations, in prose form, and in them the parallelism of the Psalms is a prominent feature. The *Gloria in excelsis*
is a beautiful example of these early hymns; but the finest example
of all is the *Te Deum* [63],* the rhythmical prose of which is (to
quote Dr Raby) "a marvellous example of an inspiration that
does not so much triumph over the rhetorical temptation which
lay so very near as soar beyond it for ever".

On first thoughts, it is somewhat surprising that Saint Hilary
of Poitiers, who was writing about the time when the *Te Deum*
was composed, abandoned the Christian prose tradition in favour
of verse when he composed his hymns. Reflection will nevertheless provide a reason for the change.

Saint Hilary's hymns are essentially didactic. He was, before

* Figures in parentheses indicate the pages where the relevant texts are
to be found.

everything else, a teacher, and his supreme object in life was to confute the Arians. His exile in Greek-speaking lands had shown him the great value of hymns for teaching the faith, and he had only to decide what was the best form in which to cast them. As Christianity was not yet a fashionable religion, but was still drawing most of its converts from the uneducated classes, verse had advantages over prose for the object which he had in view. A prose hymn like the *Te Deum*, for all its magnificence, was not easy to remember; but a metrical hymn, divided into short stanzas, was much more easily committed to memory, and its stanzas could be sung to a recurring melody.

These reasons are sufficient to account for Saint Hilary's choice of verse in preference to prose, and also for his use, in one of the hymns attributed to him, of the trochaic tetrameter catalectic, or *versus popularis*. A favourite metre of the Greek poets, it was taken over by the Latins and became very popular with the masses. Well known from its use by the Roman legions in their marching-songs, it was admirably suited to Saint Hilary's purpose. His hymns, it is true, never became popular, for they were too didactic and lacked the poetic fire; but he was the first Christian poet to write in a metre which was to clothe some of the grandest of Latin hymns. Used to great effect by Prudentius about the end of the fourth century, by Fortunatus about the end of the sixth, and by many later writers, it became the basis of the greatest Sequences of the later Middle Ages and of one of the finest hymns of Saint Thomas Aquinas, nearly a thousand years after Hilary's time. Used again by the earliest Romance poets, it has remained a favourite in European verse, religious and secular, down to the present day. It is strange that hymn-books have no specific name for the metre of *Lo! he comes with clouds descending* and *Glorious things of thee are spoken.*

The popularity which Saint Hilary failed to achieve as a hymn-writer was won by his younger contemporary, Saint Ambrose [65-6], who stands out as the greatest figure in Latin hymnody. Like his predecessor, he wrote with a didactic purpose, and chose a popular metre of the time, but his hymns are much simpler. All of them are written in iambic dimeters grouped in quatrains—

a stanza known ever since as the Ambrosian. This simplest of metres is combined with a plain, unadorned style, producing a dignified and virile effect, free from sentimentality. Exhibiting, as Archbishop Trench says, "the old Roman stoicism transmuted and glorified", Ambrose's hymns served as models to successive generations of hymn-writers. Through all the gradual changes which led from the unrhymed, strictly metrical hymn to the rhymed, accentual hymn of the Middle Ages, throughout the Renaissance, with its reversion to unrhymed hymns on a strictly quantitative basis, from the Renaissance to the present day, Saint Ambrose's supremacy has been unchallenged, and the Ambrosian stanza has been the staple of Latin hymnody, as it is—under the name of "Long Metre"—one of the two staples of English hymnody.

The disregard for quantity which has already been noticed in Commodian's verse is absent from Saint Ambrose, for Italy was more conservative linguistically than Africa. Consequently, Ambrose writes with strict regard for the quantitative principle. At the same time, his verse has a well-marked rhythm, based on accent, so that "the rhythmic syllabic character of the poetry of Ambrose marks in reality the beginnings of Romance versification, not because it was not known before him, but because of his constant adherence to the system on account of its popularity and effectiveness with the mass of the faithful".*

Surviving Saint Ambrose by some years, and forming with him the greatest trio of contemporaries that the Christian Church has ever produced, were Saint Jerome and Saint Augustine.

Saint Jerome's translation of the Bible [67, 69], completed during the early years of the fifth century, shows the changes through which written Latin had passed since the close of the classical period. Some of its characteristics, it is true, had been occasionally revealed even in classical literature, but they were regarded as the lapses of careless writers who allowed the Vulgar Latin of everyday life to penetrate into the sacred precincts of style. When they were on their guard, classical writers had been haunted by fear of using the language of the masses.

* Muller and Taylor, *A Chrestomathy of Vulgar Latin*, p. 115.

Saint Jerome, ardent Ciceronian though he was, had no such fear. He had, indeed, a fear of an entirely opposite kind, for he had received a vision in which he saw himself damned for ever for being a better Ciceronian than Christian. Consequently, the Vulgate is written in the natural, unstilted, everyday Latin of the closing years of the fourth century. Received at first with violent hostility from the people for whom it was written, and even accused of shaking the foundations of the Christian faith, the Vulgate never obtained the direct official approval of the Church. Its vast merits, however, brought it universal recognition when the older generation died out, and it had no rival for a thousand years.

The Vulgate, says Milman, "almost created a new language. The inflexible Latin became pliant and expansive, naturalising foreign Eastern imagery, Eastern modes of expression and of thought, and Eastern religious notions, most uncongenial to its own genius and character; and yet retaining much of its own peculiar strength, solidity, and majesty." On it the liturgy of the medieval Church was built, and from it the language of the medieval Church was drawn. Even when Latin had ceased to be any man's native tongue, and few could understand the artificial Latin of the classics, those who spoke a Romance language could yet understand the Vulgate with little difficulty; for Jerome's language, being of his own time, leaned in the direction of Romance. Further, it was so magnificently written that, throughout the centuries, Latin and Romance poets, both religious and secular, found in it a source of unfailing inspiration. Saint Jerome's version of the Psalms has been the most widely read collection of poetry in the world's history.

Saint Augustine's fame as a writer rests entirely on his prose works. He left, however, a didactic poem which, though of little aesthetic merit, is of considerable importance in the prehistory of Medieval Latin versification, for in it the transition from classical to medieval principles is carried farther than in Commodian's verses. We find in it, in embryo, three main features of Medieval Latin versification—accentual rhythm, isosyllabism, and rhyme. Its structure is not perfectly regular; but, generally speaking, its lines have sixteen syllables each, with a caesura in the middle, an accent on the penultimate syllable of each half-line, and a simple monorhyme in *e* or *ae*.

Tradition also ascribes to Saint Augustine the authorship of the magnificent prose lyric, the *Exsultet* [72], which, if it is not by him, is at least worthy of so great a writer.

A number of extracts from the poems of Prudentius [71], a Spanish contemporary of the great trio of Latin Fathers, were used as hymns throughout the Middle Ages and have remained in liturgical use to the present day. Their author, however, unlike Saint Ambrose, wrote with no congregation in view. His poems, strictly correct from the point of view of classical prosody, are written in a variety of metres, handled with a skill which has earned him the title of " the Virgil and Horace of the Christians ". Sometimes, as in his well-known *Corde natus ex parentis*, he uses a popular metre; but the appeal of many of his poems, even if they were widely known in his time, must have been practically limited to educated circles.

Yet, although he was not writing with a liturgical purpose, he had a didactic one. It was identical with Chénier's:

Sur des pensers nouveaux, faisons des vers antiques.

Christianity was now the established religion of the Empire, and the educated classes who were flocking into the Church needed a Christian substitute for the charms of pagan Latin literature, towards which many of them must have cast longing glances backwards. This substitute was provided by the lyrics of Prudentius, and by the poems of his contemporary Juvencus and of fifth-century writers such as Dracontius and Avitus, all of whom presented Bible stories, from both the Old Testament and the New, in the style of Virgilian epics.

The future of Latin verse, however, did not lie with the imitators of Virgil, but with the followers of Saint Ambrose. During the fifth century, the cycle of the Breviary Offices was completed, and the Rule of Saint Benedict, drawn up in the earlier part of the following century, required hymns to be sung at all the canonical hours. During the same period, the cultus of the saints grew apace. Many new festivals were instituted, and there was an increasing demand for hymns at these celebrations. Educated Christians soon ceased to be a novelty; and, as the memory of paganism receded more and more into the background, Christian poets ceased to write epics and turned increasingly to hymnography.

For about 150 years after the deaths of Saint Ambrose and Prudentius, no great Latin hymnographer arose, but a number of hymns were composed in Ambrosian stanzas. In these—in Sedulius's *A solis ortus cardine*[74] and the anonymous *Ad cenam agni providi*[75], for instance—we find Latin verse developing farther and farther away from the classical pattern. Accent is gradually replacing quantity as the metrical basis, metrical ictus and word-accent tend to fall more and more on the same syllable, and an increasing amount of assonance is introduced.

One sound practical reason for the ultimate victory of the accentual basis of Latin hymnody has been pointed out by Dom Anselm Hughes:

"Latin hymnody of the earliest periods", he says, "introduced for the first time the custom of singing stanzas or strophes to fixed recurring melodies. This was practically an innovation, for early Christian hymns written in Greek rarely had more than one or two stanzas—if, indeed, the stanza-form is evident at all in the few remaining examples. This must have created a natural demand for the change, for in most of the classical metres the number of syllables may vary: amphibrach may replace trochee, dactyl may become spondee, and so on. To sing a number of stanzas, the corresponding lines of which might contain a varying number of syllables in different verses, to a fixed recurring melody is impossible without continual adaptations and 'footnotes'; the system, if ever tried, must have been found unmanageable, and a modification of practice is therefore to be expected. To this fact, quite as much as to the individual development of poets working under Byzantine or Oriental influences, the change should probably be ascribed."

In the second half of the sixth century, the growth of the new principles is strongly evident in the hymns of Venantius Fortunatus[77], the first great Christian Latin poet since Saint Ambrose and Prudentius. His short secular poems are pretty, but it is as a writer of hymns that he shows himself a great poet. His fame is secure as the author of *Vexilla regis* and the equally famous *Pange, lingua*—both of them occasional poems. In the former, he uses the Ambrosian stanza to magnificent effect. In the latter, he uses the trochaic tetrameter catalectic. Since his time, the same metre, in its classical or later forms, has been used frequently by Latin hymn-writers and by vernacular poets, sacred and secular, down to the present day; but by no poet has it been used to more sublime effect than by Fortunatus. Written though they were before the Middle Ages opened, his two great hymns, both in matter and in manner, provide a fair test of anyone's appreciation of things medieval.

In the anonymous *Verbum supernum* [78], which probably dates from the seventh century, we find accent gaining still further ground at the expense of quantity. In the hymns of the Venerable Bede, who died in 735, the defeat of quantity is complete, for his poems are based entirely on accent.

From his time onwards, with one short interval, the new system held its ground throughout the Middle Ages. During the classical revival under Charlemagne, quantity regained its ascendancy for a while, and Latin hymnody was enriched with the *Veni, creator* and the Sapphic hymns of Rabanus Maurus and other writers, but their triumph was a short-lived one. When the great figures of the Carolingian revival passed away, accent resumed its dominion. From time to time, scholars wrote Latin verses, as was but natural, on the classical principle, sometimes—as in *Hora novissima*—with magnificent effect; but hymn-writers, great and small, continued to write rhythmical verse. When Romance verse, which was based on the same principle, began to produce rivals in the daughter-tongues of Latin, the parent lyric learned from them in turn and developed in directions which Saint Ambrose had never contemplated. Accentual Latin verse, reinforced by fully developed rhyme, held sway in both the liturgical and the secular spheres until the Middle Ages passed away. Only in the sixteenth century, when the principles of the Renaissance managed to penetrate into liturgical places, was the accentual hymn all but swept out of the Breviary, leaving only those specimens which were spared for the sake of the renown of their authors or the ardent attachment of the faithful to them after centuries of usage.

By the end of the eighth century, hymns had been incorporated into breviaries throughout the greater part of Western Europe, largely owing to the wide diffusion of the Benedictine Rule. On the other hand, the hymn had not succeeded in forcing its way into the missal, nor has it ever done so. During the ninth century, however, the Mass evolved a new feature which, in the course of time, stood in much the same relation to the Mass as the hymn did to the Office.

In the celebration of the Mass, the Epistle is followed by a prose text—generally scriptural—called the Gradual. This, in non-penitential seasons, ends with the word *Alleluia*. When church music was elaborated, the singing of the final syllable of the *Alleluia* was prolonged on a melody called the Sequence. Probably about the end of the eighth century, words were added to this melody to help the singers to remember it—a syllable to each note—and the words themselves came to be known as Sequences. This new form of composition soon outgrew its mnemonic origin, and Sequences became increasingly popular as the ninth century advanced. The texts were improved, and in time new texts and new melodies to accompany them were written simultaneously.

In spite of long-established legends to the contrary, the Sequence as a literary type most probably originated in France, but a Swiss monk, Notker of Saint Gall, who died in 912, was the first to spring to eminence as a Sequence-writer.

The earliest Sequences were written in unrhythmical prose, divided into phrases of unequal length. A striking feature in many of them, particularly in those of French origin, is that every phrase ends in *a*, thus echoing the final syllable of the *Alleluia* from which the Sequence sprang. The same monorhyme in *a* occurs in the Modenese watch-song, *O tu qui servas armis ista moenia* [85]; and Gottschalk's secular poem, *Ut quid jubes, pusiole* [83], has a monorhyme in *e*. Both of these were probably written in the second half of the ninth century, when the monorhymed Sequence in *a* was flourishing.

By the end of the ninth century, the Sequence had developed a stage further: every second phrase was tending to become the same length as the preceding phrase, and was sung to the same melody repeated. This development was perhaps suggested by the antiphony of the Office Hymn, which in its turn rested on the practical basis of giving two groups of singers a rest alternately. It introduced the subdivision of the Sequence into strophes and antistrophes which was to lead to further developments later. Sequences of this kind, with the monorhyme in *a* as a prominent feature, are typified in *Salus aeterna*[87], dating from the first half of the tenth century.

A further stage in the development of Medieval Latin rhyme is to be seen in two famous poems which probably date from the tenth century—the pilgrims' song, *O Roma nobilis*[88], and the secular poem, *O admirabile Veneris idolum*[89]. Each of these is divided into three six-line stanzas. Each stanza is in monorhyme, but the first example has two different rhymes for its three stanzas, while the second has a different rhyme for each.

O admirabile Veneris idolum occurs in one of the most famous of all collections of Medieval Latin lyrics—the *Cambridge Songs*[89–94]. Although the manuscript itself dates from about the middle of the eleventh century, it is probable that the greater part of its contents was first written between A.D. 950 and 1000. Of the forty-nine poems in this collection, more than half are on religious, didactic, or historical subjects, but the remainder are in much lighter vein, some of them too much so for previous owners of the manuscript, who made considerable erasures. A number of these lighter poems, including some of the least ecclesiastical in tone, are written in common liturgical metres, such as the *versus popularis* and the Ambrosian stanza, the celebrated *Levis exsurgit zephyrus*, with its lines rhyming regularly in pairs, being a fine example of the latter. Others, such as the *Advertite, omnes populi*, are in Sequence form, showing how well known and popular the Sequence had already become.

By the end of the tenth century, the Sequence had achieved popularity throughout Western Europe. Its popularity continued to grow during the eleventh century; and even Southern

Italy, which had not hitherto received the Sequence with open arms, produced schools of Sequence-writers.

During this century, the Sequence passed through a transitional period of development, proceeding gradually along the path from rhythmical prose to verse. The single assonance in *a* which had characterized many of the earlier Sequences was abandoned, and its place was taken by varied rhymes. At first, many of these rhymes—as in contemporary hymns and secular poems—were mere assonances, and even the genuine rhymes were not carried throughout a whole composition, nor were they symmetrically placed. Later in the century, however, we find a greater proportion of rhyme and more attempt at symmetrical placing. *Victimae paschali* [95], which still appears in the Roman Missal as the Sequence for Easter, and *Laetabundus* [97], which, despite its popularity during the Middle Ages, does not share that honour, are examples of these transitional Sequences.

Before the eleventh century ended, rhyme reached perfection outside the sphere of the Sequence. In the poems of Hildebert of Lavardin [98], who died in 1133, we find that accentual Latin verse, after a long struggle, has at length reached its destined triple goal of perfect rhythm, regular caesura, and symmetrically placed double rhymes extending through a whole poem. The substitution of double for single rhymes, however, offered a much narrower field to a poet in his search for rhymes, and made rhyming much more difficult. Hence we find, as a general rule, that Latin poets from this time onwards change their rhymes from stanza to stanza. Even if necessity had not driven them to this course, they would most probably have adopted it, as they generally used a short stanza, and the repetition of the same double rhymes at close intervals would have produced an effect of heaviness and monotony.

The hymns of Hildebert's younger contemporary, Abelard [101–2], of which about a hundred have survived, show a bold step forward in one respect and a step back in another. They were written for the use of Heloisa and her nuns, who found, as many must have found long before, that the quantitative basis of the hymns of Saint Ambrose, Prudentius and other early writers made some of them difficult to sing. Further, many texts were corrupt, and a number of feasts had no Office Hymns. In answer to Heloisa's request, Abelard wrote hymns for both seasons and festivals, and in them he showed himself a great liturgical innovator.

Until then, the great defect of the Office Hymns had been monotony of metre. The trochaic tetrameter, the Sapphic, and a few other metres occurred now and then in the yearly course, but the great majority were in the Ambrosian stanza. Abelard's metres, on the other hand, are extremely varied. His lines are of any length from four syllables to twelve, and lines of several different lengths are often combined in one stanza. This was an uncommon feature in hymns before Abelard's time, and is one in which the influence of the Sequence may perhaps be traced. His use of the accentual dactyl was also a liturgical innovation.

There is, however, one feature in which Abelard's technique is less developed than Hildebert's—he uses simple rhymes only. Considering his bold innovations in liturgical metre—so bold that his hymns, for all their beauty, never became popular, even when personal animosity was long dead—it is unlikely that he avoided double rhymes as unsuitable for ecclesiastical use; nor can his failure to use them be ascribed to inability to do so. It is more probable that he avoided them on aesthetic grounds, for double rhyme had not yet come into general favour, either in Latin or in the vernacular.

Abelard is at his greatest in *O quanta qualia*[101], which, strictly speaking, is not a hymn at all. It is one of the most beautiful, and at the same time one of the saddest, of medieval poems. On the surface, it is a meditation on the endless Sabbath calm of the life to come; but the whole pitiful story of Abelard's life, which had known no calm, can be heard in a murmur immediately beneath the surface.

Abelard's great contemporary and opponent, Saint Bernard of Clairvaux, has for centuries been credited with the authorship of the immortal poem, *Dulcis Jesu memoria*[110], but this tradition does not go back beyond the end of the thirteenth century. Hauréau, the great French medievalist, and Vacandard, the scholarly biographer of Bernard, both decided, on the evidence available, against the saint's authorship. More recently, Dom André Wilmart made a thorough investigation of the subject, which included the examination of 65 manuscripts, and arrived at the conclusion that the poem was written in England, by some Cistercian, at the end of the twelfth century. As the poem is steeped in the spirit of Bernard and contains verbal echoes of his writings, it was not unnatural that its authorship should be attributed by what Dom Wilmart calls "an innocent subterfuge" to the Abbot of Clairvaux. The earliest and best texts are all in manuscripts of English origin. Wilmart's study was published in Rome in 1941 under the title, Le "Jubilus" dit de Saint Bernard, étude avec texte; it is summarized by Dr Raby in The Hymn Society Bulletin, October 1945.

Whoever wrote Dulcis Jesu memoria, it is one of the most beautiful poems of the Middle Ages, and any praise of it here would be a presumption. Its construction is as simple as its language. Its lines have very little enjambement, and its monorhymed stanzas reproduce a favourite feature of popular poetry.

About the time of Saint Bernard's death, the Sequence, in the masterly hands of Adam of Saint Victor [113], reached the goal towards which it had long been striving. Its strophes corresponded exactly to their antistrophes; its rhythm was beautifully smooth and regular, though rhythmical licence was allowed; there was a regular caesura; and rhyme, which had become of prime importance, was exact, regularly placed, generally of two syllables, and sometimes of three. Adam's Sequences are as remarkable for their perfection of form as for their closely packed content. In particular, he has a wonderful command of rhyme, and no other Latin writer has surpassed him in the artistic use of double rhymes. Of the extremely varied metres which he used, his favourite was an elaboration of the ever-popular trochaic tetrameter catalectic. He uses it, for instance, in combination with others, in his Sequence for Saint Agnes's Day:

> Animemur ad agonem,
> Recolentes passionem
> Gloriosae virginis,

and in other Sequences he uses this metre alone. It rapidly became a prime favourite with other Sequence-writers, and remained so as long as Sequences continued to be written.

As far as regularity was concerned, the Sequence was now in no way inferior to the Office Hymn, but it differed from the latter structurally in three important respects. First, the various strophes in any one Sequence need not be homomorphic, though they often were. Secondly, whereas in the normal Office Hymn no rhyme used in one stanza was (except by coincidence) repeated in another, each strophe of a Sequence was deliberately linked to its antistrophe by the use of the same final rhyme. Thirdly, the typical Office Hymn was iambic, but the typical Sequence, once it had settled down to verse form, was trochaic. Little appears to have been written to account for this last difference, which is a very striking one. As we have seen, the Sequence began as a prose composition. When, therefore, it gradually assumed verse form, it might as well have become iambic as trochaic. Why, particularly as the Office Hymn was predominantly iambic, did it not do so?

One reason may well be that there was a desire to differentiate the Sequence from the Office Hymn. Another is that the Sequence was at first used during joyful seasons only; and the trochee is more festive than the iambic metre. Further, the Breviary was intended for the clergy, and the laity were under no obligation to be present at the recitation of the offices which, through all the medieval elaborations of the Mass, retained much of the severe Ambrosian traditions of the early Church. The Mass, on the other hand, within which the Sequence evolved, was the people's service; and the trochaic metre has a popular appeal lacking in the iambic. Finally—and this is a point to which no attention appears to have been called hitherto—the word *Alleluia*, from the singing of which the Sequence first sprang, is itself composed of two trochees. Even when this origin was forgotten, the Sequence remained liturgically attached to the *Alleluia*, and this connection was sufficient to give the Sequence its characteristic stress.

No less than in form, the Office Hymn and the Sequence differ essentially in spirit. The Office Hymn, born in the post-classical period, when quantity still lived and rhyme was almost unknown, retained much of the severity of Classical Latin, even when it adopted accent and rhyme. The Sequence, on the other hand, born when accent had replaced quantity as a living principle and when rhyme was a recognized ornament of style, is thoroughly medieval in tone.

The twelfth century, which saw liturgical Latin verse rise to great heights in the Regular Sequence, witnessed the arrival of a great new force in secular Latin verse also. Hitherto, secular Latin verse had lagged behind liturgical verse in its development. On the whole, it was confined to academical exercises in quantitative metres. Some of these, such as the tenth-century epic, *Waltharius*, had reached a high artistic level; but of lyrical poetry, particularly of the living accentual kind, there was little of value, the *Cambridge Songs* being among the few outstanding exceptions.

The promise contained in the *Cambridge Songs*, with their simple rhymes and somewhat faltering language, was more than fulfilled in those secular Latin songs of the twelfth century, some of which may have been written by the so-called "Goliards"—restless clerks who lived on the fringe of ecclesiastical society and were regarded with suspicion by the authorities of the Church. Contemporary with the troubadours and the jongleurs they are, in social standing as in other respects, the clerical counterparts of the latter rather than of the former. The Goliard, indeed, can be regarded as a sub-species of the jongleur, and evidence exists that the personnel of the two classes was to some extent interchangeable. Thus a jongleur might take Orders and then revert to his former state; or a Goliard would gradually accustom himself to lay audiences, study their tastes, and abandon his original intention of pursuing a clerical career.

The anonymous Goliard known as the Archpoet [118] was of higher social standing than most of his confreres and, as a poet, one of the greatest of his class. In his famous *Confessio Goliae*:

Aestuans intrinsecus ira vehementi,

he raised the secular Latin lyric at a bound to a level with the Victorine Sequence in technical perfection. It is a masterpiece of rhythm and rhyme, unsurpassed in Medieval Latin verse, sacred or secular. Its metre became so great a favourite with the Goliards that it is known as the Goliardic Metre. So popular did it become, indeed, that it was used also in hymnody—for instance, in John Peckham's eucharistic hymn:

> Ave, vivens hostia, veritas et vita,
> In qua sacrificia cuncta sunt finita.

The standard laid down by the Archpoet was difficult to maintain, but he found a worthy seconder in Walter of Châtillon [125], who was at the same time one of the most prolific and one of the most talented of these poets. A skilful handler of the Goliardic Metre in his satirical poems, he is perhaps at his best in the composition of pastorals, in which he exhibits a remarkable command of rhythm and double rhyme, and also rivals contemporary vernacular poets in their own sphere.

The triumph of the secular Latin lyric is maintained in the thirteenth-century anthology known as the *Carmina Burana* [176, 185, 204, 214, 218, 220], the most famous and extensive collection of Goliardic poetry. The manuscript probably dates from the last quarter of the thirteenth century, its contents being mostly of German or French origin. Quantitative poems are included, but the majority are accentual. The artistic standard varies greatly, from poems of the highest quality to little better than doggerel. Authors such as the Archpoet and Walter of Châtillon are represented, but most of the contributions are by unknown writers.

A considerable part of the manuscript is occupied by serious items, such as Crusade poems and satires against simony, but the great majority of the contents are in lighter vein—love-songs, spring-songs, begging-songs, together with other pieces which, as Dr Raby says, "are of an unmatched obscenity". The technique shows a great advance on that of the *Cambridge Songs*, and the finest pieces have a charming atmosphere of youth and grace. Their rhythm is practically perfect, elaborate and difficult rhymes are used with the greatest ease, and metres of great variety are most skilfully handled. Two features which are strongly evident in the collection are the influence of the vernacular and of ecclesiastical Latin. The former is seen in many of the *Carmina*, in *Exiit diluculo*[204], for instance—a charming little pastoral which stops short of the obscenities met with elsewhere in the collection and in many French *pastourelles* of the time. The influence of ecclesiastical Latin is to be seen mostly in the use of liturgical metres, particularly those of the Sequence, as in *Huc usque, me miseram*[176], and *O comes amoris, dolor*[214].

Yet, although secular Latin poetry of the thirteenth century shows the influence of vernacular poetry, it was more indebted to the aristocratic troubadours and trouvères than to the poets of the people. The Goliards, indeed, cared nothing for the masses. As in the time of Saint Ambrose, so in the time of Saint Francis it is to sacred rather than to secular Latin verse that we must turn to discover affinities with popular poetry. It is in the new genre of the *cantio* that we chiefly find them.

The *cantio* is the Latin counterpart of the vernacular carol, which it resembles in its simplicity and in its use of dance-measures, repetitions, and refrains. Like the carol, it is non-liturgical, but it was eminently suited for rendering by choirs at the end of Mass or the Office, in processions, or in the religious dance which, it will be remembered, still survives at Seville. It existed in embryo in such compositions as Abelard's *Christiani, plaudite*[102], but the Franciscan practice of using carols extensively for teaching religious lessons was no doubt the chief impulse that brought the *cantio* into vogue. It reached its highest level, however, in the poetry of a strong opponent of the friars, the versatile Philip the Chancellor[167-8], whose *Procedenti puero* is one of the finest compositions of its kind. The delightful *cantiones* of an anonymous monk of Tours[242-3], whose *Cantet omnis creatura* offers a close parallel to popular poetry, probably date from the closing years of the thirteenth century. In his works, as in those of Philip the Chancellor, we also find, on the other hand, poems which, departing from the general rule of Medieval Latin verse, use the same rhymes in every stanza, in the same order, thus reproducing a method of rhyming which was a great favourite with the troubadours.

The influence of popular poetry is perhaps to be seen also, to

a limited extent, in three of the four greatest Sequences of the thirteenth century—the *Veni, sancte spiritus*[147], the *Dies irae*[197], and the *Stabat mater*[206]; for, while they are among the very greatest Medieval Latin poems, they are much simpler in thought, and less elaborate in construction, than the typical Victorine Sequence of the previous century. These three great Sequences are in different metres, but the metres of all three are drawn from the ancient *versus popularis*; and they possess the common feature that their strophes, contrary to those of many Victorine Sequences, are homomorphic. In them, the Sequence attained its final form; and, as that form was also the simplest and the most easily remembered, they brought it nearer to popular poetry than it had ever been.

Of the three, the *Dies irae* is by common consent the greatest, and yet the *Veni, sancte spiritus* is the only one to which posterity has given a specific name. A masterpiece of flowing rhythm, beautifully clear and concise, it is well called the *Golden Sequence*. The *Dies irae* is a superb example of the perfect union of sound and sense. It possesses what is attributed to many a poetaster of to-day—stark realism. Not a word is superfluous or out of place in its grand monorhymed tercets. It is, moreover, thoroughly Franciscan. If its author had been a Dominican, the *Dies irae* would have been no less grand, but it would have been more objective. It would have lacked its emotional appeal, and would not have moved Dr Johnson to tears. Like the *Dies irae*, though without the awe-inspiring grandeur of the latter, the *Stabat mater* is a characteristically Franciscan product—simple, pathetic, vivid, and strongly subjective. Its beauty forced a way for it into the Roman Missal a century and a half after all Sequences but four had been ruthlessly swept out of it by the neo-classical revisers of the sixteenth century, and no other Sequence has shared in this victory. It appeals more to the masses than any other Sequence, and it is significant that the *Stabat mater* is generally sung at the Stations of the Cross—a service otherwise entirely in the vernacular, and the one which, of all the services of the Latin Church, appeals the most to the simple-hearted.

The fourth great Sequence of the thirteenth century—the

Lauda, Sion [222] of Saint Thomas Aquinas—is, with its severe dogmatic teaching and its objectiveness, as characteristically Dominican as the *Dies irae* and *Stabat mater* are Franciscan. In form, it reverts to an earlier type, to the typical Victorine Sequence with heteromorphic stanzas. It is, in fact, modelled in detail on one of Adam of Saint Victor's finest compositions. In the grandest of his Office Hymns [224]—the last great Office Hymn of the Middle Ages—Aquinas goes much farther back for a model—to the *Pange, lingua* of Venantius Fortunatus. He begins his hymn with the same words and uses the same metre of three catalectic tetrameters to each stanza. Yet there are great technical differences between the two hymns, illustrating the changes through which Latin verse had passed since the sixth century. Thus, while Fortunatus's hymn is in quantitative metre and has only sporadic, elementary rhyme, Saint Thomas's is accentual, and has regular, double rhyme, both at the end of each tetrameter and at the caesura.

Aquinas and Jacopone da Todi were the last two great writers of Medieval Latin verse, for the poets of the fourteenth century were but the pale afterglow of the glorious sunset of the thirteenth. During the interval which elapsed before the return to quantity, accentual Latin verse, both sacred and secular, was still written, written indeed in vast quantities, but, on the whole, poetical inspiration had departed from it, to enter into the new languages which had grown up from the popular Latin of an earlier age. Accentual Latin verse, however, had had a long life—so long, indeed, that its eldest descendant was already suffering from the effects of old age.

II

The gulf between literary Latin and spoken Latin which Saint Jerome bridged widened again after his death. Although he set a standard of liturgical Latin which endured for centuries, he remarked himself that "Latinitas ipsa et regionibus quotidie variatur et tempore". The popular speech passed through such revolutionary changes after his death that, by the seventh century,

the inhabitants of various parts of the Empire were conscious that they were not speaking Latin, but a different tongue, which they called *lingua romana,* or Romance.

The change was most rapid in France. In 659, an ecclesiastic was elected Bishop of Noyon because he understood both German and Romance. In 813, the Council of Tours ordered the clergy to preach, not in Latin, but in Romance, so that the people might understand them. The Oaths of Strasburg, exchanged in 842 between two grandsons of Charlemagne and their followers, provide us with a specimen of the spoken language of France at that time—the earliest monument of the French language.

Similar developments were taking place in other parts of Western Europe, the vulgar speech being everywhere termed Romance, but gradually differentiating more and more in the various provinces.

It was a long time, however, before any branch of Romance produced anything worth calling literature. Before the ninth century was ended, the Northern French vernacular produced at least one poem, but it is of no literary value. The tenth century produced a few more poems, but not until near the end of the eleventh century did a Romance language produce any literature in the strict sense of the word. Until then, literary activity, in France as elsewhere, continued to be exercised in Latin.

In France, differences of race, civilization, and political allegiance caused Romance to develop in two different directions in North and South. As a result, two different languages and literatures evolved in that country—French in the North, and Provençal, as it is generally though misleadingly called, in the South. Both literatures began with religious or didactic poetry, more prolific in the North than in the South, but the southern language was the first to produce lyrical poetry, half a century or so before the northern. The lyrical poets of the South are the troubadours, those of the North the trouvères.

The chief attraction of the poetry of the troubadours lies in its formal excellence, and in nothing is this more apparent than in their use of rhyme—an art in which they have never been surpassed. Rhyming was easy in Provençal, and the troubadours took every advantage of this fact. Of the great variety of ways in which rhyme is arranged in their poetry, only the most prominent can be described.

As we have seen, Medieval Latin poets generally use different rhymes for each stanza of the same poem. The same method is used in many Provençal poems, particularly those of early writers, the stanzas being then known as *coblas singulars* [151]. In order to knit stanzas of this kind together, they are sometimes *cap-finidas* [229]—that is to say, a word or phrase in the last line of a stanza, or a word derived from the same root, is repeated in the first line of the next. This method of giving unity to a poem was borrowed from the *chansons de geste*. It was sparingly used by the troubadours—partly, perhaps, because they considered it too easy an artifice, and partly because they found other methods of linking the stanzas of a poem together. One of these—closely allied to the one just described—was to make the first line of each stanza rhyme with the last line of the previous one, the stanzas being then called *coblas capcaudadas*. If the same head and tail rhymes were used throughout the poem, but in a different order in alternate stanzas, it became a *chanso redonda*, of which Bernart de Ventadorn's *Non es meravelha* [123] is an example.

Other poems are written in *coblas doblas* [130]—i.e. the same rhymes are used in every even stanza as in the previous stanza, and in the same order. This grouping of the stanzas into pairs may possibly be due to the influence of the Sequence, in which strophe and antistrophe have the same form, and, though they use different rhymes in all their lines but one, end with the same rhyme. An extension of this method was to use the same rhymes, in the same order, in all the stanzas, which were then called *coblas unissonans* [111]. This method was a difficult one to employ, and, for that very reason, rapidly became a favourite with the troubadours. Another method of welding the stanzas of a poem together was to use *rimas dissolutas* [107]—rhymes which find no answer in their own stanza, but keep the ear waiting until they are answered at the same place in each subsequent stanza. In some poems, there is only one of these isolated rhymes. In others, there are two or more. This method reached its climax in the *cobla estrampa*, in which all the rhymes are *dissolutas*.

The earliest troubadour, William IX[100], Duke of Aquitaine, was born in 1071 and died in 1127. His whole life was therefore included within that of Hildebert of Lavardin, in whose poems, as we have seen, double rhymes, symmetrically placed and effectively used, are met in Latin verse for the first time. William IX's versification is less elaborate than that of his successors, and yet his technique is almost perfect. From this it has been too easily concluded that earlier troubadours existed, whose works have been lost. No such assumption is necessary, however. It is enough that non-lyrical Provençal verse had been written for a considerable time, that William IX was a talented poet, and that he found models in contemporary Latin verse.

The technique of the early troubadours resembles that of contemporary Latin hymnographers in several respects. Their favourite line is the octosyllable of the Ambrosian stanza; the great majority of their stanzas are composed of lines of equal length; they are fond of writing poems in *coblas singulars*; and their poems are rhymed throughout, with none of the mere assonance which the Latin hymn and the Sequence had already abandoned. At the same time, their rhymes are almost entirely simple (masculine), as in the Latin hymn before Hildebert of Lavardin. Of William IX's eleven poems, for instance, seven are wholly or mostly in octosyllables, ten use masculine rhymes only, and five are in *coblas singulars*. His stanzas, too, are of simple construction, none of them exhibiting the tripartition which came to be considered almost essential by later troubadours.

Yet, when all is said, the lyrical poetry of the early troubadours is simple only by comparison with the extreme elaboration of their successors half a century later. We have no relics of the infancy or childhood of the Provençal lyric. When we first meet it, it stands on the threshold of manhood. It starts from the point to which accentual Latin verse had attained by a laborious evolution spread over several centuries, except that for a time double rhyme is less evident in Provençal than in Latin.

The technique of the troubadours developed greatly during

the course of the twelfth century, but two notes which had been struck by William IX are sustained in nearly all their work. First of all, their poetry is written almost exclusively for aristocratic audiences, and even those troubadours who sprang from the opposite end of the social scale to William IX make it clear that their poems are addressed to the high-born. Popular influences can be traced in Old Provençal verse, but it is a rare occurrence to meet a poem with a genuinely popular ring. The fine popular dance-song, *Coindeta sui*[171], is, characteristically, anonymous, its author being no doubt too obscure for his name to be perpetuated. The second feature in which the Provençal lyric as a whole resembles William IX's poetry is that it is overwhelmingly subjective. The troubadours generally express their own feelings or what they obviously wish their audiences to accept as such. Objective poetry, in which the author expresses the feelings of others or at least stands aloof from his theme, forms only a small part of the mass of Old Provençal verse.

Until about the middle of the twelfth century, the technique of the troubadours remained comparatively simple, but was nevertheless developing. In Marcabrun and Jaufre Rudel, the greatest Provençal poets of this period, we still find octosyllabic lines and masculine rhymes predominating; but, in both poets, we find William IX's fondness for changing his rhymes from stanza to stanza much less in evidence, and more difficult methods of rhyming in greater favour than with him. Thus, while five of William IX's eleven poems are in *coblas singulars*, only a quarter of Marcabrun's are so constructed, another quarter being in *coblas doblas*. Further, while William IX had used *coblas unissonans* in one poem only, Marcabrun uses them in twelve of his forty poems, and Rudel in four of his six.

After the middle of the twelfth century, the technique of the troubadours became more and more elaborate. The proportion of feminine rhymes to masculine rhymes increased, stanzas were more frequently composed of lines of different lengths, and, above all, the arrangement of the rhymes within the poem became more intricate. Of the thirty-seven poems of Bernart de Ventadorn, who flourished in the third quarter of the twelfth century, for instance, two only are in *coblas singulars*, ten are in *coblas doblas*, and the majority are in *coblas unissonans*. Peire Vidal, who flourished in the last quarter of the century, does not use *coblas singulars* or *coblas doblas* in any of his poems, which number nearly fifty. All of them have the same rhymes in each stanza, though not necessarily in the same order. In the poetry of Arnaut Daniel[136], about the end of the century, elaborate rhyming reaches a climax. He is fond of using rare rhymes and *rimas equivocas*, i.e. words of the same sound, but of different—sometimes only slightly different—meaning. He shows a great liking for *rimas dissolutas*, and eight of his eighteen poems are in *coblas estrampas*. He was also the inventor of the *sestina*, in which the placing of rhymes is carried, one might say, to its campanological conclusion.

Arnaut Daniel's poetry marks a climax, not merely in the use of rhyme, but also in the manipulation of the *trobar clus*—the obscure style affected by many of the troubadours. This school of poets delighted in the use of unfamiliar words, difficult rhymes, and far-fetched similes. Much of their poetry is so obscure as to be unintelligible to the modern reader, as indeed it was to their contemporaries. To Dante, Arnaut Daniel was—though not because of his obscurity—the greatest of all the troubadours. To-day, he is much less admired, except by devotees and practitioners of obscurity. These find him very much to their taste, and apparently consider him one of the few great poets whom the world produced before G. M. Hopkins.

Obscurity was probably essential to many of those who employed it, for love is the main theme of the troubadours, and their love-poems are almost always addressed to married women. By far the most important genre of Provençal poetry is the *chanso*, of which love is almost the sole theme.

The *chanso* generally, though not always, has from five to seven stanzas. The stanza has no fixed length, but eight or nine lines are the most usual. After the last stanza there is generally an envoi (*tornada*), more often two *tornadas*, and very occasionally three. The *tornada* varies in length, but is more often than not half as long as the stanzas. It has nothing in common with the refrain of popular poetry, but may perhaps be regarded as the vernacular equivalent of a Sequence-coda. In the earlier troubadours, the *tornada* merely repeats the closing thought of the last stanza in different words. In later writers, it takes the form of a dedication to a friend or protector.

Love is represented in the *chanso* as a kind of feudal obligation which no gentleman can escape. The lady is a mirror of perfection, and one kind glance from her will raise her vassal to a transport of delight, just as a reproachful glance may make him die of sorrow. The content of the Provençal love-lyric, says M. Jeanroy, is as monotonous as its form is varied: the same situations, the same sentiments, the same images are always reappearing before our eyes. Various attempts were made to break the monotony. A favourite method was for a poet to preface an account of his love-longings with a description of nature in spring or winter, but this very soon became hackneyed.

A number of troubadours, nevertheless, wrote very beautiful *chansos*. Those of Jaufre Rudel[111] are distinguished by their freshness and their freedom from the conventional phrases. His longings for his distant, unseen lady have a melancholy charm which still moves the reader and which still sets one speculating whether his love was an earthly woman or the Virgin in glory. The *chansos* of Bernart de Ventadorn[121, 123] attract one no less by their charming sincerity than by their technical skill. Not greatly appreciated by his contemporaries, he is now regarded as one of the greatest of the troubadours, perhaps as the greatest of them all, for he is one of the few among them who can still touch the heart. The eccentric Peire Vidal[132], with his genuine love for Provence, is another lyrist of high power; while Raimbaut de Vaqueiras, in his *Altas ondas que venez suz la mar*[154], breaks away from convention and gives us a haunting poem which might have been written by one of the greatest of the Romantics.

Raimbaut de Vaqueiras also provides us with an example of a sub-species of the *chanso*—the *descort*[152], which, as its name implies, aims at expressing a lack of harmony between the poet and the lady to whom it is addressed. As a means to this end, it is generally written in lines and stanzas of unequal length, like a Victorine Sequence. It will be found, indeed, that each stanza can generally be divided into two equal parts of identical construction, corresponding to the strophe and antistrophe of a Sequence. Raimbaut's *descort*, however, is unique in using different languages, instead of different metres, for its various stanzas.

Next in importance to the *chanso* in troubadour poetry comes the *sirventes*, a poem which probably owes its name to its being originally composed by a servant—a jongleur, for instance—for the benefit of his master, or in his honour. Indistinguishable from the *chanso* in metrical form, the *sirventes* differs from it entirely in subject, from which love alone is excluded. It may take the form of a reflection on current events or of a eulogy of some distinguished person, but is more often a satire—personal, literary, or political—and is at times very outspoken. Bertran de Born[133], the nobleman who is placed by Dante deep down in hell as a sower of discord in the Plantagenet family, ranks as one of the greatest writers of the political *sirventes*, and Peire Cardenal of those directed against the clergy.

The Crusade-song is an important sub-species of the *sirventes*. The period of the troubadours corresponds almost exactly with that of the Crusades and with the reconquest of the greater part of Spain from the Moors, and between thirty and forty Crusade *sirventes* have survived as witnesses to the part played by the troubadours in the struggle with Islam. Spain, owing to its geographical position, attracted their attention before Palestine, and Marcabrun's *Pax in nomine Domini*[107], the oldest Crusade *sirventes* in Provençal, was written to encourage enlistment under the King of Castile against the Moors.

Another sub-species of the *sirventes* is the *planh*, or lament. Its language is often exaggerated and its thought commonplace, but genuine emotion sometimes shines through both, as in Gaucelm Faidit's lament on Richard I[162]. It is significant, though, that of the forty *planhs* which have survived, more than thirty are elegies on feudal protectors, and that a mere three lament the deaths of any of the numerous ladies to whom the troubadours professed their devotion in the hyperbolic language of the *chanso*.

The poetical debate, or *tenso*, in which two interlocutors argue the pros and cons of a particular theme (generally in alternate stanzas constructed on the same metre and rhyme system) was a favourite genre with the troubadours, as it was with Latin poets. In some of these poems, two writers did in fact compose the stanzas attributed to them. In others—as in the Monk of Montaudon's imaginary *tensos* with the Almighty[142]—the whole poem is the work of one writer. His opponent may, in fact, be an animal, or even an inanimate object. If the opener gives his opponent a choice of positions, or if more than two characters take part in the discussion, the poem is known as a *partimen* or *joc partit*. The difficult problem discussed in a *partimen* between Saváric de Mauleon, Gaucelm Faidit, and Uc de la Bacalaria[164] is typical of both the *tenso* and the *partimen*, for they are more often than not concerned with love casuistry.

The subjective *chanso*, *sirventes*, *planh*, and *tenso* constitute by far the greater part of the Old Provençal lyric, but its objective genres, of which the *pastorela* and the *alba* are the most important, are of considerable interest.

At first glance, the *pastorela* might be taken for a subjective poem, since it is written in the first person. On closer examination, however, it becomes clear that this is a convention, and that the author is merely a narrator. The poem relates a love encounter between a courtly suitor and a shepherdess. It opens with an account of their meeting, more often than not beginning with the stock phrase, "The other day", and devotes itself mainly to a dialogue between the pair, the suitor being generally unsuccessful.

This type of poem perhaps originated in songs sung at rural feasts; but, in the form in which it has come down to us, it is, like its Latin antecedents—*Jam, dulcis amica*, for instance—and its Latin imitators—Walter of Châtillon's *Sole regente*[125] is one—thoroughly aristocratic in tone. It is found as far back as the time of Marcabrun, but, owing to its objectivity, did not make much headway until late in the thirteenth century. When it did so, it had acquired a changed metrical form, for it had undergone the influence of its French equivalent. The change is apparent if

Marcabrun's *L'autrier, jost' una sebissa*[104], with its *chanso* form, is compared with Guiraut Riquier's *L'autre jorn, m'anava*[229], in which we find the short lines and long stanzas of the Northern *pastourelle*.

The *alba*, or dawn-song, of which the Modenese watch-song, *O tu qui servas*, is in some ways a prototype, does not appear in Provençal literature until very late in the twelfth century. It probably originated as a monologue by a woman, expressing her sorrow at her lover's departure at dawn. In the next stage, which is found only in Northern France, the song of birds announcing the arrival of dawn was introduced. In the final stage, the birds are replaced by watchers, who keep guard over the lovers and wake them when dawn is at hand. The watcher's part had perhaps a prosaic origin in the cry of the night-watchman, familiar in the Middle Ages and later centuries. The *alba* was not a prolific genre, but it produced two of the finest of all Provençal poems— Guiraut de Bornelh's *Reis glorios*[130], and the anonymous *En un vergier*[151].

Another objective genre, the dance-song[171], is met in Provençal under the names *balada* and *dansa*, but, being of popular appeal, has only a few representatives, all of which, except one, are anonymous.

The golden age of Provençal poetry passed away when the Church carried out a successful crusade against the Albigensian heretics of Southern France in the early years of the thirteenth century. The crusade spelled ruin to the troubadours, for it eclipsed the quasi-independent feudal courts at which they had lived and from the life of which they had drawn inspiration. Provençal poetry began to decline rapidly and, frowned upon by the Inquisition, turned to those religious themes to which it had not paid much attention during its prime. In particular, it sang the praises of the Virgin, whose cultus was zealously fostered by the newly founded Dominican Order. The transition from exaggerated praise of mundane love to extolling the virtues of the mother of Christ was not difficult, particularly as many troubadours, though strongly anticlerical, had never been unorthodox in their beliefs. Thus Peire Cardenal[184], one of the most outspoken critics of the clergy, produced one of the most attractive religious poems in Provençal literature.

Guiraut Riquier, the last of the great troubadours, lived on until nearly the end of the thirteenth century. He tried hard to keep Provençal poetry alive by creating new genres and reviving old ones, but he realized that the day of the troubadours was over. He was a lonely singer in his later years. After his death, the writing of Provençal verse became an academic exercise; but the poetry of the troubadours had meanwhile exercised great influence in other lands.

III

It was about the middle of the twelfth century, when Adam of Saint Victor was in his prime and the early troubadours were flourishing, that the lyric made its first appearance in Northern France.

The Provençal lyric, when it first appeared, was almost fully developed, appealed almost solely to the cultured, and had a powerful duke as its first writer. The earliest French lyric, on the other hand, was comparatively primitive, both in subject and in form, and was the work of anonymous writers. Though it sang of the loves of high-born maidens, it was largely popular in its construction and its appeal. It owed nothing to the troubadours, nor had its simple, unpolished style anything in common with the elaborately polished Victorine Sequence.

One of its earliest representatives was the *chanson de toile* [115, 116], originally intended to accompany a dance, or (as its title indicates) to be sung by women while sewing or spinning. Often, indeed, the heroine—and a woman is always the central figure—is discovered sewing or spinning.

The *chanson de toile* is a lyrico-narrative poem; hence its alternative title—*chanson d'histoire*. It tells a story, but it tells it concisely and objectively. It has the objectiveness of the ballad, but eschews the ballad's discursiveness. Its theme is the love, often tragic, of a high-born maiden, and in it love is represented from the medieval woman's point of view. It is a primitive passion, far removed from the courtly love, the feudal surrender of a man to his liege-lady, which one finds invariably in the poetry of the troubadours. The construction of the *chanson de toile* is very simple. Each stanza consists of two or more lines—generally decasyllabic, with a caesura after the fourth syllable—followed by a refrain, which varies in length from a mere exclamation to two lines. A single assonance or simple rhyme runs through each stanza.

The *chanson de toile* has no counterpart in Provençal literature, but the opposite is true of three other varieties of the early French lyric—the *chanson de mal-mariée*, the *pastourelle*, and the *aube*.

The subject of the first of these [157] is indicated by its title. Its moral standard is low, marriage being regarded in it as a mere social bond and no impediment to a woman's loving where she pleases. The same standard is accepted in the two surviving Provençal poems of this class, of which the *balada*, *Coindeta sui*, is one.

The general plan of the *pastourelle* [158] is identical with that of the Provençal *pastorela*, the chief technical difference between the two being that the northern form has longer stanzas and shorter lines. A further difference is that in the *pastourelle* the shepherdess generally yields to the amorous advances made to her. Yet, while its moral standard is lower, it has an easier rhythm than the *pastorela*, and has much more freshness, largely because it keeps nearer to the popular poetry from which both forms sprang. Further, whereas the objectivity of the pastoral lyric prevented it from obtaining any great vogue in the essentially subjective poetry of the South, it found a more congenial atmosphere in the North, with the result that about 130 French examples have survived, compared with about thirty in Provençal.

The dawn-song, unlike the pastoral lyric, does not attain to as high a literary level in the North as in the South; and, while there are eleven secular *albas* in Provençal, the *aube* is rarer in early French, only four examples having survived. One of these, *Entre moi et mon ami* [159], is of a more primitive type than any surviving *alba*, as the arrival of dawn is announced in it by a lark. In a later example, *Gaite de la tor*[160], the birds have been replaced by watchers, in the Provençal style.

The *reverdie*[155], another type of the early French lyric, includes only a few poems, but some very charming ones are among them. It has been described as a *pastourelle* without the shepherdess, but M. Bédier's description of it as a spring morning's dream is more apt. The *reverdie* probably originated in popular May Day songs; but, as with the *pastourelle* and the *aube*, its surviving representatives are the product of cultured writers for sophisticated audiences.

One other type of the early French lyric must be mentioned—the short poem known as the *rondet* or *rondel*[212, 234]. This attractive genre originated in the popular dance-song, and was at first nothing but a dance-song of a single stanza, divided into two interwoven but equal parts for soloist and chorus. Adam de la Halle and other poets remodelled it and made it more artistic, and in the fourteenth and fifteenth centuries these new forms enjoyed a great vogue as the *triolet* and the *rondeau*.

In the *chanson de toile*, *chanson de mal-mariée*, *pastourelle*, *aube*, *reverdie*, and the early types of the *rondel* we have dealt with poems which are of unknown authorship, objective in character, and, though overlaid with an aristocratic veneer, ultimately of popular origin. These early lyrics first appear in an undeveloped state; but, as the twelfth century progressed and gave way to the thirteenth, they grew more and more sophisticated, their metre became more regular, and their rhyme more elaborate and exact. These changes were due, no doubt, partly to the increased skill of the poets of Northern France, but they were also due in part to the influence of the troubadours, which became increasingly felt in the North during the second half of the twelfth century.

The strong resemblance of the *pastourelle* and the *aube* to their Provençal counterparts has already been noticed, but a great part of this resemblance is probably due to their springing from a common popular origin, and it is difficult, moreover, to say, with regard to these two branches of the lyric, whether French or Provençal influenced the other more. Matters are very different, however, as soon as the name of a trouvère is found attached to a poem. The overwhelming influence of the troubadours is obvious at a glance, and the word "influence" is indeed insufficient to express the dependence of the French lyric on the Provençal from that time onward.

From the first, the trouvères wrote in the language of Northern France, not in that of the South. Most of them, no doubt, could, if they had wished, have as easily written in Provençal. Considering the prestige of the latter tongue, and the close resemblance of the poetry of the trouvères to that of the troubadours, it is in some ways surprising that they did not do so, but the fact remains that they did not. Yet, though the language is different, we find the main types of the Provençal lyric represented in the poetry of the trouvères under practically the same names—*chanson, serventois, tenson, jeu-parti*—and their form and content have changed as little as their names. The principal genre is still the *chanson*, and in it the same theme of courtly love is expressed in the same terms, with the same accompaniment of polished metre and elaborate rhyme.

There are nevertheless several interesting points of difference between the lyrical verse of the trouvères and that of the troubadours. The refrain, for instance, which is uncommon with the latter, is more frequently found in the North. The *trobar clus* is avoided, and the *senhal*, or secret pseudonym for the poet's lady, is not used. Further, the rhyming system is less elaborate. *Rimas dissolutas* are avoided, large numbers of poems have only two rhymes to the stanza, and *coblas unissonans* are less common than in Provençal. *Coblas doblas*, on the other hand, are great favourites, and are used by practically all the trouvères. Six of Conon de Béthune's ten surviving poems, for instance, are written in *coblas doblas*, as are the great majority of Thibaut of Navarre's numerous love-songs.

The earliest known trouvère is Chrétien de Troyes[128], who flourished about the same time as Bernart de Ventadorn, and in whose *chansons* we find the technique of the troubadours firmly established. He is more famous, however, as a writer of narrative poetry than as a lyrist. Soon after him comes Conon de Béthune[135], a powerful feudal lord and a writer of considerable originality and power, rising to his best in two *chansons de croisade*. Contemporary with him were Guy de Coucy [140] and Gace Brulé [148]—two poets who perhaps come nearest of all the trouvères to the writers of the courtly lyric of the South, which they imitate in close detail. The lyrics of Colin Muset [189], which belong entirely to the thirteenth century, are of outstanding interest, with more originality than those of most other trouvères. Strongly impressed with the personality of their author, they have a vagabond air which reminds one of Villon. Contemporary with Colin Muset was Gautier de Coinci [173], the chief of the clerical trouvères. His muse, however, was very different from that of the Monk of Montaudon, being entirely religious. He imitates the style of the troubadours, but not their subjects. "Let others sing of Mariette," he says, "I sing of Mary."

In Thibaut IV [195], who was both King of Navarre and Count of Champagne, we find another trouvère of outstanding ability. His lyrics are melodious and smoothly flowing, as technically correct as those of the troubadours who inspired him, and yet— as befits his two titles—they often combine elements of the more popular Northern lyric with the formal correctness of the South. Thibaut was one of the last of the trouvères who were also feudal lords. After his death in 1253, the art of poetry, following the same trend in Northern France as in the South, passed from the aristocracy to the middle classes in the cities.

The citizens of Arras had already produced, in the first half of the century, a group of poets who wrote imitations of the troubadour love-lyric. Their chief representative was Audefroi le Bâtard [177], who, after writing in the Provençal style, apparently tired of it. Turning to the earlier poetry of Northern France for further inspiration, he wrote a number of imitations of the *chanson de toile*. His imitations have a higher moral tone than their exemplars, and, with their smooth rhythm and full rhyme instead of assonance, are more polished. They have undeniable attractions, but they lack the spontaneity of the older poems, nor do their author's attempts at moral elevation always manage to avoid an absurd dénouement.

The Arras school of poetry continued to flourish throughout

the thirteenth century and produced a large number of writers. Chief among them is Adam de la Halle[234], who died about the year 1288. Famous as one of the founders of the secular French drama, he takes high rank also in the history of the lyric as the author of a number of charming *rondels* and other short poems. In these, he acts as a connecting link with the fourteenth century, in which the *rondel* and its allied forms claimed much of the attention of French lyrical poets.

Another poet whose work points forward rather than backward is Adam de la Halle's great contemporary, Rutebeuf[225], who is pre-eminently a satirical poet. We find in his verse, it is true, some of the last echoes of troubadour song, but we feel that he and Adam de la Halle are the first of a new age rather than the last of the trouvères.

When all is said, the lyrical poetry of the trouvères is little more than a close imitation of that of the troubadours. It is nevertheless an imitation which one cannot but admire.

IV

In the Iberian Peninsula, there were in the Middle Ages three Romance languages of literary importance—Castilian, Galician-Portuguese, and Catalan.

Catalan was spoken, and still is spoken, in the north-eastern part of Spain and down the east coast, and was but a variant of Provençal. In course of time, it naturally differentiated from the latter, but the difference has never been great, and Catalan poets continued for some time to write solely in the language of the troubadours. Towards the end of the thirteenth century, they incorporated a number of Catalanisms into their vocabulary, but they went no farther than that throughout the fourteenth century, even though prose-writers were by then using the ordinary spoken Catalan. It was not until the fifteenth century that they became entirely emancipated from Provençal influence.

The Catalans are eulogized by Guiraut Riquier in one of his most attractive poems, but practically the whole of Christian Spain had long been a favourite resort of the troubadours. Their visits began with William IX of Aquitaine, who went on pilgrimage to Compostela, one of the most popular shrines in all Europe. Marcabrun, Peire Vidal, the Monk of Montaudon, and Peire Cardenal are among other great troubadours who lived in Spain for long or shorter periods, and many less famous poets followed them. They were welcomed at the royal courts of both Castile and Aragon, and repaid their hospitality with Crusade-songs, *sirventes*, and other poems which reflect many aspects of the life of Spain during the twelfth and thirteenth centuries. Further, a number of Spanish poets were inspired to write Provençal poems in imitation of these foreign visitors, and between thirty and forty such writers are known by name.

Yet the direct influence of the troubadours, though great in Catalonia, was very small in Castile, and the virtual identity of their language with that of Catalonia is not sufficient to account for this. A solution is perhaps to be found in historical geography.

Both Castile and Aragon were still engaged in the reconquest of Spain from the Moors, and were advancing slowly southward. As they advanced, the configuration of the country was such that Aragon, of which Catalonia was the most important part, had less and less of its frontier exposed to the Moors. The exposed frontier of Castile, on the other hand, grew no shorter, but even lengthened, and after 1248 Castile was the only one of the two kingdoms that had any Moorish frontier.

In these circumstances, the comparative peace of Aragon provided a favourable environment for the cultivation of the Catalan lyric; but, in Castile, it was natural that poetical invention should turn rather to the warlike epic. As the genius of Old Provençal poetry is essentially lyrical—it never produced a great epic, even in its home territory—it was unsuitable for this purpose. It was further natural that the epic should be written in the language of the people. The result is, therefore, that the lyric is poorly represented in early Castilian verse, and that the first great literary monument of the language is the thoroughly national epic, *El poema de mio Cid*, written about 1140, in which the exploits of the champion of the Reconquest are told in the language of the masses.

Only two Castilian poems that can be called lyrics have survived from the twelfth century. Both are anonymous, written in rhymed octosyllabic couplets, and reveal French influence. One, an *Argument between Water and Wine*, has no literary value. The other, *La razón de amor*, takes the form of a discussion between two lovers, and, though conventional, is not without literary merit. Other lyrics of a popular kind must have been written in Castilian during the twelfth century, but the language was evidently not recognized in literary circles as a suitable medium for lyrics. Evidence for this is forthcoming from the polyglot *descort* of Raimbaut de Vaqueiras, written about the year 1200. It is significant that this poem, which contains stanzas in Provençal, French, Italian, Gascon, and Galician-Portuguese, has nothing in Castilian.

In the thirteenth century, representatives of the Castilian lyric are as scanty as in the twelfth.

The first Castilian poet whose name is known to us is Gonzalo de Berceo [182] who flourished in the first half of the century and is known to have been still alive in 1246. Most of his poems are pious narratives of the legends of the saints, but one of them contains an attractive lyric, *Eya velar*. This takes the form of a watch-song and, with its repetitions and its refrain, is semi-popular in style. Alfonso X of Castile [213–14], who outlived Gonzalo de Berceo by about forty years, wrote his prose works in Castilian, but nearly all his verse in Galician-Portuguese. In the earlier part of the fourteenth century we find the Castilian lyric firmly established, in the poems of the priest, Juan Ruiz; but, until the early years of the fifteenth century, Castilian court lyrists preferred to write in Galician-Portuguese.

V

Alfonso X probably realized that the language of the north-western part of the Peninsula, which already had a considerable and powerful lyrical tradition, was at the time better suited to lyrical use than Castilian.

Galicia was included in his kingdom, but its language was also spoken outside his dominions, in the newly founded kingdom of Portugal. Portugal began as an overflow from Galicia into Moorish lands, and until the fifteenth century Galician and Portuguese were practically the same language.

The history of Portugal as a Christian state begins in 1095, when Alfonso VI, King of Castile, Leon, and Galicia, granted the northern part of Portugal, which had been reconquered from the Moors, to Henry of Burgundy, who was to hold it in fief as a county, in recognition of his services in the reconquest. National feeling soon grew up in the county. The Portuguese stopped calling themselves Galicians, and in 1143 obtained recognition of their land as an independent country. Four years later, Lisbon was captured from the Moors. After the end of the twelfth century, they held only a narrow strip along the southern coast, and this surrendered to Portugal in 1253.

In view of the large number of references to Spain in the poetry of the troubadours, it is surprising that they make none to Portugal. The latter country nevertheless came decidedly under French influence early in its history. This is what one might expect, considering that the founder of the Portuguese monarchy was a French nobleman, who naturally brought Frenchmen with him. Others followed later, attracted by prospects of fighting the Moors and settling on the reconquered lands. They were followed by French monks, who helped to civilize the new kingdom, and by French ecclesiastics who became bishops of Portuguese sees. Long before the reconquest of Portugal, the road from France to

Galicia had been safe from Moorish attacks, and many Frenchmen had gone on pilgrimage to the renowned shrine of Santiago de Compostela—so many of them, indeed, that the pilgrims' road became known as the *camino francés*.

Before the middle of the thirteenth century, French influence was very strong in Portugal. It received further impetus in 1246, when Alfonso III, who had lived thirteen years at the French court, became King of Portugal; and it maintained its strength throughout the reign (1279–1325) of Alfonso's son Denis, who had been educated by a Frenchman, was a great patron of poetry, and was himself a poet.

The oldest surviving specimens of Galician-Portuguese poetry[161] date from the closing years of the twelfth century. National feeling had not yet become consolidated in so new and cosmopolitan a state as Portugal, and, probably for that reason, its earliest poetry presents an unusual feature. It begins with the lyric and not, as in Castile and elsewhere, with the epic.

The influence exerted by France on the Galician-Portuguese lyric during the thirteenth century, particularly during its second half, was very strong, and the troubadour lyric, decaying in its own soil, flowered again in the Peninsula. Practically every Provençal genre was imitated, and successfully imitated, from the *chanso*, *sirventes*, *tenso*, and *planh* to the more objective *pastorela* and *alba*. The troubadours' theory of courtly love reappears in the love-poems, in practically the same terms, but with the important difference that the ladies whose praises are sung are unmarried. The satire of the *sirventes* reappears in the *cantigas de escarnho* or *de maldizer*, but in these poems the satire is mostly concerned with petty personal affairs, and not with the wider interests which are ventilated in the *sirventes*.

The technique of these imitations is often remarkably good, but the metre does not attain to the perfection which it had in Provençal poetry. Rhyme is less elaborate, and is sometimes mixed with assonance, and masculine rhymes predominate. The stanzas are generally *singulars*, but *coblas doblas* and *unissonans* are sometimes found. As in Northern France, the *senhal* of troubadour poetry is not used. Another resemblance with the poetry of the trouvères is that refrains are used more than in Provençal, and indeed more than in Northern French imitations of the troubadours.

The chief representative of this imitative poetry is the *cantiga de amor*, which corresponds to the *chanso* of the troubadours. It rarely exceeds more than three stanzas in length, however, and its lines are generally of eight or ten syllables. It often ends with a *finda*—the Galician-Portuguese name for the *tornada*. Gomes Charinho's *Muytos dizem con gram coyta d'amor* [239] is a good example of the *cantiga de amor*, except that in it the poet declares that he does not intend to die for love. Another example is King Denis's *Quer' eu en maneyra de proençal* [247], in which he uses *coblas unissonans*.

Of the Galician-Portuguese presentation of the *pastorela* there are two types. In one, represented by João d'Aboim's *Cavalgava noutro dia* [203], we have an early type of the pastoral poem—one in which shepherdesses tell of their love but no male participates. In the other, represented by King Denis's *Vi oj' eu cantar d'amor* [248], we have the later type, with its encounter between a shepherdess and a suitor of higher class. In neither, however, do we find the indecencies which are so often met in the French *pastourelles* to which these poems are obviously indebted, and which are met also in their Latin equivalents. This high moral standard is characteristic of the early Galician-Portuguese love-lyric in general. Of the hundreds of extant poems, scarcely any are tainted with the indecency or immorality of so many of the compositions of the troubadours, the trouvères, and the Goliards. This remains true even of poems which are close imitations in every other respect.

The *cantiga de amor*, as we have seen, corresponds to the Provençal *chanso*. In it, the poet expresses his own emotions. In another type of the early Galician-Portuguese lyric, however— the *cantiga de amigo*—the song, though written by a man, is put into the mouth of a woman.

The *cantiga de amigo* is the most prolific and also the most important type of early Galician-Portuguese poetry. In it, the lyric of the north-western part of the Peninsula rose to its greatest height and displayed its greatest originality. Its themes vary considerably. In the *alva*[199], or dawn-song, we have the counterpart of the Provençal *alba*, but the word "dawn", almost *de rigueur* with the troubadours, is not introduced; and, as in all *cantigas de amigo*, it is the woman who speaks. In the *cantiga de romaria*[219], or pilgrimage-song, we have a love-lyric centring round one of the numerous shrines of the north-west—not, as its name might seem to imply, a devotional composition. Another variety is the *barcarola*[205, 216], or boat-song, of which, as is natural in a country possessing an extensive sea-coast and numerous rivers, there are many examples. A fourth variety is the *bailada*[205, 227], or dance-song, of which there are some splendid examples.

All these varieties of the *cantiga de amigo* have this feature in common—the singer is a woman. In technique, however, they assume different forms, according to the relative amounts of Provençal and popular influence present. In the *Meu amigo, vós morredes*[221] of João Airas, for instance, we have a poem with a refrain, but it cannot resist the temptation to end with a *finda* in troubadour style, and its theme is the well-worn troubadour theme of dying for love, dressed in correct metre and full rhyme. In João Servando's *Ora van a San Servando*[219]—a *cantiga de romaria*—on the other hand, the *finda* has been dropped. In Pero da Ponte's *Vistes, madr', o escudeiro*[192] we are conscious of less Provençal influence still, for not only is there no *finda*, but the refrain is the most striking part of the poem and has a thoroughly popular ring. Further, this popular refrain is the foundation-stone on which the rest of the poem is built. In the *bailada*, as would be expected, we get further still from troubadour influence, and nearer to popular poetry. João Zorro's *Bailemos agora*[205], for instance, is probably based on a well-known popular dance-song of the time. Equally popular in its inspiration is the *Bailad' oj', ai filha*[227] of Airas Nunes, with its monorhymed stanzas and amphibrachic metre.

We have not yet mentioned the most original of all the metrical forms assumed by the *cantiga de amigo*. This is the *cantiga* *paralelística* or *cossante**—the form which provides us with many enchanting Galician-Portuguese lyrics.

The *cossante* is a poem written in assonant couplets, with a refrain after each couplet. The final stressed vowel is always *i* in the first couplet and *a* in the second, and the same vowel is repeated in alternate couplets throughout the poem. The connection thus established between the alternate couplets is made even more intimate by the use of *leixa-pren*—i.e. the second line of the first couplet is repeated as the first line of the third, the second line of the second couplet becomes the first line of the fourth couplet, and so on throughout the poem. It is not merely the alternate couplets, however, which are intimately connected with each other, for the odd couplets are also closely linked with the even couplets. This is brought about by parallelism—the repetition of the words of the odd stanzas in a slightly different form in the even ones.

From this description, it might appear that the *cossante* is a complicated poem, of interest chiefly for its technique, but the reverse is true. The *cossante* is, in fact, extremely simple and strikingly effective.

This will be seen at once by turning to examples. The simplest and shortest of all, and at the same time one of the most effective, is Martin Codax's *barcarola, Ondas do mar de Vigo*[216], with which may be compared João Zorro's *barcarola, Per ribeira do rio*[205]. Another fine example is King Denis's famous lyric, *Ai flores, ai flores do verde pĩo*[249]. In Fernandez Torneol's *alva, Levad', amigo*[199], with its long melodious lines, we get the same striking effect from the alternation of the *i* and *a* sounds. *Eu velida non dormia*[215], by Pedro Eanes Solaz, in which part of the refrain is inserted between the lines of the couplets, is an example of an imperfect *cossante*, as the *leixa-pren* is not carried beyond the fourth stanza. It is nevertheless a very striking poem—largely, though not entirely, because of its strange refrain.

* Sr Rodrigues Lapa uses the longer title, and suggests *cantiga retornada* as an alternative. He deprecates the use of the term *cossante*, but I have used it in these pages, both because it is short and also because Mr Aubrey Bell has made it familiar to English readers.

It will be noticed from these examples that rhyme is sometimes used instead of assonance in the *cossante*, or in combination with it, and that the *cossante* line has no fixed length. Seven or eight syllables are the commonest lengths, but lines with as few as five and as many as fourteen syllables are sometimes used. It will also be noticed that the *cossante* has no fixed number of stanzas. Its machinery requires a perfect example to have an even number of couplets, and not less than four, but there is no limit to the number of couplets otherwise. As Sr Rodrigues Lapa remarks, a *cossante* could in theory go on to infinity, without varying in its essential form.

The *cossante*, with its simple themes, no doubt originated in the poetry of the people, and it remained popular in its appeal. At a first glance, even its most finished representatives might be taken as the work of popular poets, but their appearance is deceptive. Their apparent simplicity conceals the high art of skilful and cultured writers; and we find, moreover, that many of the *cossantes* were written by poets who were also skilled writers in the intricate style of the troubadours. It is very probable, too, that they owe something to liturgical influence, particularly to the Psalms.*

The fundamental principle of the Psalms (as of Hebrew poetry in general) is that the two halves of each verse are linked together by parallelism of thought. Very often, the second half merely repeats the first half in slightly different words, as in

> Praise the Lord, ye servants:
> O praise the name of the Lord.

The consecutive couplets of a *cossante* reproduce this feature; but the *cossante* comes closer in form to such psalms as Psalm 136 (Vulgate 135)[67], which have a refrain:

> O give thanks unto the God of all gods:
> *for his mercy endureth for ever.*
>
> O thank the Lord of all lords:
> *for his mercy endureth for ever....*

* Cf. Bell, *Portuguese Literature*, pp. 23–4.

[43]

Who smote great kings:
for his mercy endureth for ever.

Yea, and slew mighty kings:
for his mercy endureth for ever.

Sehon, king of the Amorites:
for his mercy endureth for ever.

And Og the king of Basan:
for his mercy endureth for ever.

As is well known, the first half of each verse of this psalm is commonly sung alternately by opposite sides of the choir, the second half, or refrain, being sung by the whole choir. While, therefore, each even verse is linked to its predecessor by parallelism, one group of voices links the odd verses together throughout the psalm, and another group of voices links the even verses. In the same way, each even couplet in a *cossante* is linked to its predecessor by parallelism, and the odd couplets are linked together by an *i* assonance, the even couplets by an *a* assonance. It is most probable that the odd couplets were originally sung by one person and the even couplets by another, the refrain being sung by a chorus.

The *cossante* was the supreme achievement of the early Portuguese poets. Unknown elsewhere, it is one of the most beautiful types of the medieval Romance lyric, into which it introduced a new strain of freshness, delicacy, and melancholy charm. Its beauty won over so staunch a protagonist of the troubadours as King Denis, with whose *cossantes* the early Galician-Portuguese lyric comes to an admirable close.

VI

The troubadours began to visit Italy during the closing years of the twelfth century, and found a ready welcome there, particularly in the North, where social life was much the same as in their native land, and where their songs could be understood with little difficulty. They were welcomed, above all, at the court of the Marquis of Montferrat, where Peire Vidal and Raimbaut de Vaqueiras both stayed before the century closed. The Albigensian Crusade carried out during the opening years of the thirteenth century scattered the troubadours and swelled the number of those who visited Italy. Not a few of them settled there permanently, and before long they had as their disciples a band of native Italian poets writing in the same language and on the same themes as themselves.

Conspicuous among these was Sordello, a native of Mantua and a prolific poet. He is chiefly famous for his *planh* on Blacatz, in which he takes the opportunity of satirizing the chief rulers of Western Europe. He died in 1269, but was by no means the last of his line; for other troubadours, both Italian and Provençal, continued to write until the end of the thirteenth century, one of the last of note being Bartolommeo Zorzi, a Venetian merchant, who died in 1290.

The first vernacular poets of Italy, then, wrote in a foreign tongue, and Italian was the last of the great Romance languages to be used in literature. There are several explanations of these two closely allied phenomena.

First of all, Provençal possessed tremendous prestige at the time as a literary medium. Secondly, it was easily understood by many educated Italians, particularly in the North. Thirdly, it was fashionable, and that would be enough to secure for it the applause of many of those who did not understand it; for it is not unreasonable to assume that there were many Italians in the early thirteenth century whose mentality was similar to that of a large part of a Covent Garden audience to-day. Another factor to be taken into account is that Italian, of all the Romance languages, bore the closest resemblance to Latin—so close, in fact, that it was not regarded as a separate language, but as a mere corruption of the classical language which Italians above all others would naturally venerate. It was a degenerate, "soft bastard Latin", unworthy of the attention of anyone with literary pretensions. Those who first used it for serious writing were no doubt regarded as daring or, rather, contemptible innovators. Innovators they certainly were; and yet they were, to a very great extent, in both the form and the matter of their poetry, influenced by the troubadours.

The main theme of Italian poetry throughout the thirteenth century is love, but there is no need to see the troubadours' influence in that. At the same time, their influence on the great bulk of Italian poetry, down to the time of Dante and later, is obvious. The amount of influence varies in different poets, and in different poems by the same writer, but its existence, though it has been minimized by some critics, cannot be denied. Some poems are almost literal translations from a Provençal original, but such instances are uncommon. It is far more usual to find an Italian poem adorned with stock Provençal epithets, and possessing an air of resemblance to troubadour poetry in general, than to find reminiscences of a particular poem.

In their treatment of love, the earliest Italian poets follow the troubadours very closely. The objects of their devotion are all alike in being the mirror of perfection and the fountain of any merit that may exist in their admirers. Each of them is a pattern of beauty, but their beauty is not described, so that we cannot distinguish one from another. In spite of their use of troubadour terminology, however, the early Italian poets' conception of love was, with some exceptions, on a higher plane from the first, being less sensual. As the thirteenth century progressed, this conception rose several planes higher, until it culminated in Dante's Beatrice; but this evolution was a gradual one, and its various steps must be traced through the works of many poets.

The technique of early Italian poetry is less elaborate than that of the troubadours, and a number of differences, largely due to the different natures of the two languages used, are apparent.

Feminine rhymes, for instance, are far commoner in Italian than in Provençal. They are, in fact, almost inevitable, owing to the great predominance of paroxytones in Italian. Again, the later troubadours show a strong preference for *coblas unissonans*. A number of Italian poets emulated them in this; but the comparative paucity of identical endings in Italian generally forced those who wrote in the latter language to use *coblas singulars*. We consequently find *coblas capfinidas* in greater favour than with the troubadours.

The favourite length for a stanza in troubadour poetry is eight or nine lines. A number of the earliest Italian poets show a similar liking for a comparatively short stanza; but, as the century progresses, the preference for a longer stanza increases, stanzas of thirteen or fourteen lines being very common, and those of sixteen or even eighteen lines being freely used. The stanzas are generally tripartite, but quadripartition is also frequent. The line, like the stanza, has no fixed length. The hendecasyllable* is, however, the favourite line, with the heptasyllable coming second and the pentasyllable third in frequency.

The favourite genre with the Italian poets of the thirteenth century was the *canzone*. In this, the arrangement of the rhymes varies considerably. Very often, two rhymes are used alternately in the first half of the stanza, and two others in the second half. Another method which is very frequently used is to open each stanza with rhymes in the order: *a b c a b c*. The number of stanzas in a *canzone* varies. In the second half of the century, five is a favourite number, and the poem frequently ends with a *comiato*, the Italian equivalent of the Provençal *tornada*; but, whereas the latter invokes a person, the *comiato* generally invokes the poem itself. As in the Provençal *chanso*, love is the main theme of the *canzone*, but is not the only theme.

Another favourite form with the early Italian poets was the *ballata*[238, 244-5], which consists of a short introductory *ripresa* of two or more lines, followed by two or more stanzas, to which is sometimes added a *comiato*. When the latter appears, it has the

---

* This term is not used in the classical sense in the present work, but is applied to any line of eleven syllables.

same metrical form and rhymes as the *ripresa.* Often, like the *comiato* of a *canzone*, it invokes the poem itself.

That the *ballata* sprang from the popular dance-song is indicated both by its title and by several of its characteristics. The stanzas represent the soloist's part, the *ripresa* the refrain sung by the chorus. Further, one of the most prominent features of the *ballata* is that the last line of each stanza rhymes with the last line of the *ripresa*, which is intended to be repeated after each stanza. The *comiato* is but a final refrain. Its use of different words from the *ripresa* is paralleled in similar poems in other Romance languages, in which the wording of the refrain often varies, to a greater or less extent, after the various stanzas.

The *ballata*, however, though it had its origin in the popular dance-song, is not, in its thirteenth-century literary form, either popular or a dance-song. It is too elaborate and too sophisticated to be either. We cannot, for instance, imagine a dance-chorus singing the *ripresa*:

> Questa rosa novella,
> Che fa piacer sua gaia giovanezza,
> Mostra che gentilezza,
> Amor, sia nata per virtù di quella;

still less the *comiato* to the same poem:

> Ballata giovincella,
> Dirai a quella ch' à bionda la trezza,
> Ch' amor per la sua altezza
> M' à comandato sia servente d' ella.

The simpler, less sophisticated *ballate* are nevertheless suited to dancing, and it seems clear that to Dante the *ballata* was intended to be danced. In his *De vulgari eloquentia*, when comparing the *canzone* with the *ballata*, he remarks that

whatever produces unaided the effect at which it aims is nobler than that which depends on outside help. *Canzoni* produce unaided the whole of the effect at which they aim, but *ballate* do not, for they need the help of the performers for whom they are written. It follows, therefore, that *canzoni* are to be considered nobler than *ballate*.

In the passage just quoted, Dante goes on to remark that, just as the *canzone* is more noble than the *ballata*, so the *ballata* is more noble than the sonnet.

The sonnet is almost certainly of Italian origin and was used by some of the earliest poets in the language, but took some time to win its way into favour. Although several varieties of structure were used by early sonnet-writers, the normal type of the Italian sonnet in the thirteenth century was what it still is to-day. It consists of fourteen hendecasyllables divided into an octave and a sestet, the octave being subdivided into two quatrains and the sestet into two tercets. The octave has two rhymes, which are either used alternately or arranged in the order *abba* in each quatrain. The sestet either has two rhymes used alternately, or three rhymes arranged *c de* in each tercet.

The *canzone*, *ballata*, and sonnet are the three great contributions of early Italian poetry to the Romance lyric. Other genres, such as the *tenzone*, *serventese*, and *discordo*, do not reach the same level. With some exceptions, they are content to copy Provençal models, which they often resemble as closely as do the corresponding poems of the trouvères. Another genre, the *contrasto*, displays more originality. It takes the form of a love-dialogue, and its origin has consequently been traced by some writers to the French *pastourelle*. It has, however, none of the introductory machinery of the latter, and its participants, moreover, both belong to the same class. The origin of the *contrasto* is rather to be sought in Italian popular poetry than in the *pastourelle* or its Provençal equivalent. The simplicity of popular poetry is a noteworthy feature, for instance, of Ciacco dell' Anguillaia's *contrasto*, *O giema leziosa* [217].

With the possible exception of the *cantilena giullaresca*, *Salva lo vescovo senato*, it is interesting to find that the earliest Italian verse which we possess occurs in two poems written, not later than the year 1202, by a Provençal, Raimbaut de Vaqueiras. In both of them, however, Italian is introduced for a special reason. One is the *descort* [152], already mentioned, in which the poet uses several different languages in order to express the disturbed state of his mind. The other is a dialogue between an amorous Provençal and a Genoese lady who, pretending not to understand his wishes fully, answers him in her own language, though a number of Provençal words are mingled with it.

Italian poetry first came into its own in Sicily, where the Provençal language was more imperfectly understood than in any other part of Italy, and where literature found a congenial home at the brilliant court of the Emperor Frederick II. To foster the writing of poetry in a language to which it was as yet unaccustomed was characteristic of the "amazing revolutionist", who may moreover have cherished a hope that the use of its national language might help to unite Italy with him against the Papacy. Frederick himself wrote love-lyrics in Italian, but he was eclipsed as a poet by such writers as his chancellor, Piero delle Vigne; his notary, Giacomo da Lentino; the almost unknown Giacomo Pugliese; and the nobleman, Rinaldo d' Aquino.

In the works of all these poets, imitation of the troubadours is balanced by the influence of popular poetry and by original features. Piero delle Vigne and Giacomo da Lentino, for instance, took part in a *tenzone*, in the approved Provençal style, on the nature of love, but both were also writers of the sonnet, which Piero was probably the first to use. In the poems of both these Italian writers, the treatment of love has already advanced beyond its conventional, sensual troubadour stage and points forward to the psychological treatment which it was to receive in Central Italy. This new feeling is apparent in Piero's *Amore, in cui disio ed ò speranza*[180], and still more in Giacomo da Lentino's charming sonnet, *Io m' agio posto*[186], in which he declares that he would not want to go to Paradise without his lady, and that he would be content if he could but gaze on her there. In his *Guiderdone aspetto avire*[187], on the other hand, we find the usual theory of courtly love—set out, it is interesting to note, in the form of a Victorine Sequence.

Giacomo Pugliese[193] similarly has his conventional "nature introductions" in troubadour style:

> Quando vegio rinverdire
> Giardino e prato e rivera,
> Gli augelletti odo bradire...,

but his poetry as a whole has an unaffected popular strain which we do not find in the troubadours; and his beautiful elegy, *Morte, perchè m' ài fatta sì gran guerra,* is written with a sincerity and a restraint which are lacking from the formal Provençal *planh.* In the poetry of Rinaldo d' Aquino [201], too, we find many conventional troubadour phrases. In others of his poems, however, we hear the voice of popular poetry, as in his *Giammai non mi conforto,* in which a girl laments the departure of her lover on a Crusade. This charming lyric, with its simple technique, moves the reader whom the more elaborate efforts of Marcabrun on the same theme leave cold.

It is going too far to say, with Gaspary, that the work of the Sicilian school has little intrinsic value, for it produced some beautiful poems and was at its best when it was freest from Provençal influence. Neither it nor its successors killed Provençal, for Provençal was already dying and would have died whether there had been Italian poetry or not. The Sicilian poets, however, did at least show that the Italian language was now capable of producing genuine poetry. Their successors built on the foundations which they had laid, and, in less than a century, Italian had not merely proved that it was capable of taking the place of Provençal, but had also produced one of the greatest poets in all literature.

The Sicilian school included many poets who were not Sicilians, and, considerably before the death of Frederick II in 1250, Italian poetry had gained a footing in other parts of the country. Its development was slow in Northern Italy, where foreign influences were strong. The result was that many poets continued to write in Provençal until the end of the thirteenth century. Others, enamoured of the *chansons de geste,* wrote adaptations or imitations of them, not in Italian, but in French, which was considered the language *par excellence* for chivalrous romances. Such Italian poetry as was written in the North was mainly narrative and directed to religious or didactic ends.

In Central Italy, however, the vernacular lyric, both religious and secular, obtained an early hold and developed rapidly.

The religious lyric was the outcome of Franciscanism, of which

Central Italy was the cradle. Saint Francis made it the vehicle for expressing his own religious fervour and also found it an excellent medium for teaching the masses. His own simple *lauda*, written in assonant prose, was elaborated by his followers, who, taking the popular song as their metrical basis, composed large numbers of *laude spirituali*, which were soon sung throughout the length and breadth of Italy. The greatest writer of these religious lyrics was Jacopone da Todi, in whose *Donna del paradiso* [207] we have the Italian religious drama of the fourteenth century in embryo.

The religious lyric of Central Italy found its natural home in Saint Francis's native Umbria. The secular lyric grew up in the great Tuscan communes, such as Florence, Pisa, Arezzo, and Siena, whose wealthy, cultured citizens took a pride in writing in their own language.

The early Tuscan poets, many of whom had probably spent some time at the court of Frederick II, continued the traditions of the Sicilian school, but were more strongly imbued with the influence of the troubadours. Direct imitation of the latter is much more frequently met in them than in the Sicilian poets, and this imitation extends to the reproduction of many of the excesses of the troubadours, such as the use of difficult and equivocal rhymes and the practice of the *trobar clus*. Their imitation of the troubadours also covered a wider field than in Sicily. Thus, while the Sicilians had confined themselves almost entirely to the love-lyric, the early Tuscans made great use of the *tenzone*, the *partimen*, and the *serventese*. Even in their use of these characteristic Provençal genres, however, they showed originality. Their *tenzoni*, for instance, are often in the form of a series of sonnets, and frequently abandon the discussion of trivialities for more important subjects. Their *serventesi*, too, often assume an entirely new metrical form, and are inspired by genuine patriotism rather than mere personal prejudice.

The greatest of these early Tuscan poets was Guittone d'Arezzo [231]. His early love-poems are crowded with Provençal expressions and with attempts to outdo the troubadours in the use of difficult and homonymous rhymes. Even in his later poems, which are more serious in tone, we find the same features, reinforced by Latinisms and imitation of the Latin word-order. His later poems nevertheless reveal the Italian lyric in a state of development. In his *canzoni*, for instance, his stanzas are longer than those of his predecessors, and he generally uses a shorter *comiato* than the Sicilian poets. Some of his religious poems reach a high level, but he is at his best in political poetry—in his poem on the battle of Montaperti, for example.

From Tuscany, the art of Italian poetry spread over the Apennines to Bologna, where Guido Guinicelli [235] was its most distinguished exponent. In his early poems, he calls Guittone d' Arezzo master, and is content to follow him in his imitation of the troubadours, including his use of homonymous rhymes and the *trobar clus*. His later poetry, however, is of a very different kind. At this time, a great revival of philosophical studies was taking place in Italy: the works of Aristotle were becoming widely known through the translation carried out at Frederick II's orders, Aquinas was engaged on his great work of reconciling the Aristotelian philosophy with Christian theology, and the University of Bologna in particular was studying philosophy with the greatest enthusiasm. The influence of this revival is strongly evident in Guinicelli's later poetry, particularly in his attitude towards love.

The troubadours made no attempt to solve the mystery of their greatest theme. They merely described its effects, time after time, in the same terms. To them, as to their immediate successors in Italy, love was merely a physical attraction; but Guinicelli raises it to a higher level, by introducing a philosophical conception of the passion, which he states in his *canzone*, *Al cor gentil ripara sempre amore* [235]. Love, he says, finds its abode in the gentle heart as naturally as the bird finds its home in the trees. It is inseparable from a gentle heart, and nature created the two at the same time. Love purifies like fire, and, where it comes, all base thoughts flee. From Guinicelli's time onwards, the beloved is still the embodiment of perfection, but she has been raised from the fleshly to the spiritual plane.

Guido Guinicelli's chief disciples were Tuscans, but his influence is to be found, together with that of Guittone d' Arezzo, in another Bolognese poet, Onesto [238], the author of a number of sonnets. He is chiefly known, however, as the writer of the lilting *ballata*, *La partenɀa che fo dolorosa*, in which we have the first example of the use of decasyllabic lines in Italian verse.

Side by side with the *laude* of Jacopone da Todi, the political poetry of Guittone d' Arezzo, and the philosophical love-lyrics of Guido Guinicelli, Italy was also producing humorous and light verse of a very striking kind. There is no need to trace its origin, as has been done, to the wealth of the Tuscan cities, or to a reaction against the extreme asceticism of the Flagellants, for human character was much the same then as it is now. Few poets, however, can have expressed their devotion to the familiar trio,

> la donna, la taverna, e 'l dado,

with such frankness and vivacity as Cecco Angiolieri [240–1] of Siena does in his brilliant sonnets. His contemporary, Folgore da San Gemignano [242], who details the pleasures of each day of the week and each month of the year in two series of sonnets, is less entertaining, but shows remarkable skill in his use of the sonnet form.

The note of humour and satire is also struck in some of the poems of the Florentine Guido Cavalcanti, whom Dante revered as the founder of the *dolce stil nuovo*; but the poem which made him famous among his contemporaries and earned for him the veneration of Dante is a *canɀone* in which he expounds the nature and origin of love. Packed as it is with the dialectic of the Bolognese philosophers, it was received with the greatest enthusiasm at the time, and was the subject of a number of commentaries. To-day, however, it is not highly regarded, for it is a dissertation on an obsolete philosophy rather than a poem. It is completely lacking in the lyrical quality which distinguishes Guinicelli's *canɀone*, *Al cor gentil*, and if Cavalcanti had written nothing else his reputation as a poet would stand low to-day.

His fame now rests mainly on his love-sonnets and, perhaps most of all, on his *ballate*, of which his *In un boschetto trovai pasturella* [244] is a beautiful example. Its setting is that of the *pastourelle*, but it has an utterly different atmosphere from its

French prototype. It belongs, indeed, to another world. The vulgar sensualism of the amorous knight has disappeared, and has been replaced by the refined love of the *dolce stil nuovo*. In Cavalcanti's hands, the pastoral lyric has attained a new life, and is clothed with a delicacy which it had never known in France. Gentleness is its distinctive note, and there is the greatest possible contrast between the crude phrasing of the older pastorals and such quiet, musical lines as:

Ed ella mi rispose dolcemente
Che sola sola per lo bosco gia.

Guido Cavalcanti's last poem, *Perch' io non spero di tornar già mai*[245], is also a *ballata*, but of a very different type. It is a beautiful lyric, and it is something much more than that. Anyone who reads it can scarcely fail to be reminded of Leconte de Lisle's fine poem, *Le cœur de Hialmar*, which is founded on a Scandinavian popular poem.* Guido Cavalcanti's *ballata* and Leconte de Lisle's poem are poles asunder in atmosphere, yet they deal with the same theme in different ways. In the French poem, the hero, who is dying on the field of battle, wishes to send to his lady some token of his undying love. He therefore bares his breast and calls on a crow to tear out his heart and take it to her:

Va, sombre messager, dis-lui bien que je l'aime,
Et que voici mon cœur. Elle reconnaîtra
Qu'il est rouge et solide et non tremblant et blême;
Et la fille d'Ylmer, Corbeau, te sourira.

In the Italian poem, the hero, who is the poet himself, is also dying and wishes to send a token of his love to his lady; but, instead of calling on a crow to tear out his heart, he commits his soul to a *ballatetta*, and bids it carry it to his lady, to stay with her for ever:

De! ballatetta mia, a la tu' amistate
Quest' anima che trema raccomando.
Menala teco, nella sua pietate,
A quella bella donna a cui ti mando.

* Leconte de Lisle probably drew also from the Spanish ballad, *¡Oh Belerma!*, for the text of which see G. le Strange, *Spanish Ballads*, Cambridge, 1920, p. 38.

We have here, then, a striking instance of that spiritualization of material things which characterizes the poetry of the *dolce stil nuovo*. One is forced to the conclusion that Cavalcanti drew his theme from popular poetry, like Leconte de Lisle; but, whereas the latter, in accordance with the general scheme of his *Poèmes barbares*, heightens the primitive barbarism of his source, his predecessor by six centuries humanizes and spiritualizes the same theme, and at the same time produces a most moving poem.

In Dante[250-3], we reach the culmination of the *dolce stil nuovo* and of the poetry of the Middle Ages. His veneration for the troubadours is recorded in his *De vulgari eloquentia* and in many passages of his greater works. Their influence, and the influence of their Italian successors, permeates his poetry and is expressed both in his style and in his thought. "One may even go so far", says Butler, "as to say that Beatrice herself is the *donna* of the troubadours and their Italian imitators, in a sublimated form." "In a sublimated form"—those are the essential words. For, while Dante's love for Beatrice is still expressed in the *canzone*, the *ballata*, and the sonnet, she is no longer an earthly being, a feudal lady, or a philosophical abstraction, but love itself personified.

VII

Dante was separated from Saint Ambrose, the founder of Romance versification, by nine centuries. During that long period, the Latin and Romance lyric underwent continuous development. It was compounded of three elements—the liturgical, the popular, and the cultured.

For the first 700 years, development was slow, and the Latin lyric held the field alone. It began with liturgical verse, and liturgical verse continued to be its mainstay. With occasional exceptions, secular Latin verse during these seven centuries did not contribute to the new technique from which Romance verse was to spring, but confined itself to the application of the dead principles of Classical Latin. It was written, not for the unlettered masses, but for the educated few. Liturgical verse, on the other hand, was intended for the masses. Consequently, Saint Ambrose wrote in a popular metre, used simple language and simple word-order, and recognized the importance of the tonic accent, on which the popular poetry of the time was based.

His successors showed the same regard for popular demands. They cultivated the simple Ambrosian metre before all others, and made considerable use of another popular form—the trochaic tetrameter. Above all, they catered for the people by neglecting the aristocratic quantitative principle more and more, and by giving increasing prominence to accent and assonance. Hence, when the eighth century arrived, the victory of accent was complete in their verse, and assonance was reinforced here and there by simple rhyme.

By this time, however, the masses no longer understood Latin. The liturgical lyric nevertheless continued to develop along the lines already laid down. During the ninth century, it was re-inforced by the Sequence, which was at first in prose, with a single assonance to all its lines. The latter feature, together with the accentual system, also appears in some of the secular poetry of the century.

By the tenth century, a considerable number of secular poems were written on the accentual system, as is shown by the *Cambridge Songs*. The liturgical lyric was strongly influencing the secular, and both were using varied rhymes instead of monorhyme. By the end of the eleventh century, the Sequence, which had achieved great popularity, had settled down to verse form.

From this time onwards, Latin verse had to compete with Provençal.

The troubadour lyric, complete with full rhyme and regular metre from the start, showed some indebtedness to liturgical poetry at first, but very rapidly developed on independent lines, becoming almost equally unconcerned with liturgical and popular themes or forms. By the middle of the twelfth century, it was firmly established. Latin verse, however, had kept pace with it, and produced the great Sequences of Adam of Saint Victor and the magnificent lyrics of the Archpoet at the very moment when the Provençal lyric was entering on its golden age. Other poets, too, had begun to write in the vernacular of Northern France, though their efforts were at first confined to the semi-popular assonant verse which the troubadours had ignored.

The second half of the twelfth century was the golden age of the troubadours. Limiting themselves mainly to love and satire, they displayed great virtuosity of technique within their chosen field. Expressing the feelings of feudal society, they cared as little as before for the Church or the masses. They achieved a great victory in Northern France, where the trouvères were for the most part content to be their imitators. Their influence spread also into the secular Latin lyric, but sacred Latin poetry was still going its own way, and was producing the *Golden Sequence* and the hymns of Guy de Bazoches.

In the early years of the thirteenth century, the foundations of the Galician-Portuguese lyric were laid, partly on a Provençal and partly on a liturgico-popular basis. The Italian lyric originated about the same time, and was strongly impregnated with the style and thought of the troubadours. After the end of the first quarter of the century, Provençal poetry suffered a sharp decline, and became but a shadow of its former self. The lyric of Northern France continued to imitate the troubadours for about a quarter of a century longer, after which it began to develop independently. The sacred Latin lyric meanwhile, in the poems of Philip the Chancellor, was borrowing a little from the troubadours, but was maintaining every inch of its strength. The secular Latin lyric also kept its vigour unimpaired, and in fact reached the zenith of its power in the *Carmina Burana*.

During the second half of the century, the Galician-Portuguese lyric enjoyed its golden age, and liturgical Latin verse produced its greatest marvels in the *Dies irae*, the *Stabat mater*, and the hymns of Saint Thomas Aquinas. The Italian lyric was meanwhile rapidly casting away most of its Provençal dress and revealing its own beauty. Its remarkable development was the chief feature of the last quarter of the century.

At the end of the century, the Italian lyric reigned supreme. Rhythmical Latin verse, which had prepared the way for the Romance lyric, had seen its greatest days, and was falling to a lower level. The troubadours, the fathers of the Romance lyric, had also had their day. The trouvères were dead, and their successors were serving an apprenticeship to new forms of verse. The Castilian lyric had scarcely been born. The early Portuguese lyric was drawing to a close in the poetry of King Denis, after whose death in 1325 an interval was to follow. In Italy, on the other hand, the lyric was now in the hands of one of the greatest poets of all ages, and had a long and glorious future before it.

Considering that Medieval Latin verse retained its prestige and its brilliance intact until the end of the thirteenth century, one might have expected its influence on the Romance lyric to have been greater than it was. There was, however, an important difference between the two, which prevented the influence of Latin from being either far-reaching or deep, viz. that Romance verse was overwhelmingly secular, Latin verse predominantly ecclesiastical. Consequently, there was a tendency for secular Latin poetry to be influenced by Romance rather than for the reverse process to take place; and liturgical Latin did all that could reasonably be expected of it when it provided the early Romance poets with examples of metrical form and polished technique.

Further, Latin was separated from Romance by a considerable linguistic gulf, whereas the various Romance languages still bore a very close resemblance to each other, as Dr Grillo shows by his comparison of a famous passage in the *Inferno*:

> Per me si va nella città dolente,
> Per me si va nell' eterno dolore,
> Per me si va tra la perduta gente.
> Giustizia mosse il mio alto fattore;
> Fecemi la divina potestate,
> La somma sapienza, e il primo amore,

with Raynouard's translation of it into Old Provençal:

> Per me si va en la ciutad dolent,
> Per me si va en l' eternal dolor,

Per me si va tras la perduta gent.
Justizia moguet el mieu alt fachor;
Fez mi la divina potestat,
La summa sapienza, e·l prim' amor,

and Littré's into Old French:

Par moi se va dans la cité dolente,
Par moi se va dans l'eternal dolor,
Par moi se va parmi la gent pullente.
Justice mut mon souverain faitor;
Et si me firent devine poestés,
Raison hautisme, e premeraine amor.

It was very easy, therefore, for the poets of one Romance language to influence or be influenced by those who wrote in another.

The troubadours, who had the advantage of coming first, have probably benefited more than most poets from the argument: *post hoc, ergo propter hoc*. There has been a tendency for their influence to be taken for granted where nothing more than coincidence can be proved. Their influence on the subjective lyric was nevertheless very great. They were for a long time the almost undisputed overlords of Northern France. In Portugal, they shared the supremacy with native and popular elements. In Italy, their rule was almost undisputed at first. At the end of the thirteenth century, it was largely disregarded in practice, but was still acknowledged in theory.

In the sphere of the objective lyric, M. Jeanroy attributes overwhelming influence to the popular poetry of France. Sr Rodrigues Lapa, in his turn, asserts that "the obvious foundation of the so-called popular poetry of the Romance languages is liturgical poetry. Only by a common musical and religious culture", he continues, "can the unity of the European lyric be explained." M. Jeanroy defends his thesis with exhaustive quotation and illustration, and Sr Rodrigues Lapa does the same. While it would be grossly impertinent to criticize the works of these learned writers, it may nevertheless be permissible to suggest that their far-reaching artillery is, to use a homely Bedfordshire phrase, "like Bishop's gun—too good"; in other words, that they have overstated their case.

Other writers have gone even farther afield—to Moorish Spain and to China, for instance—in their search for the origin of the Romance lyric. To these, Dr Raby's remarks, though predicated of the Medieval Latin lyric only, make a fitting reply:

"We do not need to search out obscure causes," he says, "to go to the East or to Spain, to wander in the northern forests, or to look for mimes and players with an ancestry stretching back to the ancient world. Two things are needed—the human spirit and a favourable environment."

By the end of the thirteenth century, the Romance languages had produced many very beautiful lyrics. None of them, however, until Dante appeared, had produced a literature which can be called great without fear of its claim to that title being questioned. Liturgical Latin, on the other hand, had done so. In both the Hymn and the Sequence it had risen—not once nor twice, but many times—to the greatest heights of sublimity, majesty, and beauty. Its finest poems will bear comparison with anything in Classical Latin. They have, moreover, as far as form is concerned, a much greater appeal than the latter to-day, because they are built on the modern accentual system instead of a dead quantitative one which only the trained ear of the few can appreciate. Catullus's lament on his dead brother moves one intensely now, after the lapse of two thousand years, but it is its subject alone which moves the average reader, for the form in which it is conveyed is wasted on him. The *Dies irae* and the *Stabat mater*, on the other hand, lose none of their effect, and cannot lose it as long as European verse is based on accent. They are among the greatest achievements, not merely of medieval poets, but of the poets of all time.

SELECTED LYRICS

with Comments

⁂

SAINT NICETAS

FOURTH CENTURY

The authorship of the *Te Deum*, the greatest prose hymn of the Latin Church, is ascribed by tradition to Saint Ambrose. Recent scholarship, however, ascribes it to Saint Nicetas, who was Bishop of Remesiana in Dacia during the latter part of the fourth century.

The hymn falls into four sections, of which the first three closely resemble each other in construction. The fourth section, consisting almost entirely of verses from the Psalter, was added later, and its line-endings lack the rhythmical *cursus* which distinguishes those of the preceding sections.

Te Deum

T E D E U M laudamus : te Dominum confitemur.
Te aeternum patrem omnis terra veneratur.
Tibi omnes angeli, tibi caeli et universae potestates,
Tibi cherubim et seraphim incessabili voce proclamant
  Sanctus, sanctus, sanctus Dominus Deus Sabaoth,
  Pleni sunt caeli et terra majestatis gloriae tuae.

Te gloriosus apostolorum chorus,
Te prophetarum laudabilis numerus,
Te martyrum candidatus laudat exercitus,
Te per orbem terrarum sancta confitetur ecclesia
  Patrem immensae majestatis,
  Venerandum tuum verum unicum filium,
  Sanctum quoque paraclitum spiritum.

Tu rex gloriae, Christe : tu patris sempiternus es filius.
Tu ad liberandum suscepisti hominem : non horruisti virginis
  uterum.
Tu devicto mortis aculeo : aperuisti credentibus regna caelorum.

Tu ad dexteram Dei sedes in gloria patris : judex crederis esse
   venturus.
   Te ergo quaesumus tuis famulis subveni : quos pretioso
   sanguine redemisti.
   Aeterna fac cum sanctis tuis gloria munerari.

Salvum fac populum tuum, Domine : et benedic hereditati tuae.
Et rege eos et extolle illos usque in aeternum.
Per singulos dies benedicimus te.
Et laudamus nomen tuum in saeculum et in saeculum saeculi.
Dignare, Domine, die isto sine peccato nos custodire.
Miserere nostri, Domine : miserere nostri.
Fiat misericordia tua, Domine, super nos : quemadmodum
   speravimus in te.
In te, Domine, speravi : non confundar in aeternum.

SAINT AMBROSE
c. 340 — † 397

SAINT AMBROSE, the great Bishop of Milan and stern opponent of Arianism,
was the first Christian Latin writer of outstanding importance in Italy and the
virtual founder of Latin hymnody in Western Europe. Of the large number
of hymns attributed to him, it is probable that he wrote eighteen. All these
are written in the same metre and have several strongly marked characteristics in common.

Splendor paternae gloriae, one of his finest hymns, is made up, like all his
authentic hymns, of eight stanzas, with a pause in the sense at the end of
each stanza and a more pronounced pause after each second stanza. This
suggests that the hymn was written for antiphonal singing—a practice
which Ambrose introduced into Western Europe and which greatly impressed Saint Augustine before his conversion. As in the following hymn,
a considerable amount of assonance is noticeable. This is commonly regarded as accidental, but there seems too much of it for that to be so.

Intende, qui regis Israel contains several lines of nine syllables and other
evidence of Ambrose's adherence to classical principles; e.g. conflict between word-accent and metric ictus. The first stanza, taken almost verbatim
from the Psalms, was omitted later in liturgical use, probably because of the
difficulty experienced in singing it when elision was abandoned.

Morning Hymn

SPLENDOR paternae gloriae,
De luce lucem proferens,
Lux lucis et fons luminis,
Dies dierum illuminans,

Verusque sol illabere,
Micans nitore perpeti,
Jubarque sancti spiritus
Infunde nostris sensibus.

Votis vocemus et patrem,
Patrem perennis gloriae,
Patrem potentis gratiae,
Culpam releget lubricam.

Informet actus strenuos,
Dentem retundat invidi,
Casus secundet asperos,
Donet gerendi gratiam.

Mentem gubernet et regat
Casto fideli corpore,
Fides calore ferveat,
Fraudis venena nesciat.

Christusque nobis sit cibus,
Potusque noster sit fides;
Laeti bibamus sobriam
Ebrietatem spiritus.

Laetus dies hic transeat,
Pudor sit ut diluculum,
Fides velut meridies;
Crepusculum mens nesciat.

Aurora cursus provehit;
Aurora totus prodeat,
In patre totus filius,
Et totus in verbo pater.

Christmas Eve

INTENDE, qui regis Israel,
Super cherubin qui sedes,
Appare Ephrem coram, excita
Potentiam tuam et veni.

Veni, redemptor gentium,
Ostende partum virginis;
Miretur omne saeculum,
Talis decet partus Deo.

Non ex virili semine,
Sed mystico spiramine,
Verbum Dei factum est caro,
Fructusque ventris floruit.

Alvus tumescit virginis,
Claustrum pudoris permanet,
Vexilla virtutum micant,
Versatur in templo Deus.

Procedat e thalamo suo,
Pudoris aula regia,
Geminae gigans substantiae,
Alacris occurrat viam.

Egressus ejus a patre,
Regressus ejus ad patrem,
Excursus usque ad inferos,
Recursus ad sedem Dei.

Aequalis aeterno patri
Carnis tropaeo accingere,
Infirma nostri corporis
Virtute firmans perpeti.

Praesepe jam fulget tuum
Lumenque nox spirat novum,
Quod nulla nox interpolet
Fideque jugi luceat.

THE VULGATE

c. 400

SOPHRONIUS EUSEBIUS HIERONYMUS was born in Dalmatia about 340 or a few years earlier, of Christian parents, and was educated at Rome under the celebrated grammarian, Donatus. Much of his time was spent in the East, where he embraced the ascetic life. He settled finally at Bethlehem, where he founded a monastery, finished his translation of the Bible (afterwards known as the Vulgate), and died.

Saint Jerome translated the Psalter three times. The first translation, which was little more than a correction of the Old Latin texts, is known as the Roman Psalter. The second, from Origen's Hexaplar text, is known as the Gallican Psalter. This version was preferred to Jerome's final translation direct from the Hebrew, and is the one which is found in current editions of the Vulgate.

The Psalm, *Confitemini Domino*, has an unusual form. It has the parallelism which is the basis of Hebrew poetry, but the two halves of each distich are separated by a refrain. The text is arranged here with the first verse printed separately as a proem, the remaining verses being printed in pairs. The verse, *Qui dat escam omni carni*, has been moved eight places up from its usual position.

Of the many magnificent lyrics included in the Old Testament outside the Psalter, Saint Jerome's version of the *Song of Songs*, of which a small part is given on page 69, has probably exercised more influence over the Latin and Romance lyric than any other part of the Vulgate.

Psalm

CONFITEMINI Domino quoniam bonus:
quoniam in aeternum misericordia ejus.

Confitemini Deo deorum:
quoniam in aeternum misericordia ejus.

Confitemini Domino dominorum:
quoniam in aeternum misericordia ejus.

Qui facit mirabilia magna solus:
quoniam in aeternum misericordia ejus.

Qui fecit caelos in intellectu:
quoniam in aeternum misericordia ejus.

Qui firmavit terram super aquas:
quoniam in aeternum misericordia ejus.

Qui fecit luminaria magna:
quoniam in aeternum misericordia ejus.

Solem in potestatem diei:
quoniam in aeternum misericordia ejus.

Lunam et stellas in potestatem noctis:
quoniam in aeternum misericordia ejus.

Qui percussit Aegyptum cum primogenitis eorum:
quoniam in aeternum misericordia ejus.

Qui eduxit Israel de medio eorum:
quoniam in aeternum misericordia ejus.

In manu potenti et brachio excelso:
quoniam in aeternum misericordia ejus.

Qui divisit mare rubrum in divisiones:
quoniam in aeternum misericordia ejus.

Et eduxit Israel per medium ejus:
quoniam in aeternum misericordia ejus.

Et excussit Pharaonem et virtutem ejus in mari rubro:
quoniam in aeternum misericordia ejus.

Qui traduxit populum suum per desertum:
quoniam in aeternum misericordia ejus.

Qui dat escam omni carni:
quoniam in aeternum misericordia ejus.

Qui percussit reges magnos:
quoniam in aeternum misericordia ejus.

Et occidit reges fortes:
quoniam in aeternum misericordia ejus.

Sehon regem Amorrhaeorum:
quoniam in aeternum misericordia ejus.

Et Og regem Basan:
quoniam in aeternum misericordia ejus.

Et dedit terram eorum hereditatem:
quoniam in aeternum misericordia ejus.

Hereditatem Israel servo suo:
quoniam in aeternum misericordia ejus.

Quia in humilitate nostra memor fuit nostri:
quoniam in aeternum misericordia ejus.

Et redemit nos ab inimicis nostris:
quoniam in aeternum misericordia ejus.

Confitemini Deo caeli:
quoniam in aeternum misericordia ejus.

Confitemini Domino dominorum:
quoniam in aeternum misericordia ejus.

Love-dialogue

Sponsa. EGO flos campi:
et lilium convallium.

Sponsus. Sicut lilium inter spinas:
sic amica mea inter filias.

Sponsa. Sicut malus inter ligna silvarum:
sic dilectus meus inter filios.
Sub umbra illius quem desideraveram sedi:
et fructus ejus dulcis gutturi meo.
Introduxit me in cellam vinariam:
ordinavit in me caritatem.
Fulcite me floribus,
stipate me malis:
quia amore langueo.

Laeva ejus sub capite meo:
et dextera illius amplexabitur me.

Sponsus. Adjuro vos, filiae Jerusalem,
per capreas cervosque camporum:
ne suscitetis neque evigilare faciatis dilectam,
quoadusque ipsa velit.

Sponsa. Vox dilecti mei:
ecce iste venit,
saliens in montibus,
transiliens colles.
Similis est dilectus meus capreae:
hinnuloque cervorum.
En ipse stat post parietem nostrum:
respiciens per fenestras,
prospiciens per cancellos.
En dilectus meus loquitur mihi:

Sponsus. Surge, propera,
amica mea, columba mea, formosa mea,
et veni.
Jam enim hiems transiit:
imber abiit et recessit.
Flores apparuerunt in terra nostra:
tempus putationis advenit,
vox turturis audita est in terra nostra.
Ficus protulit grossos suos:
vineae florentes dederunt odorem suum.
Surge, amica mea, speciosa mea:
et veni.

PRUDENTIUS

348—*c.* 410

A URELIUS C LEMENS P RUDENTIUS, a Spaniard, spent most of his life in the civil service in his native province, but it is evident from his writings that he knew Rome well. Although he remained a layman all his life, his poems deal entirely with religious subjects, and are remarkable for their clearness of style and their mastery of varied metres. His versification is quantitatively correct, but he uses a number of new words and revives a number of obsolete ones. His poems show the influence of his rhetorical training and a fondness for alliteration and word-play.

The hymn *Cultor Dei*, used as an Office Hymn in the Sarum and other medieval breviaries, consists of the final stanzas of *Ades, pater supreme*, one of the twelve poems in Prudentius's *Cathemerinon*, his most important work. It is in catalectic iambic dimeters, grouped in quatrains, with practically no assonance, such little of it as there is being probably accidental.

The Sign of the Cross

CULTOR Dei, memento
  Te fontis et lavacri
  Rorem subisse sanctum,
Te chrismate innotatum.

Fac, cum vocante somno
Castum petis cubile,
Frontem locumque cordis
Crucis figura signet.

Crux pellit omne crimen,
Fugiunt crucem tenebrae;
Tali dicata signo
Mens fluctuare nescit.

Procul, o procul, vagantum
Portenta somniorum!
Procul esto pervicaci
Praestigiator astu!

O tortuose serpens,
Qui mille per meandros
Fraudesque flexuosas
Agitas quieta corda,

Discede, Christus hic est.
Hic Christus est, liquesce.
Signum quod ipse nosti
Damnat tuam catervam.

Corpus licet fatiscens
Jaceat recline paulum,
Christum tamen sub ipso
Meditabimur sopore.

?SAINT AUGUSTINE OF HIPPO
354 — † 430

The lighting of the Paschal Candle has figured among the Easter Eve ceremonies of the Latin Church from at least the fourth century, and has always been performed by a deacon who, in early times, had to compose his own form of benediction for the occasion. The beautiful prose lyric still used in the Roman rite has Saint Augustine for its traditional author. In it, a striking effect is produced by the use of repetition and of the rhythmical *cursus* which has already been noticed in the *Te Deum*. In the two excerpts given here, the cadences are about equally divided between those where the stress falls on the second and fifth syllables from the end (*cursus planus*), the second and seventh from the end (*cursus velox*), and the third and sixth from the end (*cursus tardus*).

The Blessing of the Paschal Candle

EXSULTET jam angelica turba caelorum.
 Exsultent divina mysteria:
  et pro tanti regis victoria tuba insonet salutaris.
Gaudeat et tellus tantis irradiata fulgoribus:
 et aeterni regis splendore illustrata totius orbis se sentiat amisisse caliginem.
Laetetur et mater ecclesia tanti luminis adornata fulgoribus:
 et magnis populorum vocibus haec aula resultet....

Haec sunt enim festa paschalia:

> in quibus verus ille agnus occiditur, cujus sanguine postes
> fidelium consecrantur.

Haec nox est:

> in qua primum patres nostros filios Israel eductos de Aegypto
> mare rubrum sicco vestigio transire fecisti.

Haec igitur nox est:

> quae peccatorum tenebras columnae illuminatione purgavit.

Haec nox est:

> quae hodie per universum mundum in Christo credentes a
> vitiis saeculi et caligine peccatorum segregatos reddit gratiae,
> sociat sanctitati.

Haec nox est:

> in qua destructis vinculis mortis Christus ab inferis victor
> ascendit.

Nihil enim nobis nasci profuit: nisi redimi profuisset.

O mira circa nos tuae pietatis dignatio.

O inaestimabilis dilectio caritatis:

> ut servum redimeres, filium tradidisti.

O certe necessarium Adae peccatum:

> quod Christi morte deletum est.

O felix culpa:

> quae talem ac tantum meruit habere redemptorem.

O vere beata nox:

> quae sola meruit scire tempus et horam in qua Christus ab
> inferis resurrexit....

SEDULIUS

SEDULIUS is a shadowy figure whose very nationality is doubtful. Practically all that can be stated of him with any approach to certainty is that, like most early Christian poets, he was educated in the public schools, and that he lived at Rome during the middle part of the fifth century.

The hymn, *A solis ortus cardine*, consists of the opening stanzas of his alphabetical poem on the life of Christ. Very different opinions have been expressed about its literary merits, but it has kept its place in the Roman Breviary to this day—largely, perhaps, because of the beautiful melody to which it is sung.

It is written in Ambrosian stanzas on the quantitative basis, but examination of it shows that the accentual system, which was to be the basis of medieval verse, had made progress since Saint Ambrose's time. In his hymns, the contrast between metric ictus and word-accent, so characteristic of Classical Latin, is strongly evident. In Sedulius, this contrast is not nearly so common. One finds, indeed, that ictus and word-accent frequently coincide. Further, Sedulius's hymn shows a great advance in the amount of assonance introduced, as is obvious at a glance. In eleven of the fourteen couplets the lines are assonant, and three whole stanzas have a single assonance.

Christmas

A SOLIS ortus cardine
Ad usque terrae limitem
Christum canamus principem,
Natum Maria virgine.

Beatus auctor saeculi
Servile corpus induit
Ut, carne carnem liberans,
Non perderet quod condidit.

Clausae puellae viscera
Caelestis intrat gratia:
Venter puellae bajulat
Secreta quae non noverat.

Domus pudici pectoris
Templum repente fit Dei:
Intacta nesciens virum
Verbo creavit filium.

Enixa est puerpera
Quem Gabriel praedixerat,
Quem matris alvo gestiens
Clausus Johannes senserat.

Faeno jacere pertulit,
Praesepe non abhorruit,
Parvoque lacte pastus est
Per quem nec ales esurit.

Gaudet chorus caelestium
Et angeli canunt Deum;
Palamque fit pastoribus
Pastor creator omnium.

ANONYMOUS

Ad cenam agni

c. 500 — 550

The hymn, *Ad cenam agni*, sometimes ascribed to Saint Ambrose and sometimes to as late a time as the seventh century, can probably be awarded, for technical reasons, to the earlier half of the sixth century. It shows the same features as *A solis ortus cardine*, but they are carried farther. Nearly all the couplets, for instance, have a simple rhyme.

Stolis in the second line is to be scanned *istolis*. From the second century onwards, in some parts of the Empire, an *i* was prefixed to initial *s* when the latter was followed by a consonant, and by the fourth century this practice was widespread.

Easter

AD cenam agni providi,
Stolis albis candidi,
Post transitum maris rubri
Christo canamus principi.

Cujus sacrum corpusculum
In ara crucis torridum,
Cruore ejus roseo
Gustando vivimus Deo,

Protecti paschae vespero
A devastante angelo,
Erepti de durissimo
Pharaonis imperio.

Jam pascha nostrum Christus est,
Qui immolatus agnus est;
Sinceritatis azyma
Caro ejus oblata est.

O vera digna hostia,
Per quam fracta sunt tartara,
Redempta plebs captivata,
Reddita vitae praemia.

Consurgit Christus tumulo,
Victor redit de barathro,
Tyrannum trudens vinculo,
Et reserans paradisum.

Quaesumus, auctor omnium,
In hoc paschali gaudio,
Ab omni mortis impetu
Tuum defendas populum.

VENANTIUS FORTUNATUS

c. 530 — † 609

VENANTIUS FORTUNATUS, a native of Italy, after various wanderings settled at Poitiers, where he became chaplain to a community of nuns recently founded by Saint Radegund, to whom a number of his poems are addressed.

His *Pange, lingua* was written to celebrate the reception by Saint Radegund of a relic of the cross, sent to her by the Emperor, as was also his *Vexilla regis*. Very fittingly, it has for centuries formed part of the Roman rite for the veneration of the cross on Good Friday. It is written in catalectic trochaic tetrameters, but with metric ictus and word-accent frequently falling on the same syllable, and a number of its lines are assonant.

It will be noticed that elision, which was gradually disregarded in Latin verse, is still necessary in lines 6 and 8, and that the letter *h*, regarded as a vowel in Classical Latin, is in line 9 (as frequently in Medieval Latin verse) treated as a consonant to avoid elision.

The Triumph of the Cross

PANGE, lingua, gloriosi proelium certaminis,
Et super crucis tropaeo dic triumphum nobilem,
Qualiter redemptor orbis immolatus vicerit.

De parentis protoplasti fraude factor condolens,
Quando pomi noxialis morte morsu corruit,
Ipse lignum tunc notavit, damna ligni ut solveret.

Hoc opus nostrae salutis ordo depoposcerat,
Multiformis perditoris arte ut artem falleret
Et medellam ferret inde hostis unde laeserat.

Quando venit ergo sacri plenitudo temporis,
Missus est ab arce patris natus, orbis conditor,
Atque ventre virginali carne factus prodiit.

Vagit infans inter arta conditus praesepia,
Membra pannis involuta virgo mater alligat,
Et pedes manusque crura stricta pingit fascia.

[77]

Lustra sex qui jam peracta tempus implens corporis,
Se volente, natus ad hoc, passioni deditus
Agnus in crucis levatur immolandus stipite.

Hic acetum, fel, arundo, sputa, clavi, lancea;
Mite corpus perforatur; sanguis, unda profluit,
Terra, pontus, astra, mundus quo lavantur flumine.

Crux fidelis, inter omnes arbor una nobilis,
Nulla talem silva profert flore, fronde, germine,
Dulce lignum dulce clavo dulce pondus sustinens.

Flecte ramos, arbor alta, tensa laxa viscera,
Et rigor lentescat ille quem dedit nativitas,
Ut superni membra regis mite tendas stipite.

Sola digna tu fuisti ferre pretium saeculi,
Atque portum praeparare nauta mundo naufrago,
Quem sacer cruor perunxit fusus agni corpore.

ANONYMOUS

Verbum supernum

?SEVENTH CENTURY

The anonymous hymn, *Verbum supernum*, written in Ambrosian stanzas, is sometimes ascribed to the sixth century and even to the fifth, but its technique points to a later date. In it, accent has to a great extent replaced quantity, and all its stanzas are in monorhyme or in rhymed couplets.

Advent Hymn

VERBUM supernum prodiens,
A patre olim exiens,
Qui natus orbi subvenis
Cursu declivi temporis,

Illumina nunc pectora
Tuoque amore concrema,
Audita ut praeconia
Sint pulsa tandem lubrica.

Judexque cum post aderis
Rimari facta pectoris,
Reddens vicem pro abditis
Justisque regnum pro bonis,

Non demum artemur malis
Pro qualitate criminis,
Sed cum beatis compotes
Simus perennes caelibes.

ANONYMOUS

Ave, maris stella

EIGHTH CENTURY

The famous hymn to the Virgin, *Ave, maris stella*, is first found in manuscripts dating from the eighth century. In it, quantity has been entirely
replaced by accent, and nearly all its couplets are rhymed. The hymn is in
trochaic metre, and much of its charm is due to its simplicity. Each line is
of six syllables, and only six words have more than two syllables each.

Hymn for the Annunciation

AVE, maris stella,
  Dei mater alma
    Atque semper virgo,
Felix caeli porta.

Sumens illud *Ave*
Gabrielis ore,
Funda nos in pace,
Mutans nomen Evae.

Solve vincla reis,
Profer lumen caecis,
Mala nostra pelle,
Bona cuncta posce.

Monstra te esse matrem;
Sumat per te precem
Qui pro nobis natus
Tulit esse tuus.

Virgo singularis,
Inter omnes mitis,
Nos culpis solutos
Mites fac et castos.

Vitam praesta puram,
Iter para tutum,
Ut videntes Jesum
Semper collaetemur.

Sit laus Deo patri,
Summum Christo decus,
Spiritui sancto
Honor tribus unus.

ANONYMOUS

A solis ortu usque ad occidua

c. 814

The author of this Lament on Charlemagne was perhaps a monk of the Italian monastery of Bobbio, which was founded by Saint Columban and other Irishmen early in the seventh century and for long maintained direct connection with Ireland. Alliteration—a favourite device with Irish poets —occurs in several places in the poem, and Saint Columban is invoked in it.

The Lament is not a great poem, but is noteworthy as a Latin forerunner of the Provençal *planh* and for its effective use of a refrain. It is in accentual iambic trimeters, with a pause after the fifth syllable in the classical manner. The same metre was used in hymns, e.g. in the *Aurea luce et decore roseo* attributed to Elpis, wife of Boethius. There is little rhyme or assonance in the poem; and, as in accentual Latin verse in general, there is no elision.

Lament

A SOLIS ortu usque ad occidua
Littora maris planctus pulsat pectora.
Heu mihi misero.

Ultra marina agmina tristitia
Tetigit ingens cum moerore nimio.
Heu mihi misero.

Franci, Romani atque cuncti creduli
Luctu punguntur et magna molestia.
   Heu mihi misero.

Infantes, senes, gloriosi praesules,
Matronae plangunt detrimentum Caesaris.
   Heu mihi misero.

Jamjam non cessant lacrimarum flumina,
Nam plangit orbis interitum Karoli.
   Heu mihi misero.

Pater communis orphanorum omnium,
Peregrinorum, viduarum, virginum,
   Heu mihi misero.

Christe, caelorum qui gubernas agmina,
Tuo in regno da requiem Karolo.
   Heu mihi misero.

Hoc poscunt omnes fideles et creduli,
Hoc sancti senes, viduae et virgines.
   Heu mihi misero.

Imperatorem jam serenum Karolum
Telluris tegit titulatus tumulus.
   Heu mihi misero.

Spiritus sanctus, qui gubernat omnia,
Animam suam exaltet in requiem.
   Heu mihi misero.

Vae tibi, Roma, Romanoque populo
Amisso summo glorioso Karolo.
   Heu mihi misero.

Vae tibi, sola formosa Italia,
Cunctisque tuis tam honestis urbibus.
   Heu mihi misero.

Francia diras perpessa injurias
Nullum jam talem dolorem sustinuit,
Heu mihi misero,

Quando augustum facundumque Karolum
In Aquisgrani glebis terrae tradidit.
Heu mihi misero.

Nox mihi dira jam retulit somnia,
Diesque clara non adduxit lumina,
Heu mihi misero,

Quae cuncti orbis Christiano populo
Vexit ad mortem venerandum principem.
Heu mihi misero.

O Columbane, stringe tuas lacrimas,
Precesque funde pro illo ad Dominum.
Heu mihi misero.

Pater cunctorum, misericors Dominus,
Ut illi donet locum splendidissimum.
Heu mihi misero.

O Deus cunctae humanae militiae
Atque caelorum, infernorum Domine,
Heu mihi misero,

In sancta sede cum tuis apostolis
Suscipe pium, O tu Christe, Karolum.
Heu mihi misero.

GOTTSCHALK
c. 805 — † 869

GOTTSCHALK, a German nobleman, entered the famous monastery of Fulda under pressure, and became a keen student of the works of Saint Augustine. He was condemned for expressing heretical opinions on the doctrine of predestination, and, refusing to recant, died excommunicate.

His poem, *Ut quid jubes*, was written from exile, in reply to a young monk who had asked him to write a song. It is constructed entirely on the accentual principle, the first two lines in each stanza being iambic, the rest trochaic. It is rhymed throughout, with double rhymes in several places, but all the lines end in *-e*. Considering the varied rhymes used in earlier poems, and Gottschalk's skill, one might have expected them in a poem of this length. Gottschalk was perhaps influenced by the contemporary Sequence, which was monorhymed for a special reason.

In answer to a request for a song

UT quid jubes, pusiole,
Quare mandas, filiole,
Carmen dulce me cantare,
Cum sim longe exsul valde
Intra mare?
O cur jubes canere?

Magis mihi, miserule,
Flere libet, puerule,
Plus plorare quam cantare
Carmen tale, jubes quale,
Amor care.
O cur jubes canere?

Mallem, scias, pusillule,
Ut velles tu, fratercule,
Pio corde condolere
Mihi atque prona mente
Conlugere.
O cur jubes canere?

Scis, divine tyruncule,
Scis, superne clientule,
Hic diu me exsulare,
Multa die sive nocte
    Tolerare.
  O cur jubes canere?

Scis, captivae plebiculae
Israeli cognomine
Praeceptum in Babylone
Decantare extra longe
    Fines Judae.
  O cur jubes canere?

Non potuerunt utique,
Nec debuerunt itaque
Carmen dulce coram gente
Alienae nostri terrae
    Resonare.
  O cur jubes canere?

Sed quia vis omnimode,
Consodalis egregie,
Canam patri filioque
Simul atque procedente
    Ex utroque.
  Hoc cano ultronee.

Benedictus es, Domine,
Pater, nate, paraclite,
Deus trine, Deus une,
Deus summe, Deus pie,
    Deus juste.
  Hoc cano spontanee.

Exsul ego diuscule,
Hoc in mare sum, Domine,
Annos nempe duos fere
Nosti fore, sed jam jamque
Miserere.
Hoc rogo humillime.

Interim cum pusione
Psallam ore, psallam mente,
Psallam voce, psallam corde,
Psallam die, psallam nocte,
Carmen dulce
Tibi, rex piissime.

ANONYMOUS

O tu qui servas

c. 900

The watch-song, *O tu qui servas*, with its curious blending of pagan
mythology and invocations of saints, was written at Modena, probably between 892 and 900, when the city was threatened with a Hungarian invasion.
It is written in the metre of the earlier Lament on Charlemagne, with a
strong pause after the fifth syllable; but, like a contemporary Sequence, it
is monorhymed throughout in *a*, except for two lines, which rhyme together and have an internal rhyme.
This poem is a prototype, in some respects, of the Provençal *alba*.

Watch-song

O TU qui servas armis ista moenia,
Noli dormire, moneo, sed vigila.
Dum Hector vigil exstitit in Troïa,
Non eam cepit fraudulenta Grecia:
Prima quiete dormiente Troïa
Laxavit Sinon fallax claustra perfida.

Per funem lapsa occultata agmina
Invadunt urbem et incendunt Pergama.
Vigili voce avis anser candida
Fugavit Gallos ex arce Romulea,
Pro qua virtute facta est argentea
Et a Romanis adorata ut dea.

Nos adoremus celsa Christi numina:
Illi canora demus nostra jubila.
Illius magna fisi sub custodia
Haec vigilantes jubilemus carmina.
Divina, mundi rex Christe, custodia,
Sub tua serva haec castra vigilia.

Tu murus tuis sis inexpugnabilis,
Sis inimicis hostis tu terribilis.
Te vigilante nulla nocet fortia,
Qui cuncta fugas procul arma bellica.
Tu cinge nostra haec, Christe, munimina,
Defendens ea tua forti lancea.

Sancta Maria, mater Christi splendida,
Haec cum Johanne, theotocos, impetra,
Quorum hic sancta venerantur pignora
Et quibus ista sunt sacrata limina.
Quo duce victrix est in bello dextera
Et sine ipso nihil valent jacula.

Fortis juventus, virtus audax bellica,
Vestra per muros audiantur carmina;
Et sit in armis alterna vigilia,
Ne fraus hostilis haec invadat moenia.
Resultet echo: "Comes, eja, vigila",
Per muros: "Eja", dicat echo: "Vigila."

ANONYMOUS

Salus aeterna

c. 900—950

The anonymous *Salus aeterna* illustrates the structure of the early prose
Sequences. It is made up of six pairs of strophes and antistrophes, followed
by a coda. Except that the third antistrophe has a phrase more than its
strophe, and the sixth antistrophe an extra syllable, each strophe has the
same number of syllables as its antistrophe, and the same number in each
phrase. The phrases vary in length from three syllables to nine, and all but
one end in *a.*

Advent Sequence

SALUS aeterna,
Indeficiens mundi vita;

Lux sempiterna,
Et redemptio vere nostra;

Condolens humana
Perire saecla,
Per temptantis numina,
Non linquens excelsa
Adisti ima,
Propria clementia.

Mox tua spontanea
Gratia
Assumens humana,
Quae fuerant perdita
Omnia
Salvasti terrea,
Ferens mundo gaudia.

Tu animas et corpora
Nostra, Christe, expia,

Ut possideas lucida
Nosmet habitacula.

Adventu primo justifica,

In secundo nosque libera;

Ut, cum facta
Luce magna,
Judicabis omnia,

Compti stola
Incorrupta
Nosmet tua subsequamur

Mox vestigia
Quocumque visa.

[87]

ANONYMOUS
O Roma nobilis
TENTH CENTURY

The fine poem, *O Roma nobilis*, probably written at Verona some time in the tenth century, is a song for pilgrims to the tombs of Saint Peter and Saint Paul at Rome. Its construction is very regular. Each stanza has six lines, written on one rhyme, the same rhyme being used in the first and last stanzas. Each line is an accentual dactylic tetrameter, with a strong pause after the second foot. This metre was a favourite both in secular Medieval Latin verse and in hymnody.

Pilgrims' song

O ROMA nobilis, orbis et domina,
Cunctarum urbium excellentissima,
Roseo martyrum sanguine rubea,
Albis et virginum liliis candida,
Salutem dicimus tibi per omnia,
Te benedicimus: salve per saecula.

Petre, tu praepotens caelorum claviger,
Vota precantium exaudi jugiter.
Cum bis sex tribuum sederis arbiter,
Factus placabilis judica leniter.
Teque petentibus nunc temporaliter
Ferto suffragia misericorditer.

O Paule, suscipe nostra precamina,
Cujus philosophos vicit industria.
Factus oeconomus in domo regia
Divini muneris appone fercula,
Ut, quae repleverit te sapientia,
Ipsa nos repleat tua per dogmata.

ANONYMOUS
O admirabile Veneris idolum

TENTH CENTURY

This poem, like *O Roma nobilis*, was probably written at Verona during the tenth century, perhaps by the same author. It is constructed on exactly the same plan, except that each stanza has a different rhyme and the second stanza an extra line. In content, it is very different from *O Roma nobilis*, being a clerk's lament on the abduction of a favourite acolyte. It is found in the *Cambridge Songs*. Either the third or the fourth line of the second stanza, as Sir Stephen Gaselee remarks, "may be an addition by an early copyist who wished to show his learning".

Song

O ADMIRABILE Veneris idolum,
Cujus materiae nihil est frivolum,
Archos te protegat, qui stellas et polum
Fecit, et maria condidit et solum.
Furis ingenio non sentias dolum:
Clotho te diligat, quae bajulat colum.

Salvato puerum non per hypothesim,
Sed firmo pectore deprecor Lachesim,
Sororem Atropos, ne curet haeresim.
Neptunum comitem habeas et Thetim,
Cum vectus fueris per fluvium Thesim.
Quo fugis, amabo, cum te dilexerim?
Miser quid faciam, cum te non viderim?

Dura materies ex matris ossibus
Creavit homines jactis lapidibus,
Ex quibus unus est iste puerulus,
Qui lacrimabiles non curat gemitus.
Cum tristis fuero, gaudebit aemulus:
Ut cerva rugio, cum fugit hinnulus.

ANONYMOUS

Advertite, omnes populi

TENTH CENTURY

The *Cambridge Songs* include a number of light secular poems in liturgical dress. One of the most interesting of these is a cleverly written version of a well-known folk-tale. It tells how the wife of a Swabian, during his absence at sea, gives birth to a child by another man. On her husband's return, she tells him that the child was the offspring of some snow which she had swallowed. Five years later, the Swabian goes to sea again, taking the "snow-child" with him, and sells him into slavery. On his return, he tells his wife that the child melted away under the tropical sun.

The story is cast in the form of a prose Sequence of the late tenth century. It consists of five strophes and antistrophes, with a coda. The last two strophes are identical in form, the others of different forms, but each strophe corresponds exactly in length with its antistrophe, phrase for phrase. There is no rhyme.

Burlesque Sequence

ADVERTITE,
Omnes populi,
Ridiculum;
Et audite quomodo
Suevum mulier
Et ipse illam
Defraudaret.

Constantiae
Civis Suevulus
Trans aequora
Gazam portans navibus
Domi conjugem
Lascivam nimis
Relinquebat.

Vix remige
Triste secat mare,
Ecce subito

Orta tempestate,
Furit pelagus,
Certant flamina,
Tolluntur fluctus,
Post multaque exsulem
Vagum littore
Longinquo notus
Exponebat.

Nec interim
Domi vacat conjux.
Mimi aderant,
Juvenes sequuntur.
Quos et immemor
Viri exsulis
Excepit gaudens,
Atque nocte proxima
Praegnans filium
Injustum fudit
Justo die.

Duobus
Volutis annis
　　Exsul dictus
　　Revertitur.
　　Occurrit
Infida conjux,
　　Secum trahens
　　Puerulum.
Datis osculis
Maritus illi,
"De quo", inquit, "puerum
　　Istum habeas?
　　Dic, aut extrema
　　Patieris."

　　At illa
Maritum timens
　　Dolos versat
　　In omnia.
　　"Mi", tandem,
"Mi conjux", inquit,
　　"Una vice
　　In Alpibus,
Nive sitiens
Exstinxi sitim.
Inde, ergo gravida
　　Istum puerum
　　Damnoso foetu
　　Heu gignebam."

Anni post haec quinque
Transierunt aut plus,
Et mercator vagus
Instauravit remos :
Ratim quassam reficit,
　　Vela alligat,

Et nivis natum
　　Duxit secum.

Transfretato mari
Producebat natum,
Et pro arrabone
Mercatori tradens,
Centum libras accipit,
　　Atque vendito
　　Infante dives
　　Revertitur.

Ingressusque domum
Ad uxorem ait:
"Consolare conjux,
Consolare cara.
Natum tuum perdidi,
　　Quem non ipsa tu
　　Me magis quidem
　　Dilexisti.

Tempestate orta
Nos ventosus furor
In vadosas syrtes
Nimis fessos egit,
Et nos omnes graviter
　　Torret sol at il-
　　Le nivis natus
　　Liquescebat."

　　Sic perfidam
Suevus conjugem
　　Deluserat.
Sic fraus fraudem vicerat:
　　Nam quem genuit
　　Nix, recte hunc sol
　　Liquefecit.

ANONYMOUS
Jam, dulcis amica
TENTH CENTURY

The anonymous *Jam, dulcis amica*, one of the most famous of Medieval
Latin love-songs, is from the *Cambridge Songs*. Its metre is irregular, most
of the lines having nine syllables, the others ten. The trochaic foot pre-
dominates, but iambic, dactylic, and anapaestic feet also occur. All the lines
rhyme by couplets, some of the rhymes being double.

The poem, which anticipates the French *pastourelle* in more than its date,
is in dialogue form, the sixth and eighth stanzas being spoken by the
woman, the remainder by the man. Many of its phrases are drawn from the
Song of Songs, from which the eighth stanza is taken almost verbatim.

Love-dialogue

"JAM, dulcis amica, venito,
Quam sicut cor meum diligo;
Intra in cubiculum meum,
Ornamentis cunctis onustum.

Ibi sunt sedilia strata
Et domus velis ornata;
Floresque in domo sparguntur,
Herbaeque fragrantes miscentur.

Est ibi mensa apposita,
Universis cibis onusta;
Ibi clarum vinum abundat
Et quicquid te, cara, delectat.

Ibi sonant dulces symphoniae,
Inflantur et altius tibiae;
Ibi puer et docta puella
Pangunt tibi carmina bella.

Hic cum plectro citharam tangit,
Illa melos cum lyra pangit;
Portantque ministri pateras
Pigmentatis poculis plenas."

"Non me juvat tantum convivium
Quantum post dulce colloquium,
Nec rerum tantarum ubertas
Ut dilecta familiaritas."

"Jam nunc veni, soror electa
Et prae cunctis mihi dilecta,
Lux meae clara pupillae
Parsque major animae meae."

"Ego fui sola in silva,
Et dilexi loca secreta;
Frequenter effugi tumultum,
Et vitavi populum multum."

"Karissima, noli tardare;
Studeamus nos nunc amare;
Sine te non potero vivere :
Jam decet amorem perficere.

Quid juvat deferre, electa,
Quae sunt tamen post facienda?
Fac cita quod eris factura;
In me non est aliqua mora."

ANONYMOUS
Levis exsurgit zephyrus
TENTH CENTURY

The charming love-song, *Levis exsurgit zephyrus*, is found only in the *Cambridge Songs*. It is written in accentual Ambrosian stanzas, rhyming by couplets, the last two stanzas being in monorhyme. Sometimes called *planctus monialis*, it is quite likely to have been written by a nun. Nuns certainly wrote love-songs, as we find that they were forbidden to do so by a capitulary of Charlemagne dating from 789.

Love-song

LEVIS exsurgit zephyrus,
   Et sol procedit tepidus;
   Jam terra sinus aperit,
Dulcore suo diffluit.

Ver purpuratum exiit,
Ornatus suos induit;
Aspergit terram floribus,
Ligna silvarum frondibus.

Struunt lustra quadrupedes,
Et dulces nidos volucres;
Inter ligna florentia
Sua decantant gaudia.

Quod oculis dum video
Et auribus dum audio,
Heu, pro tantis gaudiis
Tantis inflor suspiriis.

Cum mihi sola sedeo,
Et haec revolvens palleo,
Si forte caput sublevo,
Nec audio nec video.

Tu saltim, veris gratia,
Exaudi et considera
Frondes, flores, et gramina;
Nam mea languet anima.

WIPO

fl. 1030

The Burgundian priest, Wipo, who was chaplain to the Emperor Conrad II, is generally credited with the authorship of the fine Easter Sequence, *Victimae paschali.*

Its construction is typical of the transitional Sequences of the eleventh century. It is written in rhythmical prose, the various phrases of each strophe and its antistrophe corresponding exactly. The single *a* assonance of *Salus aeterna* has been replaced by varied assonances in the first half of the poem, and by double rhymes in the second half. The predominance of lines of seven and eight syllables points forward to the regular Sequences of the twelfth century.

Contrary to *Salus aeterna*, *Victimae paschali*, like German Sequences in general, has no coda. On the other hand, in common with many other early German Sequences, it has a proem. In later versions, the question:

> *Dic nobis, Maria,*
> *Quid vidisti in via?*

is repeated before *Angelicos testes* and again before *Surrexit Christus*. The three answers to the question were in course of time allocated to three soloists, the remainder of the text being sung by a chorus. Used in this way at the Easter Sepulchre ceremonies, *Victimae paschali* played an important part in the foundation of the liturgical drama.

Easter Sequence

VICTIMAE paschali laudes
Immolent Christiani.

Agnus redemit oves:
Christus innocens patri
Reconciliavit peccatores.

Mors et vita duello
Conflixere mirando:
Dux vitae mortuus regnat vivus.

Dic nobis, Maria,
Quid vidisti in via?
"Sepulcrum Christi viventis
Et gloriam vidi resurgentis;

Angelicos testes,
Sudarium et vestes;
Surrexit Christus spes mea,
Praecedet suos in Galilaea."

Credendum est magis soli
Mariae veraci
Quam Judaeorum turbae fallaci.

Scimus Christum surrexisse
Ex mortuis vere.
Tu nobis, victor rex, miserere.

ANONYMOUS
Laetabundus

ELEVENTH CENTURY

We have another example of the transitional Sequences of the eleventh century in *Laetabundus*, in which development has been carried, in some respects, farther than in *Victimae paschali*. It is no longer in rhythmical prose, but in verse. The rhyming is not yet carried all through, nor is it symmetrically placed, but its placing is approaching symmetry. Other features of the poem herald the approach of the regular Sequence of the twelfth century. Thus there is neither proem nor coda, the trochaic foot is used almost throughout, the last line of each strophe is shorter than the others, and there is a decided tendency for a monorhyme to run through each strophe and a different monorhyme through each antistrophe, with the exception of the last lines. These end in *a* throughout, reminding one of the single assonance of earlier Sequences like *Salus aeterna*.

Laetabundus was particularly popular in England and France. Evidence of its popularity is to be found, *inter alia*, in the existence of parodies, such as *Or hi parra* [146].

Christmas Sequence

LAETABUNDUS
Exsultet fidelis chorus:
Alleluia.

Regem regum
Intactae profudit thorus,
Res miranda.

Angelus consilii
Natus est de virgine,
Sol de stella.

Sol occasum nesciens,
Stella semper rutilans,
Semper clara.

Sicut sidus radium,
Profert virgo filium
Pari forma.

Neque sidus radio,
Neque mater filio
Fit corrupta.

Cedrus alta Libani
Conformatur hyssopo
Valle nostra.

Verbum, mens altissimi,
Corporari passum est
Carne sumpta.

Isaïas cecinit,
Synagoga meminit;
Nunquam tamen desinit
Esse caeca.

Si non suis vatibus,
Credat vel gentilibus
Sibyllinis versibus
Haec praedicta.

Infelix, propera:
Crede vel vetera.
Cur damnaberis,
Gens misera?

Quem docet littera
Natum considera.
Ipsum genuit
Puerpera.

HILDEBERT

1056—✝ 1133

HILDEBERT OF LAVARDIN, Bishop of Le Mans and in his old age
Archbishop of Tours, is one of the most important figures in the literature
of the Middle Ages. A man of excellent taste, with a profound veneration
for the past glories of Rome and steeped in the Latin classics, he wrote
quantitative verses and prose letters practically faultless from the classical
standpoint. At the same time, he was a master of accentual Latin verse,
which in his hands attained its fully developed form, with regularly placed
double rhymes and a regular caesura. His famous *Me receptet Sion illa*,
which forms the concluding section of a longer poem, provides an excellent
illustration of his polished technique. With regard to the rhyme in the
last couplet, J. M. Neale asserts that "the mediaeval pronunciation of
Alleluia gave to the penultimate syllable the sound of *i*, not as we do, of
u", but I do not know his authority for this statement.

The Heavenly Jerusalem

ME receptet Sion illa,
    Sion David urbs tranquilla,
    Cujus faber auctor lucis,
Cujus portae lignum crucis,
Cujus claves lingua Petri,
Cujus cives semper laeti,
Cujus muri lapis vivus,
Cujus custos rex festivus,
In hac urbe lux solennis,
Ver aeternum, pax perennis;
In hac odor implens caelos,
In hac semper festum melos;
Non est ibi corruptela,
Non defectus, non querela;
Non minuti, non deformes,
Omnes Christo sunt conformes.

Urbs caelestis, urbs beata
Super petram collocata;

Urbs in portu satis tuto,
De longinquo te saluto;
Te saluto, te suspiro,
Te affecto, te requiro.
Quantum tui gratulantur,
Quam festive convivantur,
Quis affectus eos stringat,
Aut quae gemma muros pingat,
Quis calcedon, quis jacynthus,
Norunt illi qui sunt intus.
In plateis hujus urbis
Sociatus piis turbis
Cum Moyse et Elia
Pium cantem Alleluia.

WILLIAM IX OF AQUITAINE

1071 — † 1127

WILLIAM IX, Duke of Aquitaine and Count of Poitou, the earliest of the troubadours, was a man of loose living and was several times excommunicated. His licentious adventures are commemorated in his verse, but the poem given here is in a very different strain. Formerly supposed to have been written by him before setting out on a Crusade, it is now believed to refer to a pilgrimage which he was planning to Compostela, and which he carried out in 1117.

Its technique is characteristic of the early Provençal lyric. It is written in Ambrosian stanzas with masculine rhymes. The first three lines of each stanza are in monorhyme, the rhyme changing from stanza to stanza, but the final lines rhyme together throughout the poem. This arrangement of rhymes was extremely common in popular dance-songs, and remained so for centuries. The recurrent rhyme at the end of each stanza gave an easy cue to the chorus to begin their refrain, which ended with the same rhyme. The present poem, however, like the great majority of Old Provençal poems, has no refrain. On the other hand, it has a common feature of troubadour poetry—a *tornada*.

Pos de chantar is a *vers*—a genre which appears to differ only in name from the *chanso*, the latter term being more popular with the later troubadours.

Vers

Pos de chantar m'es pres talenz,
Farai un vers, don sui dolenz:
Mais non serai obedienz
En Peitau ni en Lemozi.

Qu'era m'en irai en eisil;
En gran paor, en gran peril,
En guerra laissarai mon fil,
E faran li mal siei vezin.

Lo departirs m'es aitan grieus
Del seignoratge de Peitieus.
En garda lais Folcon d'Angieus
Tota la terra e son cozi.

Si Folcos d'Angieus no·l socor,
E·l reis de cui ieu tenc m'onor,
Faran li mal tut li plusor,
Felon Gascon et Angevi.

Si ben non es savis ni pros,
Cant ieu serai partiz de vos,
Vias l'auran tornat en jos,
Car lo veiran jov' e mesqui.

Mercè quier a mon compaignon;
S'anc li fi tort qu'il m'o perdon;
Et ieu prec en Jesu del tron,
Et en romans et en lati.

De proeza e de joi fui,
Mais ara partem ambedui;
Et eu irai m'en a scellui
On tut peccador troban fi.

Mout ai estat cuendes e gais,
Mas nostre Seigner no·l vol mais;
Ar non puesc plus soffrir lo fais,
Tant soi aprochatz de la fi.

Tot ai guerpit cant amar sueill,
Cavalaria et orgueill;
E pos Dieu platz, tot o acueill,
E prec li que·m reteng' am si.

Toz mos amics prec a la mort
Que vengan tut e m'onren fort,
Qu'eu ai avut joi e deport
Loing e pres et e mon aizi.

Aissi guerpisc joi e deport
E vair e gris e sembeli.

ABELARD
1079 — † 1142

The story of Abelard's brilliant but unhappy career, and of his love for Heloisa, is too well known to need more than passing mention here. His numerous hymns, written for the use of Heloisa and her nuns at the Abbey of the Paraclete, are in a great variety of metres. In *O quanta qualia*, his best known hymn, he uses the accentual dactyl to great effect. The poem is written in quatrains, the lines of which rhyme in couplets. As in all his hymns, the rhymes are simple. In his *Christiani, plaudite*, he uses an uncommon trochaic metre, with two interwoven rhymes to each stanza. As in the *cantiones* of the thirteenth century, a refrain is embedded in the stanzas.

The Sabbath

O QUANTA qualia sunt illa sabbata
Quae semper celebrat superna curia!
Quae fessis requies, quae merces fortibus,
Cum erit omnia Deus in omnibus!

Vere Jerusalem est illa civitas,
Cujus pax jugis est summa jucunditas,
Ubi non praevenit rem desiderium,
Nec desiderio minus est praemium.

Quis rex, quae curia, quale palatium,
Quae pax, quae requies, quod illud gaudium,
Hujus participes exponant gloriae,
Si quantum sentiunt possint exprimere.

Nostrum est interim mentem erigere,
Et totis patriam votis appetere,
Et ad Jerusalem a Babylonia
Post longa regredi tandem exsilia.

Illic molestiis finitis omnibus
Securi cantica Sion cantabimus,
Et juges gratias de donis gratiae
Beata referet plebs tibi, Domine.

Illic ex sabbato succedet sabbatum,
Perpes laetitia sabbatizantium,
Nec ineffabiles cessabunt jubili
Quos decantabimus et nos et angeli.

Perenni Domino perpes sit gloria,
Ex quo sunt, per quem sunt, in quo sunt omnia;
Ex quo sunt, pater est; per quem sunt, filius;
In quo sunt, patris et filii spiritus.

Easter

CHRISTIANI, plaudite,
  (*Resurrexit Dominus*)
  Victo mortis principe
Christus imperat.
Victori occurrite,
  Qui nos liberat.

Superato zabulo,
  (*Resurrexit Dominus*)
Spoliato barathro
  Suos eruit;
Stipatus angelico
  Coetu rediit.

Fraus in hamo fallitur,
(*Resurrexit Dominus*)
Quae dum carne vescitur
  Circumposita,
Virtute transfigitur
  Carni insita.

Captivatis inferis,
(*Resurrexit Dominus*)
Ditatisque superis
  Caelum jubilat;
Hymnis, psalmis, canticis,
  Terra resonat.

Deo patri gloria,
(*Resurrexit Dominus*)
Salus et victoria
  Christo Domini,
Par honor per saecula
  Sit spiritui.

MARCABRUN
fl. 1130—1148

MARCABRUN, one of the earlier troubadours, is distinguished from all others by a pronounced misogynism. One of the first exponents of the deliberately obscure style which reached a climax in the works of Arnaut Daniel, he could be admirably clear when he liked, as in the two poems given here.

The first of these, *L'autrier, jost' una sebissa*, is the oldest pastoral poem in any Romance language. It is written in *coblas doblas*, with two rhymes to each stanza, the second being retained throughout. It will also be noticed that the fourth line of each stanza ends with the key-word, *vilana*. The lines are seven-syllabled, all with feminine endings.

Marcabrun's Crusade-song, *Pax in nomine Domini*, was probably written in 1147, to bring recruits to the army of Alfonso VII of Castile in his expedition against the Almohades. The Pope had given to the expedition the status and privileges usually limited to a Palestinian crusade; and Marcabrun, in vigorous style, points out the advantage of having so near at hand a *lavador*, or washing-place, where men may be cleansed from their sins by fighting in the cause of God.

The versification of the poem is interesting. Each stanza has nine lines and six rhymes, this being the only poem in which Marcabrun uses so many in one stanza. Variety is introduced by the employment of one short line in each stanza, which is composed otherwise of octosyllables. The rhymes are all masculine, and the key-word, *lavador*, occurs as a rhyme-word in the same position in each stanza. Three of the rhymes are *dissolutas*, and the poem is written in *coblas doblas*, except that the order of the last two rhymes is changed in alternate stanzas. Only one fresh rhyme is introduced after the first stanza.

Pastorela

L'AUTRIER, jost' una sebissa,
    Trobei pastora mestissa,
    De joy e de sen massissa;
E fon filha de vilana:
Cap' e gonel' e pelissa
Vest e camiza treslissa,
Sotlars e caussas de lana.

Ves leis vinc per la planissa:
"Toza", fi·m eu, "res faitissa,
Dol ai gran del ven que·us fissa."
"Senher", so dis la vilana,
"Merce Deu e ma noyrissa,
Pauc m'o pretz si·l vens m'erissa
Qu' alegreta sui e sana."

"Toza", fi·m eu, "causa pia,
Destoutz me suy de la via
Per far a vos companhia,
Quar aitals toza vilana
No pot ses plazen paria
Pastorgar tanta bestia
En aital luec, tan soldana."

"Don", dis ela, "qui que·m sia,
Ben conosc sen o folia;
La vostra parelharia,
Senher", so dis la vilana,
"La on se tanh si s'estia,
Que tals la cuj' en bailia
Tener, no n'a mas l'ufana."

"Toza de gentil afaire,
Cavaliers fon vostre paire
Que·us engenret en la maire,
Tan fo·n corteza vilana,
C'on plus vos gart m'etz belaire,
E per vostre joy m'esclaire,
Si fossetz un pauc humana."

"Senher, mon linh e mon aire
Vey revertir e retraire
Al vezoig e a l'araire.
Senher", so dis la vilana,
"Mas tals se fai cavalgaire
C'atrestal deuria faire
Los seis jorns de la setmana."

"Toza", fi·m eu, "gentils fada
Vos adastret, quan fos nada,
D'una beutat esmerada
Sobre tot' autra vilana.
E seria·us ben doblada
Si·m vezi' una vegada
Sobiran e vos sotrana."

"Senher, tan m'avetz lauzada
Pois en pretz m'avetz levada,
Qu'ar vostr' amor tan m'agrada,
Senher", so dis la vilana,
"Per so n'auretz per soudada
Al partir 'bada, fol, bada',
E la muz' a meliana."

"Toza, felh cor e salvatge
Adomesg' om per usatge.
Ben conosc, al trespassatge,
Qu'ab aital toza vilana
Pot hom far ric companhatge
Ab amistat de coratge,
Quan l'us l'autre non engana."

"Don, hom cochatz de folatge
Jur' e pliu e promet gatge.
Si·m fariatz homenatge;
Senher", so dis la vilana,
"Mas ges, per un pauc d'intratge
No vuelh mon despiuzelhatge
Camjar, per nom de putana."

"Toza, tota creatura
Revertis a sa natura:
Parelhar parelhadura
Devem, eu e vos, vilana,
A l'abric lonc la pastura,
Que mielhs n'estaretz segura
Per far la causa doussana."

"Don, oc; mas segon dreitura
Cerca fols la folatura,
Cortes cortez' aventura,
E·l vilas ab la vilana;
En tal loc fai sen fraitura
On hom non garda mezura,
So ditz la gens anciana."

"Belha, de vostra figura
No·n vi autra plus tafura
Ni de son cor plus trefana."

"Don, lo cavecs vos ahura,
Que tals bad' en la peintura
Qu'autre n'espera la mana."

Crusade-song

Pax in nomine Domini!
　　Fetz Marcabrus lo vers e·l so.
　　　　Aujatz que di:
Cum nos a fait per sa doussor
Lo seingnorius celestiaus
Probet de nos un lavador
C'anc, fors outramar, no·n fo taus
En de lai enves Josaphas;
E d'aqest de sai vos conort.

Lavar de ser e de maiti
Nos deuriam, segon razo;
　　　　Ie·us o afi.
Chascus a del lavar legor;
Domentre q'el es sas e saus,
Deuria anar al lavador,
Que·ns es verais medicinaus;
Que s'abans anam a la mort
D'aut desus aurem alberc bas.

Mas escarsedatz e no-fes
Part joven de son compaigno.
　　　　A! cals dols es
Que tuich volon lai li plusor
Don lo gazains es enfernaus.
S'anz non correm al lavador
C'aiam la bocha ni·ls huoills claus,
Non i a un d'orguoill tant gras
C'al morir non trob contrafort.

Qe·l seigner que sap tot qant es,
E sap tot cant er e c'anc fo,
　　　　Nos hi promes

Honor e nom d'emperador;
E·il beutatz sera, sabetz caus
De cels qu'iran al lavador?
Plus que l'estela gauzignaus,
Ab sol qe vengem Dieu del tort
Qe·ill fant sai, e lai vas Domas.

Probet del lignatge Caï,
Del primeiran home fello,
      A tans aissi
C'us a Dieu non porta honor.
Veirem qui·ll er amics coraus;
C'ab la vertut del lavador
Nos sera Jhesus comunaus,
E tornem los garssos atras
Q'en agur crezon et en sort.

Cil luxurios corna-vi,
Coita-disnar, bufa-tizo,
      Crup-en-cami
Remanran inz el folpidor.
Dieus vol los arditz e·ls suaus
Asajar a son lavador,
E cil gaitaran los ostaus
E trobaran fort contrafort:
So per q'ieu a lor anta·ls chas.

En Espaigna e sai lo marques
E cill del Temple Salamo
      Sofron lo pes
E·l fais de l'orguoill paganor,
Per que jovens cuoill avol laus.
E·l critz per aqest lavador
Versa sobre·ls plus rics captaus,
Fraitz, faillitz, de proeza las,
Que non amon joi ni deport.

Desnaturat son li Frances,
Si de l'afar Dieu dizon no,
Q'ie·us ai comes.
Antiocha, pretz e valor
Sai plora Guiana e Peitaus.
Dieus, seigner, al tieu lavador
L'arma del comte met en paus;
E sai gart Peitieus e Niort
Lo segner qui ressors del vas.

ANONYMOUS

? 12TH CENTURY

SAINT BERNARD OF CLAIRVAUX is the traditional author of *Dulcis Jesu memoria*, a small part of which—not the whole of it, as is implied by Sir Stephen Gaselee and Dr E. J. Martin—is known as the *Rosy Sequence*.

From the point of view of form, the poem is not a Sequence at all, as it is written in Ambrosian stanzas—the Office Hymn form *par excellence*—and its stanzas are not grouped in pairs, either by form or by thought; but part of it was adopted as a Sequence because it met the demands of a particular period.

Every age has its favourite devotion. To-day it is the "Little Flower", a few years ago it was Saint Joan of Arc, at the end of the fifteenth century it was the Name of Jesus. When the feast of the Holy Name was instituted about the year 1500, the beauty of *Dulcis Jesu memoria* and its obvious suitability caused a departure from tradition, and the first seven and last two of its forty-two stanzas were adopted at Salisbury as a Sequence for the new feast. Some of these stanzas, with others from the same poem, found a more liturgically correct home among the Office Hymns of the Sarum Breviary and still appear in the Roman Breviary.

The versification of the *Rosy Sequence* is typical of the whole poem from which it is taken. Each stanza is in monorhyme. In the third stanza, the rhyme is treble. In the others, it is two-syllabled, but is not double in the ordinary sense, as the eighth syllable in each line is stressed in theory only. The text given here is taken without change from the Sarum Gradual of 1532, except that, in the seventh stanza, *Maria* has been substituted for an obvious misprint in the original. This poem is generally quoted with its first two words in reverse order.

The Rosy Sequence

DULCIS Jesu memoria
Dans vera cordis gaudia,
Et super mel et omnia
Ejus dulcis praesentia.

Nil canitur suavius,
Nil auditur jucundius,
Nil cogitatur dulcius
Quam Jesus, Dei filius.

Jesu, spes paenitentibus,
Quam pius es petentibus,
Quam bonus te quaerentibus,
Sed quid invenientibus!

Jesu, dulcedo cordium,
Fons vere, lumen mentium,
Excedis omne gaudium
Et omne desiderium.

Nec lingua potest dicere,
Nec litterae exprimere;
Expertus novit tenere
Quid sit Jesum diligere.

Jesum quaeram in lectulo,
Clauso cordis cubiculo;
Privatim et in publico
Quaeram amore sedulo.

Cum Maria diluculo
Jesum quaeram in tumulo;
Cordis clamore querulo,
Mente quaeram, non oculo.

Jesus ad patrem rediit,
Regnum caeleste subiit;
Cor meum a me transiit,
Post Jesum simul abiit.

Jam prosequamur laudibus
Hymnis Jesum et precibus,
Ut nos donet caelestibus
Cum justis frui sedibus.

JAUFRE RUDEL

fl. 1150

Practically all that is known for certain about the life of the troubadour
Jaufre Rudel is that he was Seigneur, or Prince, of Blaye, and that he was
in Palestine in 1148. The well-known story of his falling in love with the
Countess of Tripoli without seeing her, of his becoming a crusader in
order to see her, and of his dying in her arms is a legend, evidently drawn
from his poems, in which he speaks of his love for a distant lady in Saracen
lands, and of his desire to become a pilgrim in order to see her.

His six poems are all of very simple construction. His lines would all be
termed octosyllabic in English, and his rhymes, as with all the early
troubadours, are generally masculine.

The *chanso, Lanquan li jorn,* which is one of his most attractive poems,
is written in *coblas unissonans,* with four rhymes, the last rhyme of each
stanza being *dissoluta.* It will be noticed that the word *lonh*—the key-word
of the poem—occurs as a rhyme twice in each stanza. The stanzas are tripartite, each of them consisting of two *pedes* of two lines each, followed by
a *cauda* of three lines. Tripartition of the stanza is almost a rule among
Rudel's successors.

Chanso

LANQUAN li jorn son lonc en may,
M'es belhs dous chans d'auzelhs de lonh;
E quan mi suy partitz de lay,
Remembra·m d'un' amor de lonh.
Vau de talan embroncx e clis,
Si que chans ni flors d'albespis
No·m platz plus que l'yverns gelatz.

Be tenc lo senhor per veray,
Per qu'ieu veirai l'amor de lonh;
Mas per un ben que m'en eschay,
N'ai dos mals, quar tant m'es de lonh.
Ai! car me fos lai pelegris,
Si que mos fustz e mos tapis
Fos pels sieus belhs huelhs remiratz!

Be·m parra joys quan li querray,
Per amor Dieu, l'alberc de lonh:
E, s'a lieys platz, alberguarai
Pres de lieys, si be·m suy de lonh.
Adoncs parra·l parlamens fis,
Quan drutz lonhdas er tan vezis
Qu'ab bels digz jauzira solatz.

Iratz e gauzens m'en partray,
S'ieu ja la vey, l'amor de lonh:
Mas non sai quoras la veyrai,
Car trop son nostras terras lonh.
Assatz hi a pas e camis,
E per aisso no·n suy devis;
Mas tot sia cum a Dieu platz!

Ja mais d'amor no·m jauziray
Si no·m jau d'est'amor de lonh,
Que gensor ni melhor no·n sai
Ves nulha part, ni pres ni lonh.
Tant es sos pretz verais e fis
Que lay el reng dels Sarrazis
Fos hieu per lieys chaitius clamatz!

Dieus que fetz tot quant ve ni vai
E formet sest'amor de lonh
Mi don poder, que cor ieu n'ai,
Qu'ieu veya sest'amor de lonh,
Verayamen, en tals aizis,
Si que la cambra e·l jardis
Mi resembles tos temps palatz!

Ver ditz qui m'apella lechay
Ni deziron d'amor de lonh,
Car nulhs autres joys tan no·m play
Cum jauzimens d'amor de lonh.
Mas so qu'ieu vuelh m'es atahis,
Qu'enaissi·m fadet mos pairis
Qu'ieu ames e no fos amatz.

Mas so q'ieu vuoill m'es atahis.
Totz sia mauditz lo pairis
Qe·m fadet q'ieu non fos amatz!

ADAM OF SAINT VICTOR

c. 1110 — 1180

Nothing is known of the life of Adam, the most prolific of all Sequence-
writers, except that he was probably a Breton and that he became a canon
of the Abbey of Saint Victor, near Paris, about 1130. His *Sequence for
Saint Agnes's Day* provides an excellent example of his style. It is perfectly regular in every respect, with double rhymes throughout. The *a*
rhyme which ended every strophe of *Laetabundus* has been replaced by
varied rhymes, but the antiphony has been made very apparent by the use
(with one exception) of the same end-rhyme for each strophe and the
corresponding antistrophe. Otherwise, practically every strophe is in
monorhyme, a different monorhyme being used for the antistrophe. A few
lines are dactylic or iambic, but the great majority are trochaic. It will be
noticed that most of the strophes are composed of two or more trochaic
lines of eight syllables, followed by one of seven syllables.

Sequence for Saint Agnes's Day

ANIMEMUR ad agonem,
Recolentes passionem
Gloriosae virginis.
Contrectantes sacrum florem,
Respiremus ad odorem
Respersae dulcedinis.

Pulchra, prudens, et illustris,
Jam duobus Agnes lustris
Addebat triennium.
Proles amat hanc praefecti,
Sed ad ejus virgo flecti
Respuit arbitrium.

Mira vis fidei,
Mira virginitas,
Mira virginei
Cordis integritas.

Sic Dei filius
Nutu mirabili
Se mirabilius
Prodit in fragili.

Languet amans, cubat lecto,
Languor notus fit praefecto,
    Maturat remedia.

Offert multa, spondet plura,
Periturus peritura,
    Sed vilescunt omnia.

Nudam prostituit
Praeses flagitiis,
Quam Christus induit
Comarum fimbriis
Stolaque caelesti.

Caelestis nuntius
Assistit propius;
Cella libidinis
Fit locus luminis:
Turbantur incesti.

Caecus amans indignatur,
Et irrumpens praefocatur
    A maligno spiritu.

Luget pater, lugent cuncti,
Roma flevit pro defuncti
    Juvenis interitu.

Suscitatur ab Agnete,
Turba fremit indiscrete:
    Rogum parant virgini.

Rogus ardens reos urit,
In furentes flamma furit,
    Dans honorem numini.

Grates agens salvatori,
Guttur offert haec lictori;
Nec ad horam timet mori,
    Puritatis conscia.

Agnes, agni salutaris
Stans ad dextram, gloriaris,
Et parentes consolaris,
    Invitans ad gaudia.

Ne te flerent ut defunctam,
Jam caelesti sponso junctam,
His sub agni forma suam
Revelavit atque tuam
    Virginalem gloriam.

Nos ab agno salutari
Non permitte separari,
Cui te totam consecrasti,
Cujus ope tu curasti
    Nobilem Constantiam.

Vas electum, vas honoris,
Incorrupti flos odoris,
Angelorum grata choris,
Honestatis et pudoris
    Formam praebes saeculo.

Palma fruens triumphali,
Flore vernans virginali,
Nos indignos speciali
Fac sanctorum generali
    Vel subscribi titulo.

ANONYMOUS
Lou samedi a soir
MID-TWELFTH CENTURY

This simple but fine poem is typical of the early French *chanson de toile*. Its lines show a mixture of assonance and full rhyme, with the unusual feature that each even stanza uses the same monorhyme as the preceding stanza. As in the early French epics, the lines are decasyllabic. The caesura, however, which in the epics generally falls after the fourth syllable, here falls after the sixth.

Chanson de toile

Lou samedi a soir, fat la semainne,
Gaiete et Orïour, serors germainnes,
Main et main vont bagnier a la fontainne.
    Vante l'ore et li raim crollent:
    Ki s'antraimment soweif dorment.

L'anfes Gerairs revient de la cuitainne,
S'ait chosie Gaiete sor la fontainne,
Antre ses bras l'ait pris, soueif l'a strainte.
    Vante l'ore et li raim crollent:
    Ki s'antraimment soueif dorment.

"Quant avras, Orrïour, de l'ague prise,
Reva toi an arriere, bien seis la vile:
Je remanrai Gerairt ke bien me priset."
    Vante l'ore et li raim crollent:
    Ki s'antraimment soweif dorment.

Or s'en vat Orïous teinte et marrie;
Des euls s'an vat plorant, de cuer sospire,
Cant Gaie sa serour n'anmoinnet mie.
    Vante l'ore et li raim crollent:
    Ki s'antraimment soweif dorment.

"Laise", fait Orïour, "com mar fui nee!
J'ai laxiet ma serour an la vallee:
L'anfes Gerairs l'anmoine an sa contree."
    Vante l'ore et li raim crollent:
    Ki s'antraimment soweif dorment.

L'anfes Gerairs et Gaie s'an sont torneit:
Lor droit chemin ont pris vers la citeit.
Tantost com il i vint, l'ait espouseit.
    Vante l'ore et li raim crollent:
    Ki s'antraimment soweif dorment.

ANONYMOUS
Bele Doette
MID-TWELFTH CENTURY

Bele Doette is another fine *chanson de toile*. It exemplifies M. Jeanroy's
remark that the poems of this class are "épiques par le sujet, lyriques par le
rythme, dramatiques par le procédé d'exposition". The lines are again
decasyllabic, but the caesura falls after the fourth syllable.

Chanson de toile

BELE Doette as fenestres se siet,
Lit en un livre, mais au cuer ne l'en tient.
De son ami Doon li ressovient,
Q'en autres terres est alez tornoier.
    E or en ai dol.

Uns escuiers as degrez de la sale
Est dessenduz, s'est destrossé sa male.
Bele Doette les degrez en avale,
Ne cuide pas oïr novele male.
    E or en ai dol.

Bele Doette tantost li demanda:
"Ou est mes sires, que ne vi tel pieça?"
Cil ot tel duel que de pitié plora.
Bele Doette maintenant se pasma.
  E or en ai dol.

Bele Doette s'est en estant drecie,
Voit l'escuier, vers lui s'est adrecie;
En son cuer est dolante et correcie
Por son seignor, dont ele ne voit mie.
  E or en ai dol.

Bele Doette li prist a demander:
"Ou est mes sires, cui je doi tant amer?"
"En non Deu, dame, nel vos quier mais celer:
Morz est mes sires, ocis fu au joster,
  E or en ai dol."

Bele Doette a pris son duel a faire:
"Tant mar i fustes, cuens Do, frans, debonaire.
Por vostre amor vestirai je la haire,
Ne sor mon cors n'avra pelice vaire;
  E or en ai dol:
Por vos devenrai nonne en l'eglyse saint Pol.

Pos vos ferai une abbaïe tele
Qant iert li jors que la feste iert nomeie,
Se nus i vient qui ait s'amor fauseie,
Ja del mostier ne savera l'entreie,
  E or en ai dol:
Por vos devenrai nonne a l'eglise saint Pol."

Bele Doette prist s'abaiie a faire,
Qui mout est grande et ades sera maire:
Toz cels et celes vodra dedanz atraire
Qui por amor sevent peine et mal traire.
  E or en ai dol:
Por vos devenrai nonne a l'eglise saint Pol.

THE ARCHPOET

BORN *c.* 1130

The great Goliard known as the Archpoet, whose real name is not known, was of knightly birth and stood high in the favour of Rainald, Archbishop of Cologne and Chancellor to the Emperor Frederick Barbarossa. His *Confessio Goliae*, perhaps the most widely known of all secular poems in Medieval Latin, was written, as internal evidence shows, between 1162 and 1165. It is in the Goliardic metre—monorhymed quatrains with trochaic lines of thirteen syllables each and a caesura after the seventh syllable.

The Goliard's Confession

Aestuans intrinsecus ira vehementi,
In amaritudine loquor meae menti.
Factus de materia levis elementi,
Folio sum similis de quo ludunt venti.

Cum sit enim proprium viro sapienti
Supra petram ponere sedem fundamenti,
Stultus ego comparor fluvio labenti
Sub eodem aere nunquam permanenti.

Feror ego veluti sine nauta navis,
Ut per vias aeris vaga fertur avis.
Non me tenent vincula, non me tenet clavis,
Quaero mei similes et adjungor pravis.

Mihi cordis gravitas res videtur gravis;
Jocus est amabilis dulciorque favis.
Quicquid Venus imperat, labor est suavis,
Quae nunquam in cordibus habitat ignavis.

Via lata gradior more juventutis,
Implico me vitiis, immemor virtutis.
Voluptatis avidus magis quam salutis,
Mortuus in anima, curam gero cutis.

Praesul discretissime, veniam te precor:
Morte bona morior, dulci nece necor.
Meum pectus sauciat puellarum decor,
Et quas tactu nequeo saltem corde moechor.

Res est arduissima vincere naturam,
In aspectu virginis mentem esse puram;
Juvenes non possumus legem sequi duram,
Leviumque corporum non habere curam.

Quis in igne positus igne non uratur?
Quis Papiae demorans castus habeatur,
Ubi Venus digito juvenes venatur,
Oculis illaqueat, facie praedatur?

Si ponas Hippolytum hodie Papiae,
Non erit Hippolytus in sequenti die.
Veneris in thalamos ducunt omnes viae,
Non est in tot turribus turris Alethiae.

Secundo redarguor etiam de ludo,
Sed, cum ludus corpore me dimittat nudo,
Frigidus exterius mentis aestu sudo,
Tunc versus et carmina meliora cudo.

Tertio capitulo memoro tabernam:
Illam nullo tempore sprevi neque spernam,
Donec sanctos angelos venientes cernam,
Cantantes pro mortuis requiem aeternam.

Meum est propositum in taberna mori,
Ut sint vina proxima morientis ori.
Tunc cantabunt laetius angelorum chori:
"Sit Deus propitius huic potatori."

Poculis accenditur animi lucerna,
Cor imbutum nectare volat ad superna.
Mihi sapit dulcius vinum de taberna,
Quam quod aqua miscuit praesulis pincerna.

Ecce, meae proditor pravitatis fui,
De qua me redarguunt servientes tui;
Sed eorum nullus est accusator sui,
Quamvis velint ludere saeculoque frui.

Jam nunc in praesentia praesulis beati,
Secundum dominici regulam mandati,
Mittat in me lapidem, neque parcat vati,
Cujus non est animus conscius peccati.

Sum locutus contra me quicquid de me novi,
Et virus evomui quod tam diu fovi.
Vita vetus displicet, mores placent novi:
Homo videt faciem, sed cor patet Jovi.

Jam virtutes diligo, vitiis irascor,
Renovatus animo spiritu renascor.
Quasi modo genitus novo lacte pascor,
Ne sit meum amplius vanitatis vas cor.

Electe Coloniae, parce paenitenti,
Fac misericordiam veniam petenti,
Et da paenitentiam culpam confitenti.
Feram quicquid jusseris animo libenti.

Parcit enim subditis leo, rex ferarum,
Et est erga subditos immemor irarum.
Et vos idem facite, principes terrarum:
Quod caret dulcedine nimis est amarum.

BERNART DE VENTADORN

fl. 1150—1180

According to legend, Bernart de Ventadorn was the son of a stoker at the castle of the Viscount of Ventadorn, from which he had to flee for making love to the Viscountess. After spending some time at the court of that great protectress of troubadours, Eleanor of Aquitaine, he retired to the Abbey of Dalon, in Limousin, where he died.

His *chansos*, conspicuous for their melody, sincerity, and technical skill, entitle him to rank among the greatest of the troubadours.

In *Quant l'erba fresqu' e·l fuelha par* he uses the conventional "nature introduction" of Provençal poetry, but nevertheless displays a genuine appreciation of nature. The first half of each stanza is in octosyllables, the second half in decasyllables. Until then, the decasyllabic line had been rarely used outside the epic, and had never been used by William IX, Marcabrun, or Jaufre Rudel. The stanzas are *unissonans*, and the four rhymes all masculine.

The next poem, *Non es meravelha*, a charming song, is a *chanso redonda*. Its lines are octosyllabic and all its rhymes masculine.

Chanso

QUANT l'erba fresqu' e·l fuelha par
E la flors botona el verjan,
E·l rossinhols autet e clar
Leva sa votz e mou son chan,
Joy ai de luy e joy ai de la flor
E joy de me e de midons major;
Daus totas partz suy de joy claus e sens,
Mas sel es joys que totz autres joys vens.

Ailas! cum muer de cossirar,
Que manhtas vetz en cossir tan:
Lairo m'en poirian portar,
Que re no sabria que·s fan.
Per Dieu, amors, be·m trobas vensedor:
Ab paucs d'amics e ses autre senhor.
Quar una vetz tant midons non destrens
Abanz qu'ieu fos del dezirier estens?

Meravil me cum puesc durar
Que no·lh demostre mon talan.
Quan ieu vey midons ni l' esgar,
Li sieu belh huelh tan ben l'estan,
Per pauc me tenc quar ieu vas lieys no cor;
Si feira ieu, si no fos per paor,
Qu'anc no vi cors miels talhatz ni depens
Ad ops d'amar sia tan greus ni lens.

Tant am midons e la tenh char,
E tant la dopt' e la reblan
Qu'anc de mi no·lh ausei parlar,
Ni re no·lh quier ni re no·lh man.
Pero ilh sap mon mal e ma dolor,
E quan li plai, mi fai ben et honor,
E quan li plai, ieu me'n sofert ab mens,
Per so c'a lieis no·n aveigna blastens.

S'ieu saubes la gent enquantar,
Miei enemic foran enfan,
Que ja us no saubra triar
Ni dir ren que·ns tornes a dan;
Adoncs sai ieu que vira la gensor
E sos belhs huelhs e sa fresca color,
E baizera·lh la boca en totz sens,
Si que d'un mes hi paregra lo sens.

Ben la volgra sola trobar,
Que dormis, o·n fezes semblan,
Per qu'ieu l'embles un dous baizar,
Pus no valh tan qu'ieu lo·lh deman.
Per Dieu, dona, pauc esplecham d'amor;
Vai se·n lo temps e perdem lo melhor;
Parlar degram ab cubertz entresens,
E pus no·ns val arditz, valgues nos gens.

Ben deuri' hom dona blasmar,
Quan trop vay son amic tarzan,
Que longua paraula d'amar
Es grans enueitz e par d'enjan,
Qu'amar pot hom e far semblan alhor,
E gen mentir lai on non a autor.
Bona domna, ab sol qu'amar mi dens,
Ja per mentir ieu no serai atens.

Messatgier, vai, e no me·n prezes mens,
S'ieu del anar vas midons suy temens.

Chanso redonda

Non es meravelha s'ieu chan
Mielhs de nulh autre chantador,
Que plus mi tra·l cors ves amor
E mielhs sui faitz a son coman.
Cor e cors e saber e sen
E fors' e poder hi ai mes;
Si·m tira ves amor lo fres
Que ves autra part no m'aten.

Ben es mortz qui d'amor non sen
Al cor qual que doussa sabor;
E que val viure ses valor
Mas per enueg far a la gen?
Ja Dombredieus no·m azir tan
Qu'ieu ja pueis viva jorn ni mes,
Pus que d'enueg serai mespres
Ni d'amor non aurai talan.

Per bona fe e ses enjan
Am la plus belha e la melhor;
Del cor sospir e dels huelhs plor,
Quar tan l'am ieu, per que hi ai dan.

Ieu que·n puesc mais, s'amors mi pren,
E las carcers en que m'a mes
No pot claus obrir mas merces,
E de merce no i trop nien?

Aquest' amors me fier tan gen
Al cor d'una doussa sabor.
Cen vetz muer lo jorn de dolor
E reviu de joy autras cen.
Ben es mos mals de bel semblan,
Que mais val mos mals qu'autre bes;
E pus mos mals aitam bos m'es,
Bos er lo bes apres l'afan.

Ai Dieus! car si fosson trian
D'entrels fals li fin amador,
E·l lauzengier e·l trichador
Portesson corns el fron denan!
Tot l'aur del mon e tot l'argen
Hi volgr' aver dat, s'ieu l'agues,
Sol que ma dona conogues
Aissi cum ieu l'am finamen.

Quant ieu la vey, be m'es parven
Als huelhs, al vis, a la color,
Quar aissi tremble de paor
Cum fa la fuelha contra·l ven.
Non ai de sen per un efan,
Aissi sui d'amor entrepres;
E d'ome qu'es aissi conques,
Pot domna aver almorna gran.

Bona domna, re no·us deman
Mas que·m prendatz per servidor,
Qu'ie·us servirai cum bo senhor,
Cossi que del guazardon m'an.

Ve·us m'al vostre comandamen,
Francx cors humils, gais e cortes!
Ors ni leos non etz vos ges,
Que·m aucizatz, s'a vos mi ren.

A mon Cortes, lai ont ylh es,
Tramet lo vers, e ja no·l pes
Quar n'ai estat tan longamen.

WALTER OF CHÂTILLON

BORN *c.* 1135

WALTER OF CHÂTILLON—also known as Walter of Lille, from his native city—was a Canon of Reims and later of Amiens, and served for a time in the English Chancery under Henry II.

His pastoral, *Sole regente*, is a fine example of the genre, and presents a close formal parallel with the French *pastourelle*. Its resemblance in subject-matter is equally striking, particularly to the less seemly specimens of the lay product. It has three double rhymes to each stanza, the second persisting throughout the poem.

Pastoral

SOLE regente lora
Poli per altiora,
Quaedam satis decora
Virguncula
Sub ulmo patula
Consederat,
Nam dederat
Arbor umbracula.

Quam solam ut attendi,
Sub arbore descendi
Et Veneris ostendi
Mox jacula,

Dum noto singula
Caesariem
Et faciem,
Pectus et oscula.

"Quid", inquam, "absque pari
Placet hic spatiari,
Dyones apta lari
Puellula?
Nos nulla vincula,
Si pateris,
A Veneris
Disjungent copula."

Virgo decenter satis
Subintulit illatis:
"Haec, precor, omittatis
    Ridicula;
  Sum adhuc parvula,
    Non nubilis
    Nec habilis
  Ad haec opuscula.

Hora meridiana
Transit, vide Tytana.
Mater est inhumana.
    Jam pabula
  Spernit ovicula.
    Regrediar,
    Ne feriar
  Materna virgula."

"Signa, puella, poli
Considerare noli.
Restant immensa soli
    Curricula,
  Placebit morula,
    Ni temere
    Vis spernere
  Mea munuscula."

"Muneribus oblatis
Me flecti ne credatis,
Non frangam castitatis
    Repagula.
  Non haec me fistula
    Decipiet,
    Nec exiet
  A nobis fabula."

Quam mire simulantem
Ovesque congregantem
Pressi nil reluctantem
    Sub pennula;
  Flore et herbula

    . . . .
      . . . .

Praebente cubicula.

GUY DE BAZOCHES

c. 1140 — † 1203?

GUY DE BAZOCHES, a secular canon of Châlons who took part in the second Crusade, wrote Sequences in the Victorine style and other poems in varied metres. His use of double rhyme is masterly, as in the following poem.

The Nativity

QUI cuncta condidit
   In sapientia
      Per ejus reddidit
Nobis auxilia,
Quae prima perdidit
Insipientia,
Per illam reparans
Quos serpens perdidit
A Deo separans.

Haec domum similis
Scrutanti feminae
Quae testae fragilis
Accenso lumine
Apparens humilis
Drachmam in homine
Repperit decimam,
Regis imagine
Fulgentem animam.

Sol veri luminis
Quem virgo concipit,
De carne virginis
Dum carnem accipit,
Naturam hominis

Non culpam suscipit,
Et necessariam
Poenam non recipit
Sed voluntariam.

Merito numinis
Fit homo socius
Per ipsum luminis
Lumen, ut alius
Non esset hominis
Quam Dei filius,
Et idem hominum
Mediator pius
Esset ad Dominum.

Carnem ingenitus
Sumere potuit
Ut unigenitus,
Sed non oportuit:
Quia qui genitus
Et non qui genuit
Humano generi
Et mitti debuit
Et homo fieri.

[[127]]

Cur datum filio	Illud angelicum
Carnem ut sumeret,	Igitur gloriae
Quae dignos odio	Cantemus canticum
Caros efficeret,	Regi justitiae,
Est item ratio,	Qui misit unicum
Prolis acciperet	Ut ejus hodie
Ne nomen alius,	Nos a miseria
Vel idem fieret	Redderet gratiae
Pater et filius.	Misericordia.

CHRÉTIEN DE TROYES
fl. 1160—1180

CHRÉTIEN DE TROYES, the earliest of the trouvères, was a protégé of
Marie de Champagne, a grand-daughter of William IX of Aquitaine, who
was an admirer of Provençal poetry and sought to introduce its theories
into Northern France.

Chrétien is chiefly famous as a writer of Arthurian romances, and wrote
few lyrics. Provençal influence, on both subject and form, is strongly
evident in the following *chanson*, which is in *coblas doblas*, with octosyllabic
lines and two masculine rhymes to each stanza.

Chanson

D'AMORS, qui m'a tolu a moi
N'a soi ne me viaut retenir,
Me plaing einsi qu'adés otroi
Que de moi face son pleisir;
Et si ne me repuis taisir,
Que ne m'an plaingne, et di por quoi:
Car ciaus qui la traïssent voi
Sovant a lor joie venir,
Et j'i fail par ma bone foi.

S'amors por eshaucier sa loi
Viaut ses anemis convertir,
De sans li vient, si con je croi,
Qu'as suens ne puet ele faillir;

Et je, qui ne me puis partir
De celi vers cui me soploi,
Mon cuer, qui suens est, li anvoi;
Mes de neant la cuit servir
Se ce li rant que je li doi.

Dame, de ce que vostre hon sui,
Dites moi, se gre m'an savez.
Nenil, se j'onques vos conui,
Ainz vos poise, quant vos m'avez.
Et puis que vos ne me volez,
Donc sui je vostre par enui;
Mes se ja devez de nului
Merci avoir, si me sofrez,
Car je ne puis servir autrui.

Onques del bevraje ne bui
Don Tristans fu anpoisonez,
Mes plus me fet amer que lui
Fins cuers et bone volantez.
Bien an doit estre miens li grez,
Qu'ains de rien esforciez n'an fui,
Fors de tant, que mes iauz an crui,
Par cui sui an la voie antrez,
Don ja n'istrai, n'ains n'i recrui.

Cuers, se ma dame ne t'a chier,
Ja mar por ce t'an partiras;
Toz jorz soies an son dangier,
Puis qu'anpris et comancié l'as.
Ja, mon los, planté n'ameras,
Ne por chier tans ne t'esmaiier.
Biens adoucist par delaiier,
Et quant plus desirré l'avras,
Tant iert plus douz a l'essaiier.

Merci trovasse, au mien cuidier,
S'ele fust an tot le conpas
Del monde, la ou je la quier.
Mes je croi qu'ele n'i est pas.
Onques ne fin, onques ne las
De ma douce dame proiier.
Pri et repri sanz esploitier,
Come cil qui ne set a gas
Amors servir ne losangier.

GUIRAUT DE BORNELH

fl. 1165 — 1200

GUIRAUT DE BORNELH, a troubadour of humble origin, is said by his Provençal biographer to have been present at the siege of Acre, but little is known with certainty about his life. His popularity is shown by the large number of his poems which have survived, and by the title, "Master of the Troubadours", conferred upon him by writers of the thirteenth and fourteenth century.

Although he was a professed opponent of the *trobar clus*, many of his poems are very obscure, and as a result his reputation stands lower than it did. He nevertheless deserves a high place in the roll of Provençal poets as the author of the magnificent *alba*, *Reis glorios*. In this poem, Guiraut makes the watcher a friend of the lover. The whole *alba* is uttered by the watcher, except the last stanza, in which the lover replies. The poem is in decasyllabic *coblas doblas*, each stanza consisting of a couplet with a masculine rhyme, a second couplet with a feminine rhyme, and a short refrain.

Alba

"REIS glorios, verais lums e clartatz,
Deus poderos, senher, si a vos platz,
Al meu companh siatz fizels ajuda,
Qu'eu non lo vi, pois la noitz fon venguda,
Et ades sera l'alba.

Bel companho, si dormetz o veillatz?
Non dormatz plus, suau vos ressidatz,
Qu'en orien vei l'estela creguda
Qu'amena·l jorn, qu'eu l'ai ben coneguda,
  Et ades sera l'alba.

Bel companho, en chantan vos apel:
Non dormatz plus, qu'eu aug chantar l'auzel
Que vai queren lo jorn per lo boscatge,
Et ai paor que·l gilos vos assatge,
  Et ades sera l'alba.

Bel companho, issetz al fenestrel
Et regardatz las ensenhas del cel:
Conoisseretz si·us soi fizels messatge;
Si non o faitz, vostres n'er lo dampnatge,
  Et ades sera l'alba.

Bel companho, pos me parti de vos,
Eu no·m dormi, ni·m moc de genolhos;
Anz preguei Dieu, lo filh Santa Maria,
Que·us mi rendes per leial companhia,
  Et ades sera l'alba.

Bel companho, la foras als peiros
Mi prejavatz qu'eu no fos dormilhos,
Enans veilles tota noit tro al dia.
Ara no·us platz mos chans ni ma paria,
  Et ades sera l'alba."

"Bel dos companh, tan soi en ric sojorn
Qu'eu no volgra mais fos alba ni jorn,
Car la gensor que anc nasques de maire
Tenc e abras, per qu'eu non prezi gaire
  Lo fol gelos ni l'alba."

PEIRE VIDAL

fl. 1175 — 1205

So many grotesque stories are told of the life of Peire Vidal—of his dressing in a wolf-skin and being hunted by hounds, for instance, or of his claim to be Emperor of Byzantium and travelling with an imperial throne in his baggage—that one would not be surprised to find in his poetry the worst eccentricities of the *trobar clus.*

His verse, however, is very clear, melodious, and graceful, and entitles him to rank among the greatest of the troubadours. The personal note is very strong in his *chansos,* as in the following example, which breathes a local patriotism not often encountered in troubadour poetry. It is in *coblas unissonans,* with heptasyllabic lines. Three of its four rhymes are feminine, and each stanza ends with a *rima dissoluta.*

Chanso

AB l'alen tir vas me l'aire
Qu'eu sen venir de Proensa:
Tot quant es de lai m'agensa,
Si que, quan n'aug ben retraire,
Eu m'o escout en rizen
E·n deman per un mot cen:
Tan m'es bel quan n'aug ben dire.

Qu'om no sap tan dous repaire
Com de Rozer tro qu'a Vensa,
Si com clau mars e Durensa,
Ni on tan fis jois s'esclaire;
Per qu'entre la franca gen
Ai laissat mon cor jauzen
Ab leis que fa·ls iratz rire.

Qu'om no pot lo jorn mal traire
Qu'aja de leis sovinensa,
Qu'en leis nais jois e comensa.
E qui qu'en sia lauzaire,
De ben qu'en diga no·i men;
Que·l melher es ses conten
E·l genser qu'el mon se mire.

E s'eu sai ren dir ni faire,
Ilh n'aja·l grat, que sciensa
M'a donat e conoissensa
Per qu'eu sui gais e chantaire.
E tot quan fauc d'avinen
Ai del seu bel cors plazen,
Neis quan de bon cor consire.

BERTRAN DE BORN

c. 1140 — † 1214

BERTRAN DE BORN, a nobleman of Limousin, is the hero of an entertaining story according to which he supplied the besiegers of his castle with
provisions and asked them in return to be good enough to remove their
battering-ram from a weak part of his wall. The besiegers, however, were
ungentlemanly enough to put to good use the information which they had
gained from their obliging opponent. After spending much time helping
the fratricidal strife between the sons of Henry II of England, Bertran
retired, like Bernart de Ventadorn, to the Abbey of Dalon, where he died.

As a writer, he is chiefly famous for his *sirventes*, a genre in which he is
unsurpassed. His main theme is the glories of war. The following example
is called a *miei-sirventes*, or half *sirventes*, as it has only three stanzas. It is
written in decasyllabic *coblas unissonans*, with two *tornadas*, two of its three
rhymes being masculine. Probably written in 1195, it expresses Bertran's
pleasure at the prospect of war between Philippe-Auguste of France on the
one side and Richard Cœur de Lion and Alfonso VIII of Castile on the
other.

Miei-sirventes

MIEI-SIRVENTES vuolh far dels reis amdos,
    Qu'en brieu veirem qu'aura mais chavaliers:
    Del valen rei de Castela, n'Anfos,
Qu'auch dir que ve e volra soudadiers;
Richartz metra a muois et a sestiers
Aur et argen, e te·s a benananza
Metr' e donar, e no vol s'afiansa,
Anz vol guerra mais que qualha esparviers.

S'amdui li rei son pro ni coratjos,
En brieu veirem champs jonchatz de quartiers
D'elms e d'escutz e de brans e d'arzos
E de fendutz per bustz tro als braiers ;
Et arratge veirem anar destriers
E per costatz e per pechs mainta lanza,
E gauch e plor e dol et alegranza;
Lo perdr' er grans e·l gazanhs er sobriers.

Trompas, tabors, senheras e penos
Et entresenhs e chavals blancs e niers
Veirem en brieu, que·l segles sera bos,
Que om tolra l'aver als usuriers,
E per chamis non anara saumiers
Jorn afiatz, ni borges ses doptanza,
Ni merchadiers qui venha de ves Franza;
Anz sera rics qui tolra volontiers.

Mas si·l reis ve, ieu ai en Dieu fianza
Qu'ieu serai vius o serai per quartiers;

E si sui vius, er mi grans benananza,
E si ieu muoir, er mi grans deliuriers.

CONON DE BÉTHUNE
c. 1150 — † 1219 OR 1220

CONON DE BÉTHUNE, one of the greatest of the trouvères, was a prominent figure in French feudal society during the latter part of the twelfth
century. In 1189 he set out on the third Crusade, but appears to have returned home in the same year. He played a leading part in the fourth
Crusade, taking part in the capture of Constantinople in 1203 and the
establishment there of the Latin Empire, of which he became regent shortly
before his death.

The following Crusade-song, written shortly before 1189, is one of the
best of its class. Though written on conventional lines, it is a vigorous
poem, and was taken as a model by later writers. It is written in *coblas
doblas*, with decasyllabic lines, and with one masculine and one feminine
rhyme to each stanza.

Chanson de Croisade

Aｈｉ! amors, com dure departie
　　Me convenra faire de la millor
　　Ki onques fust amee ne servie!
Dieus me ramaint a li par sa douçour,
Si voirement con j'en part a dolor!
Las! k'ai je dit? Ja ne m'en part je mie!
Se li cors va servir nostre Signor,
Mes cuers remaint del tot en sa baillie.

Por li m'en vois sospirant en Surie,
Car je ne doi faillir mon creator.
Ki li faura a cest besoig d'aïe,
Saiciés ke il li faura a grignor;
Et saicent bien li grant et li menor
Ke la doit on faire chevallerie
Ou on conquiert Paradis et honor
Et pris et los et l'amor de s'amie.

Dieus est assis en son saint iretaige;
Ore i parra con cil le secorront
Cui il jeta de la prison ombraje,
Quant il fu mis ens la crois ke Turc ont.
Honi soient tot chil ki remanront,
S'il n'ont poverte ou viellece ou malaige!
Et cil ki sain et jone et riche sont
Ne poevent pas demorer sans hontaige.

Tot li clergié et li home d'eaige
Qui ens ausmogne et ens biens fais manront
Partiront tot a cest pelerinaige,
Et les dames ki chastement vivront
Et loiauté feront ceaus ki iront;
Et s'eles font par mal consel folaige,
A lasques gens mauvaises le feront,
Car tot li boin iront en cest voiaige.

Ki chi ne velt avoir vie anuieuse
Si voist por Dieu morir liés et joieus,
Car cele mors est douce et savereuse
Dont on conquiert le resne presïeus,
Ne ja de mort n'en i morra uns sels,
Ains naistront tot en vie glorïeuse;
Et saiciés bien, ki ne fust amereus,
Mout fust la voie et boine et deliteuse.

Dieus! tant avons esté preus par huiseuse,
Or i parra ki a certes iert preus;
S'irons vengier la honte dolereuse
Dont chascuns doit estre iriés et honteus;
Car a no tans est perdus li sains lieus
Ou Dieus soffri por nos mort angoisseuse.
S'or i laissons nos anemis morteus,
A tos jors mais iert no vie honteuse.

ARNAUT DANIEL
fl. 1180—1210

ARNAUT DANIEL was a contemporary and probably a friend of Bertran de Born. The story of how, when at a loss for inspiration, he overheard a rival composing a song, learned it by heart, and won a wager between them by singing it first is well known.

In his celebrated *sestina*, *Lo ferm voler*, assonance, but not rhyme, is present in each stanza. The first stanza has six different rhyme-words, which are used again in each subsequent stanza by taking them in the order: 6, 1, 5, 2, 4, 3, from the preceding stanza. The lines are of ten syllables each, plus a feminine ending, except that the first line of each stanza has seven syllables with a feminine ending. One may admire the skill with which he juggles with such an unpromising combination of words as "enters", "nail", "soul", "rod", "uncle", and "chamber", but it is difficult to be moved by a poem which declares: "I never loved more, or so much, the sister of my uncle."

Sestina

LO ferm voler qu'el cor m'intra
No·m pot jes becs escoissendre ni ongla
De lausengier, qui pert per mal dir s'arma;

E car non l'aus batr' ab ram ni ab verga,
Sivals a frau, lai on non aurai oncle,
Jauzirai joi, en vergier o dinz cambra.

    Quan mi soven de la cambra
On a mon dan sai que nuills hom non intra,
Anz me son tuich plus que fraire ni oncle,
Non ai membre no·m fremisca, neis l'ongla,
Aissi cum fai l'enfas denant la verga,
Tal paor ai que·ill sia trop de m'arma.

    Del cors li fos, non de l'arma,
E cossentis m'a celat dins sa cambra.
Que plus mi nafra·l cor que colps de verga,
Car lo sieus sers lai on ill es non intra;
Totz temps serai ab lieis cum carns et ongla,
E non creirai chastic d'amic ni d'oncle.

    Anc la seror de mon oncle
Non amei plus ni tant, per aquest'arma.
C'aitant vezis cum es lo detz de l'ongla,
S'a lei plagues, volgr'esser de sa cambra:
De mi pot far l'amors qu'inz el cor m'intra
Mieills a son vol c'om fortz de frevol verga.

    Pois flori la seca verga
Ni d'en Adam mogron nebot ni oncle,
Tant fina amors cum cella qu'el cor m'intra
Non cuig qu'anc fos en cors, ni eis en arma.
On qu'ill estei, fors en plaza o dinz cambra,
Mos cors no·is part de lieis tant cum ten l'ongla.

    C'aissi s'enpren e s'enongla
Mos cors en lei cum l'escorssa en la verga;
Qu'il m'es de joi tors e palaitz e cambra,
E non am tant fraire, paren, ni oncle:
Qu'en paradis n'aura doble joi m'arma,
Si ja nuills hom per ben amar lai intra.

Arnautz tramet sa chansson d'ongla e d'oncle
A grat de lieis que de sa verg' a l'arma,
Son Desirat, cui pretz en cambra intra.

ANONYMOUS

Verbum bonum

? LATE TWELFTH CENTURY

The beautiful Sequence, *Verbum bonum et suave*, which enjoyed remarkable
popularity during the later Middle Ages, has been ascribed to various dates,
from the eleventh century to the thirteenth. Its form is typical of the later
Sequence. Each strophe is a *versus popularis* with its first half trebled, and
the rhymes are arranged in the order: *a a a b, c c c b* in each pair of stanzas.

Sequence for the Annunciation

VERBUM bonum et suave
Personemus, illud *Ave*
Per quod Christi fit conclave
Virgo, mater, filia.

Per quod *Ave* salutata
Mox concepit fecundata
Virgo, David stirpe nata,
Inter spinas lilia.

Ave, veri Salomonis
Mater, vellus Gedeonis,
Cujus magi tribus donis
Laudant puerperium.

Ave, solem genuisti,
Ave, prolem protulisti,
Mundo lapso contulisti
Vitam et imperium.

ANONYMOUS

Ave, mater verbi summi,
Maris portus, signum dumi,
Aromatum virga fumi,
 Angelorum domina.

Supplicamus, nos emenda,
Emendatos nos commenda
Tuo nato ad habenda
 Sempiterna gaudia.

ANONYMOUS
Vinum bonum
THIRTEENTH CENTURY

Parody in the Middle Ages was carried to a point which is almost incredible
to-day. Even the Mass was parodied, and the parody performed in church
on such occasions as the Feast of Fools.

One of the cleverest of Medieval Latin parodies is a Drunkard's Mass,
opening with "Introibo ad altare Bacchi". An indecent parody of a Collect
is preceded by the Versicle: "Dolus vobiscum", the Response: "Et cum
gemitu tuo", and the exhortation "Potemus". The Sequence, given here,
is a parody of *Verbum bonum et suave.*

Sequence for a Drunkard's Mass

VINUM bonum cum sapore
 Bibit abbas cum priore,
 Et conventus de pejore
Bibit cum tristitia.

Ave, felix creatura,
Quam produxit vitis pura;
Omnis mensa stat secura
 In tua praesentia.

Felix venter quem intrabis,
Felix quicquid tu rigabis,
Felix lingua quam lavabis,
 Et beata labia.

〚 139 〛

O quam felix in calore,
O quam flagrans in ardore,
O quam placens es in ore,
    Dulce linguae vinculum!

Supplicamus: hic abunda,
Omnis turba sit facunda,
Sic cum voce nos jucunda
    Personemus gaudia.

Monachorum grex devotus,
Clerus omnis, mundus totus
Bibunt adaequales potus
    Et nunc et in saecula.

GUY DE COUCY
fl. 1186—† 1203

The trouvère Guy de Coucy, generally called "le châtelain de Coucy",
took part in Crusades during the period 1186–1203, and, according to
Villehardouin, died at sea in the latter year.

His poems, both in sentiment and in technique, are closely modelled on
the Provençal *chanso*, but are more than mere imitations, having a charm of
their own. The following example is in *coblas ternas*, i.e. the stanzas are
grouped into threes by the use of the same rhymes. This elaboration of the
cobla dobla had been used by a few of the troubadours. The lines, except for
a final line of six syllables, are decasyllabic, and there is one masculine and
one feminine rhyme to each stanza.

Chanson

LI noviaus tens et mais et violete
  Et rosignols me semont de chanter,
    Et mes fins cuers me fait d'une amourete
Si douz present que ne l'os refuser.
Or me laist Dieus en tel honor monter,
Que cele ou j'ai mon cuer et mon penser
Tiegne une foiz entre mes braz nuëte,
    Ainz que voise outre mer.

Au comencier la trovai si doucete:
Ja ne cuidai por li mal endurer;
Mais ses douz vis et sa fresche bouchete
Et si bel oel, vair et riant et cler,
M'orent ainz pris, que m'osasse doner.
Se ne me veut retenir ou quiter,
Mieuz aim a li faillir, si me promete,
      Qu'a une autre achiever.

De mil sospirs, ke je li doi par dete,
Ne me veut ele un seul quite clamer,
Ne fausse amors ne lait ke s'entremete,
De moi laissier dormir ne reposer.
S'ele m'ocit, mains avra a garder;
Je ne m'en sai vengier fors au plourer;
Car cui amors destruit et desirete
      Ne s'en set ou clamer.

Sor tote joie est cele coronee,
Ki d'amors vient. Dieus, i faudrai je don?
Oïl, par Dieu, teus est ma destinee
Et tel destin m'ont doné li felon;
Si sevent bien k'il font grant mesprison:
Car ki ce tout, dont ne puet faire don,
Il en conquiert anemis et mellee,
      Ni fait se perdre non.

Las! pour quoi l'ai de mes ieus regardee,
La douce rien, ki Fausse Amie a non?
Ele me rit et je l'ai tant ploree;
Si doucement ne fu trahiz nus hon.
Tant con fui miens, ne me fist se bien non,
Mais or sui suens, si m'ocit sens raison
Et por itant que de cuer l'ai amee:
      N'i set autre ocoison.

Si coiement est ma dolors celee
K'a mon semblant ne la reconoist on;
Se ne fussent la genz maleüree,
N'eüsse pas sospiré en pardon:
Amors m'eüst doné son guerredon.
Mais en cel point, que dui avoir mon don,
Lor fu m'amors ensegniee et mostree.
            Ja n'aient il pardon!

THE MONK OF MONTAUDON
fl. 1180 — 1210

In the front rank of writers of the *tenso* stands an anonymous monk, known to his contemporaries simply as "the Monk of Montaudon". He appears to have entered the monastic life at Aurillac, and became Prior of Montaudon, but spent a great part of his life wandering round France and Spain, enjoying the patronage of the nobles and of Richard I of England and Alfonso II of Aragon.

Apparently he spent too much time away from the monastery to please his brethren, but he turns the tables neatly on them in his *tenso*, *L'autrier fuy en paradis*. In this poem, the Almighty rebukes him for returning to the cloister, and urges him to go out again into the world. "I like your songs and jests", says the Almighty, "for the world is all the better for them, and Montaudon gains by them." He asks why the monk does not go to visit King Richard, who is so generous with his money. This provides the monk with an opportunity of rebuking the Almighty. "O Lord", he answers, "I would gladly have visited him, if it were not for you; for it was you who allowed him to be taken prisoner."

The *tenso* has the same form as the *chanso*. The present example is in *coblas unissonans*, with seven-syllabled lines and three rhymes, two being masculine and the third feminine.

Tenso

L'AUTRIER fuy en paradis,
    Per qu'ieu suy guays e joyos,
    Quar tan mi fo amoros
Dieus, a cui tot obezis—

Terra, mars, vals e montanha;
E·m dis: "Morgue, quar venguis?
Ni cum estay Montaudos,
Lai on as major companha?"

"Senher, estat ai aclis
En claustra un an o dos,
Per qu'ai perdut los baros;
Sol quar vos am e·us servis,
Me fan lor amor estranha.
En Randos, cuy es Paris,
No·m fo anc fals ni gignos,
El e mos cors crey que·n planha."

"Mongue, ges ieu no grazis
S'estas en claustra rescos
Ni vols guerras ni tensos
Ni pelei' ab tos vezis,
Per que·l bailia·t remanha;
Ans am ieu lo chant e·l ris,
E·l segles en es plus pros
E Montaudos y guazanha."

"Senher, ieu tem que falhis,
S'ieu fas coblas ni cansos,
Qu'om pert vostr'amor e vos
Qui son escient mentis,
Per que·m part de la barguanha.
Pel segle que no·m n'ahis,
Me torney a las leysos,
E·n laissey l'anar d'Espanha."

"Mongue, be mal o fezis
Que tost non anies coitos
Al rey cuy es Olairos,
Qui tant era tos amis;
Per que lau que t'o afranha;
Ha! quans bos marcx d'esterlis
Aura perdutz els tieus dos,
Qu'el te levet de la fanha."

"Senher, ieu l'agra ben vis,
Si per mal de vos no fos,
Quar anc sofris sas preizos;
Mas la naus dels Sarrazis
No·us membra ges cossi·s banha;
Quar si dinz Acre·s culhis,
Pro i agr'enquer Turcx fellos;
Folhs es qui·us sec en mesclanha."

ANONYMOUS
Seignors, or entendez
c. 1200

The anonymous wassail-song, *Seignors, or entendez a nus*, long preserved
in a manuscript (now lost) at the British Museum, dates from the closing
years of the twelfth century or the early years of the thirteenth. It is
written in the Anglo-Norman dialect of French. Each stanza has three
masculine rhymes, the third serving as a link between stanza and refrain.
The metre is octosyllabic, with two half-lines included in each stanza.

Wassail-song

SEIGNORS, or entendez a nus:
De loing sumes venuz a vous
Quere Noël;
Car l'em nus dit que en cest hostel
Soleit tenir sa feste anvel
A hicest jur.
Deus doint a tuʒ cels joie d'amurs
Qui a danʒ Noël ferunt honors.

Seignors, je vus di ben por veir
Que danz Noël ne velt aveir
Si joie non,
E replenie sa maison
De pain, de char, e de peison
Por faire henor.
Deu doint a tuʒ cés joie d'amurs
Qui a danʒ Noël ferunt honors.

Seignors, il est crié en l'ost
Que cil qui despent bien e tost
      E largement,
E fet les granz henors sovent,
Deu li duble quanque il despent,
      Por faire henor.
Deu doint a tuʒ cels joie d'amurs
Qui a danʒ Noël ferunt honors.

Seignors, escriez le malveis,
Car vus nel troverez jameis
      De bone part.
Botun, batun, ferun gruinard,
Car tot dis a le quer cuuard
      Por feire henor.
Deu doint a tuʒ cels joie d'amurs
Qui a danʒ Noël ferunt honors.

Noël beit bien le vin engleis
E le gascoin e le franceys
      E l'angevin;
Noël fait beivere son veisin,
Si qu'il se dort le chief enclin
      Sovent le jor.
Deu doint a tuʒ cels joie d'amurs
Qui a danʒ Noël ferunt honors.

Seignors, je vus di par Noël
E le sire de cest hostel:
      Car bevez ben.
E jo primes beverai le men,
E pois après chescon le soen,
      Par mon conseil.
Si je vus di a trestoz: "Wesseil";
Dehaiz eit qui ne dira: "Drincheyl."

ANONYMOUS
Or hi parra
c. 1200

An Anglo-Norman drinking-song, *Or hi parra*, was contained in the same manuscript as the foregoing. It is based on the favourite Sequence, *Laetabundus*[97], of which it uses the last line of each strophe. It reproduces the form of *Laetabundus* exactly, except that it is regularly rhymed (the rhymes being arranged as in the *Golden Sequence* opposite) and that the sixth and second lines from the end have each an extra syllable.

Drinking-song

O R hi parra:
  La cerveyse nos chauntera
   Alleluia.

   Qui que en beyt,
 Si tele seyt com estre deyt,
   Res miranda.

  Bevez quant l'avez en poing:
  Ben est droit, car mut est loing
   Sol de stella.

  Bevez bien e bevez bel:
  El vos vendra del tonel
   Semper clara.

  Bevez bel e bevez bien,
  Vos le vostre e jo le mien,
   Pari forma.

  De ço soit bien porveü:
  Qui auques la tient al fu
   Fit corrupta.

  Riches genz si funt lur bruit;
  Fesom nus nostre deduit
   Valle nostra.

Beneyt soit li bon veisin
Qui nus dune payn e vin,
    Carne sumpta.

E la dame de l'ostal,
Ki nus fait chere real,
Ja ne pusse ele par mal
    Esse caeca.

Mut nus dune volentiers
Bon beivres e bons mangiers:
Meuz waut que autres muliers
    Haec praedicta.

Or bewom al dereyn
Par meitez e par pleyn,
Que ne seüm demeyn
    Gens misera.

Nostre tone ne vuit,
Kar pleine est de bon fruit,
E si ert tute nuit
    Puerpera.

STEPHEN LANGTON (*c.* 1150—† 1228)
OR
POPE INNOCENT III (*c.* 1160—† 1216)

The authorship of the great Sequence, *Veni, sancte spiritus*, has been ascribed to many different writers, but is most probably to be credited either to Stephen Langton, Archbishop of Canterbury, or to Pope Innocent III. Its stanzas, like those of *Verbum bonum*[138], are homomorphic, but the *Golden Sequence* departs from the normal type of late Sequence in two important respects: first, its lines are all of the same length; and secondly, the antiphony is obscured by the use of the same final rhyme to all the strophes.

The Golden Sequence

VENI, sancte spiritus,   Veni, pater pauperum;
Et emitte caelitus   Veni, dator munerum;
Lucis tuae radium.   Veni, lumen cordium.

Consolator optime,
Dulcis hospes animae,
Dulce refrigerium.

In labore requies,
In aestu temperies,
In fletu solatium.

O lux beatissima,
Reple cordis intima
Tuorum fidelium.

Sine tuo numine
Nihil est in lumine,
Nihil est innoxium.

Lava quod est sordidum,
Riga quod est aridum,
Sana quod est saucium;

Flecte quod est rigidum,
Fove quod est frigidum,
Rege quod est devium.

Da tuis fidelibus
In te confidentibus
Sacrum septenarium.

Da virtutis meritum,
Da salutis exitum,
Da perenne gaudium.

GACE BRULÉ

† c. 1220

Little is known of the life of Gace Brulé, a knight of Champagne, and a prolific trouvère strongly influenced by the troubadours. In the poem here given he rises above his usually conventional standard, particularly in the opening. It is written in *coblas doblas*, with one masculine and one feminine rhyme to each stanza, the lines varying in length from five syllables to eight.

Chanson

LES oisillons de mon païs
   Ai oïz en Bretaigne;
   A lor chant m'est il bien a vis
Qu'en la douce Champaigne
   Les oï jadis,
   Se n'i ai mespris.
Il m'ont en si dous penser mis
Qu'a chançon fere me sui pris
   Tant que je parataigne
Ce qu'amours m'a lonc tens promis.

De longue atente m'esbahis
   Sanz ce que je m'en plaigne;
Ce me tout le gieu et le ris;
   Nus cui amours destraigne
     N'est d'el ententis.
     Mon cors et mon vis
Truis si mainte fois entrepris
Qu'un fol semblant i ai apris.
   Qui qu'en amor mespraigne,
Ainc, certes, plus ne li mesfis.

En besant mon cuer me ravi
   Ma douce dame gente;
Trop fu fous quant il me guerpi
   Pour li qui me tormente.
     Las! ains nel senti,
     Quant de moi parti;
Tant doucement le me toli
Qu'en sospirant le trest a li;
   Mon fol cuer atalente,
Mais ja n'avra de moi merci.

D'un beser dont me membre si
   M'est avis, en m'entente,
Qu'il n'est hore, ce m'a traï,
   Qu'a mes levres nel sente.
     Quant elle souffri
     Ce que je la vi,
De ma mort que ne me gari!
Elle set bien que je m'oci
   En ceste longue atente,
Dont j'ai le vis teint et pali.

Puis que me tout rire et juer
   Et fet morir d'envie,
Trop souvent me fet comparer
   Amours sa compeignie.

GACE BRULÉ

Las! n'i os aler,
Car pour fol sembler
Me font cil faus proiant d'amer.
Morz sui quant jes i voi parler;
Que point de tricherie
Ne puet nus d'eus en li trouver.

ANONYMOUS

Entre moi et mon ami

LATE TWELFTH CENTURY

Entre moi et mon ami belongs to the earlier type of *aube*, as a woman is the
only speaker, and the coming of dawn is announced by a lark. Neither this
nor the later *Gaite de la tor* contains the word "dawn", the presence of
which is characteristic of the Provençal *alba*.

Aube

ENTRE moi et mon ami,
En un bois k'est les Betune,
Alanmes juant mardi
Toute la nuit a la lune,
Tant k'il ajorna
Et ke l'aloue chanta,
Ke dit: "Amis, alons an";
Et il respont doucement:
"*Il n'est mie jors,*
Saverouȝe au cors gent;
Si m'ait amors,
L'alouette nos mant."

Adont se trait pres de mi,
Et je ne fui pas anfrune;
Bien trois fois me baisa il,
Ainsi fis je lui plus d'une,
K'ainz ne m'anoia.

Adonc vosessiens nous la
Ke celle nuis durast sant,
Mais ke plus n'alast disant:
"*Il n'est mie jors,*
Saverouʒe au cors gent;
Si m'ait amors,
L'alouette nos mant."

ANONYMOUS

En un vergier

LATE TWELFTH CENTURY

In some Provençal dawn-songs, there is a dialogue between two lovers, or between one of them and a watcher. In others, only one of the three characters speaks. The anonymous *alba*, *En un vergier*—one of the most beautiful of all Provençal lyrics—belongs to the latter class, the lady being the speaker. It is written in monorhymed decasyllabic tercets, with a refrain. In the latter, the word *alba* appears, as in all Provençal poems of this genre except one.

Alba

EN un vergier, sotz folha d'albespi
Tenc la dompna son amic costa si,
Tro la gaita crida que l'alba vi.
Oi Deus, oi Deus, de l'alba! tan tost ve.

"Plagues a Deu ja la noitz non falhis,
Ni·l meus amics lonh de mi no·s partis,
Ni la gaita jorn ni alba no vis!
Oi Deus, oi Deus, de l'alba! tan tost ve.

Bels dous amics, baizem nos eu e vos
Aval els pratz on chanto·ls auzellos;
Tot o fassam en despeit del gilos.
Oi Deus, oi Deus, de l'alba! tan tost ve.

Bels dous amics, fassam un joc novel,
Ins el jardi on chanton li auzel,
Tro la gaita toque son caramel.
Oi Deus, oi Deus, de l'alba! tan tost ve.

Per la douss' aura qu'es venguda de lai,
Del meu amic bel e cortes e gai,
Del seu alen ai begut un dous rai.
Oi Deus, oi Deus, de l'alba! tan tost ve."

La dompna es agradans e plazens,
Per sa beutat la gardon mantas gens,
Et a son cor en amor leialmens.
Oi Deus, oi Deus, de l'alba! tan tost ve.

RAIMBAUT DE VAQUEIRAS

c. 1155 — † 1207?

RAIMBAUT DE VAQUEIRAS, the son of a poor knight of Provence, spent a considerable part of his life in Italy, at the court of Boniface II of Mont-ferrat. He accompanied the latter on the Crusade of 1202, and was probably killed with him, fighting against the Bulgarians.

Two of his poems are written partly in Italian. One of these is a *tenso* with a Genoese lady. The other, given here, is a *descort*—an unusual one, as has been already indicated. It contains a stanza each in Provençal, Italian, French, Gascon, and Galician-Portuguese, with a *tornada* composed of two lines from each of these languages in turn.

The second of Raimbaut's poems given here is of a type unusual in Old Provençal, as a woman is the speaker. It thus reminds one of the Galician-Portuguese *cantiga de amigo.*

Descort

ERAS quan vey verdeyar
Pratz e vergiers e boscatges,
Vuelh un descort comensar
D'amor, per qu'ieu vauc aratges;
Qu'una domna·m sol amar,
Mas camjatz l'es sos coratges,
Per qu'ieu fauc dezacordar
Los motz e·ls sos e·ls lenguatges.

Io son quel que ben non aio,
Ni jamai non l'averò,
Ni per april, ni per maio,
Si per madona non l'ò:
Certo que en so lengaio
Sa gran beutà dir non so,
Çhu fresca qe flor de glaio;
Per qe no me·n partirò.

Belle douce dame chiere,
A vos mi doin e m'otroi:
Je n'avrai mes joi' entiere
Si je n'ai vos e vos moi.
Mot estes male guerriere
Si je muer par bone foi;
Mes ja par nulle maniere
No·m partrai de vostre loi.

Dauna, io mi rent a bos,
Coar sotz la mes bon' e bera
Q'anc hos, e gaillard' e pros,
Ab que no·m hossetz tan hera.
Mout abetz beras haissos
E color hresq' e noera.
Boste son, e si·bs agos
No·m destrengora hiera.

Mas tan temo vostro preito
Todo·n son escarmentado.
Por vos ei pen' e maltreito
E meo corpo lazerado;
La noit, can jac' en meu leito,
So mochas vetz resperado;
E car nonca m'aprofeito
Falid' ei en meu cuidado.

[153]

Belhs cavaliers, tant es car
Lo vostr' onratz senhoratges
Que cada jorno m'esglaio.
Oi me! lasso, que farò
Si cele que j'ai plus chiere
Me tue, ne sai por quoi?
Ma dauna, he que dey bos
Ni peu cap santa Quitera,
Mon corasso m'avetz treito
E, mot gen favlan, furtado.

Chanso

ALTAS ondas que venez suz la mar,
  Que fai lo vent çay e lay demenar,
  De mon amic savez novas comtar,
Qui lay passet? no lo vei retornar.
        Et oy, Deu d'amor!
Ad hora·m dona joy et ad hora dolor.

Oy, aura dolza, qui venez deves lai
On mon amic dorm e sejorn' e jai,
Del dolz aleyn un beure m'aportai.
La bocha obre, per gran desir qu'en ai.
        Et oy, Deu d'amor!
Ad hora·m dona joy et ad hora dolor.

Mal amar fai vassal d'estran païs,
Car en plor tornan e sos jocs e sos ris.
Ja non cudey mon amic me tenys
Qu'eu li doney ço que d'amor me quis.
        Et oy, Deu d'amor!
Ad hora·m dona joy et ad hora dolor.

ANONYMOUS
Volez vos que je vos chant

LATE TWELFTH OR EARLY THIRTEENTH CENTURY

The fairyland atmosphere of this *reverdie* is reminiscent of English ballads like *Thomas the Rhymer*:

> "Her skirt was o' the grass-green silk,
> Her mantle o' the velvet fine;
> At ilka tett o' her horse's mane
> Hung fifty siller bells and nine."

Its lines show a mixture of assonance and full rhyme. It will be noticed that each stanza falls into two equal parts, that the last line of each half is shorter than the others, and that the majority of the rhymes run in the order: *a a b, c c b*. The versification is therefore similar to that of Sequences of the last or stanzaic type, such as the *Stabat mater*.

Reverdie

VOLEZ vos que je vos chant
Un son d'amors avenant?
    Vilain nel fist mie;
Ainz le fist un chevalier
Soz l'onbre d'un olivier
    Entre les braz s'amie.

Chemisete avoit de lin
Et blanc pelicon hermin,
    Et bliaut de soie;
Chauces out de jaglolai
Et solers de flors de mai,
    Estroitement chaucade.

Cainturete avoit de fueille
Qui verdist quant li tens mueille,
    D'or ert boutonade;
L'aumosniere estoit d'amor,
Li pendant furent de flor;
    Par amors fu donade.

Et chevauchoit une mule;
D'argent ert la ferreüre,
     La sele ert dorade;
Sus la crope par derriers
Avoit planté trois rosiers
     Por fere li onbrage.

Si s'en vet aval la pree;
Chevaliers l'ont encontree,
     Biau l'ont saluade.
"Bele, dont estes vos nee?"
"De France sui la loee,
     Du plus haut parage.

Li rosignox est mon pere,
Qui chante sor la ramee
     El plus haut boscage.
La seraine ele est ma mere,
Qui chante en la mer salee
     El plus haut rivage."

"Bele, bon fussiez vos nee,
Bien estes enparentee
     Et de haut parage.
Pleüst a Deu nostre pere
Que vos me fussiez donee
     A fame esposade!"

ANONYMOUS

Pancis amerouʒement

LATE TWELFTH OR EARLY THIRTEENTH CENTURY

With some irregularities, the stanzas of the following example of the *chanson de mal-mariée* are *unissonans*, with four rhymes to each stanza, and seven syllables to the line. The poem, in which three women speak, adopts the usual attitude of early French poetry towards marriage.

Chanson de mal-mariée

PANCIS amerouzement
   De Tornai parti l'autrier;
   En un pre lons un destour
Vi trois dames ombroier,
Mariees de novel.
Chascune ot un vert chapel.
La moinnee a dit ansi:
"Je servirai mon mari
Lealment en leu d'ami."

Li ainnee an ot irour,
Se li dit sans atargier:
"Damedex vos dont mal jour!
Nos volez vos asaier?
Au cuer ne m'est mie bel."
Dou poing an son haterel
L'ala maintenant ferir.
"Je ferai novel ami
An despit de mon mari."

La moienne par baudour
Fu vestue au tens d'esté
D'un riche drap de colour,
D'un vert qui fait a louer.

En avoit robe et mantel
Et chantoit cest chant novel,
Si ke je l'ai bien oï:
"S'on trovast leal ami,
Ja n'eüsse pris mari."

ANONYMOUS
De Saint Quentin
LATE TWELFTH OR EARLY THIRTEENTH CENTURY

In the following example of the Old French *pastourelle*, the stanzas, as in many others, are *unissonans*. There are three full rhymes, the third of which rhymes with the end of the refrain. As in most *pastourelles*, the lines are short, varying in length from seven syllables to three.

Pastourelle

DE Saint Quentin a Cambrai
    Chevalchoie l'autre jour.
    Les un boisson esgardai,
Touse i vi de bel atour.
    La colour
Ot freche com rose en mai.
    De cuer gai
    Chantant la trovai
    Ceste chansounete:
"*En non Deu, j'ai bel ami,*
    Cointe et joli,
    Tant soie je brunete."

Vers la pastoure tornai
Quant la vi en son destour.
Hautement la saluai
Et di: "Deus vos doinst bon jour
    Et honour.

Celle ke ci trové ai,
    Sens delai
  Ses amis serai."
Dont dist la doucete:
"En non Deu, j'ai bel ami,
    Cointe et joli,
  Tant soie je brunete."

Deles li seoir alai
Et li priai de s'amour.
Celle dist: "Je n'amerai
Vos ne autrui par nul tour,
    Sens pastour,
Robin, ke fiencié l'ai.
    Joie en ai,
  Si en chanterai
Ceste chansonnete:
'En non Deu, j'ai bel ami,
    Cointe et joli,
  Tant soie je brunete.'"

ANONYMOUS

Gaite de la tor

EARLY THIRTEENTH CENTURY

The anonymous *aube*, *Gaite de la tor*, which dates from the opening years of the thirteenth century, shows the influence of the troubadours, and yet is strongly original. It is dramatic in form, as it consists entirely of a dialogue between a lover and two watchers. The first watcher, who is a friend of the lover, utters the first half of each of the first five stanzas. The second watcher, who appears to be an ordinary night-watchman, utters the second half of the same stanzas, beginning each time with a fourfold blast on his horn. In the last two stanzas the lover answers him, his answer being punctuated by the watchman's horn.

The stanzas are *unissonans*, with three full rhymes. The lines vary in length from four syllables to seven.

Aube

"GAITE de la tor,
      Gardez entor
Les murs, se Deus vos voie!
      C'or sont a sejor
      Dame et seignor,
Et larron vont en proie."
"Hu et hu et hu et hu!
      Je l'ai veü
La jus soz la coudroie.
Hu et hu et hu et hu!
      A bien pres l'ocirroie."

"D'un douz lai d'amor
      De Blancheflor,
Compains, vos chanteroie,
      Ne fust la poor
      Del traïtor
Cui je redotteroie."
"Hu et hu et hu et hu!
      Je l'ai veü
La jus soz la coudroie.
Hu et hu et hu et hu!
      A bien pres l'ocirroie."

"Compainz, en error
      Sui, k'a cest tor
Volentiers dormiroie.
      N'aiez pas paor!
      Voist a loisor,
Qui aler vuet par voie."
"Hu et hu et hu et hu!
      Or soit teü,
Compainz, a ceste voie.
Hu et hu! bien ai seü
      Que nous en avrons joie."

"Ne sont pas plusor
      Li robeor;
N'i a c'un, que je voie,
      Qui gist en la flor
      Soz covertor,
Cui nomer n'oseroie."
"Hu et hu et hu et hu!
      Or soit teü,
Compainz, a ceste voie.
Hu et hu! bien ai seü
      Que nous en avrons joie."

"Cortois ameor,
      Qui a sejor
Gisez en chambre coie,
      N'aiez pas freor,
      Que tresq'a jor
Poëz demener joie."
"Hu et hu et hu et hu!
      Or soit teü,
Compainz, a ceste voie.
Hu et hu! bien ai seü
      Que nous en avrons joie."

"Gaite de la tor,
      Vez mon retor
De la, ou vos ooie;
      D'amie et d'amor
      A cestui tor
Ai ceu, que plus amoie."
"Hu et hu et hu et hu!"
      "Pou ai geü
En la chambre de joie."
"Hu et hu!" "Trop m'a neü
      L'aube qui me guerroie.

Se salve l'onor
Au criator
Estoit, tot tens voudroie,
Nuit feïst del jor;
Ja mais dolor
Ne pesance n'avroie."
"Hu et hu et hu et hu!"
"Bien ai veü
De biauté la monjoie."
"Hu et hu!" "C'est bien seü.
Gaite, a Deu tote voie!"

SANCHO I OF PORTUGAL
1154 — † 1211

The earliest surviving poem in the Galician-Portuguese language probably dates from 1189. The second earliest is the following *cantiga de amigo* attributed to Sancho I, King of Portugal from 1185 to 1211. It has been conjectured that it was written between 1194 and 1199, when Sancho was building the fortress of Guarda as an outpost against the Moors, and that the speaker is his mistress, Maria Paez. The poem is generally printed in four-lined stanzas, as in the original manuscript, the lines ending with *vivo*, *amigo*, *tarda*, and *Guarda*; but I follow here the arrangement of O. Nobiling.

Cantiga de amigo

Ai eu coitada!
Como vivo en gram cuidado
Por meu amigo
Que ei alongado!
Muito me tarda
O meu amigo na Guarda.

Ai eu coitada!
Como vivo en gram desejo
Por meu amigo
Que tarda e non vejo!
Muito me tarda
O meu amigo na Guarda.

GAUCELM FAIDIT

fl. 1180—1220

According to his Provençal biographer, Gaucelm Faidit was the son of a citizen of Uzerche and, having lost all his money at the gaming-table, was forced to sing for his living. Greatly addicted to eating and drinking, the biographer continues, he became fat beyond measure, and his wife became as fat as he. Like Raimbaut de Vaqueiras, he was protected by Boniface II of Montferrat, and followed him on the Fourth Crusade, but returned alive.

His lament on the death of Richard I of England in 1199—the only *planh* of which the melody has come down to us—is written, like most of its kind, in decasyllabic lines. Its stanzas are *unissonans*, with four rhymes, one of which is feminine. It resembles other *planhs* in its exaggerated language, but contains a number of very fine lines.

Planh

FORTZ chauza es que tot lo major dan
E·l major dol, las! qu'ieu anc mais agues,
    E so don dei tostemps planher ploran,
M'aven a dir en chantan e retraire;
Car selh qu'era de valor caps e paire,
Lo rics valens Richartz, reys dels Engles,
Es mortz. Ai Dieus! quals perd' e quals dans es!
Quant estrangz motz! quan salvatge a auzir!
Ben a dur cor totz hom qu'o pot suffrir.

Mortz es lo reys, e son passat mil an
Qu'anc tan pros hom no fo, ni no·l vi res,
Ni mais non er nulhs hom del sieu semblan,
Tan larcs, tan pros, tan arditz, tals donaire;
Qu'Alichandres, lo reys qui venquet Daire,
No cre que tan dones ni tan mezes,
Ni anc Charles ni Artus tan valgues,
Qu'a tot lo mon se fes, qui·n vol ver dir,
Als us duptar et als autres grazir.

[162]

Meravil me del fals secgle truan
Co i pot estar savis hom ni cortes,
Pus ren no i val belh ditz ni fait prezan.
E donc, per que s'esfors' om pauc ni guayre?
Qu'era nos a mostrat mortz que pot faire;
Qu'a un sol colp a lo mielhs del mon pres,
Tota l'onor, totz los gaugz, totz los bes;
E pus vezem que res no i pot guandir,
Ben deuri' om meins duptar a murir.

A! senher reys valens, e que faran
Huei mais armas ni fort tornei espes
Ni ricas cortz ni belh don aut e gran,
Pus vos no i etz, qui n'eratz capdelaire?
Ni que faran li liurat a maltraire,
Silh qui s'eran el vostre servir mes,
Qu'atendion que·l guazardos vengues?
Ni que faran cilh, que·s degran aucir,
Qu'aviatz faitz en gran ricor venir?

Longa ira e avol vida auran
E tostemps dol, qu'enaissi lor es pres;
E Sarrazi, Turc, Payan, e Persan,
Que·us duptavon mais qu'ome nat de maire,
Creisseran tan d'erguelh e lur afaire
Que plus tart n'er lo sepulcres conques;
Mas Dieus o vol, que, s'il non o volgues
E vos, senher, visquessetz, ses falhir
De Suria los avengr' a fugir.

Huei mais non ai esperansa que i an
Reys ni princeps que cobrar lo saubes;
Pero tug silh qu'el vostre loc seran
Devon gardar cum fos de pretz amaire
E qual foron vostre dui valen fraire—
Lo joves reys e·l cortes coms Gaufres;
E qui en loc remanra de vos tres,
Ben deu aver aut cor e ferm cossir
De comensar totz bos faitz e fenir.

Ai! senher Dieus, vos qu'etz vers perdonaire,
Vers Dieus, vers hom, vera vida, merces!
Perdonatz li, que ops e cocha l'es;
E non gardetz, senher, al sieu falhir,
E membre vos com vos anet servir.

SAVARIC DE MAULEON (†1231?), GAUCELM FAIDIT (*fl.* 1180—1220) AND UC DE LA BACALARIA

SAVARIC DE MAULEON held high office, both in France and in England, under King John, who rewarded him with an English peerage. The subject of the *partimen* between him, Gaucelm Faidit, and Uc de la Bacalaria is an interesting one. A lady has three suitors. She gives the first of them an amorous glance, gently squeezes the hand of the second, and presses the foot of the third. Who is the most favoured of the three?

The poem is in octosyllabic lines, with thirteen lines and six masculine rhymes to each stanza. Like most of its kind, it is in *coblas unissonans.*

Partimen

"GAUCELM, tres jocs enamoratz
Partisc a vos et a n'Hugo,
E chascus prendetz lo plus bo,
E laissatz me cal que·us voillatz:
Una dompna a tres prejadors,
E destreingn la tant lor amors
Que, quan tuich trei li son denan,
A chascun fai d'amor semblan;
L'un esgard' amorosamen,
L'autr' estreing la man dousamen,
Al tertz caucïa·l pe rizen.
Digatz a cal, pois aissi es,
Fai major amor de totz tres."

"Seign' en Savaric, ben sapchatz
Que l'amics receup plus gent do,
Que franchamen, ses cor felo,
Es dels huoills plazens esgardatz.

Del cor mou aquella doussors,
Per qu'es cen tans majer honors;
E del man tenir dic aitan
Que non li ten ni pro ni dan,
C'aital plazer comunalmen
Fan dompnas per acuillimen;
E del cauciar non enten
C'anc la dompn' amor li fezes,
Ni·l deu per amor esser pres."

"Gaucelm, vos dizetz so qu·eus platz
For que non mantenetz razo;
Q'en l'esgardar non conosc pro
A l'amic que vos razonatz,
E si l'i enten es follors,
C'uoill esgardon lui et aillors
E nuill autre poder non an.
Mas, qand la blancha mas ses gan
Estreing son amic dousamen
L'amors mou del cor e del sen.
E·n Savarics, que part tant gen,
Mantega·l cauciar cortes
Del pe, q'ieu no·l mantenrai ges."

"N'Hugo, pois lo mieills me laissatz,
Mantenrai lo ses dir de no;
Don dic que·l cauciars que fo
Faitz del pe fon fin' amistatz,
Celada dels lausengadors;
E par ben, pos aital socors
Pres l'amic rizen chaucian,
Que l'amors es ses tot engan.
E, qui·l tener de la man pren
Per major amor, fai nonsen.
E d'en Gaucelm no m'es parven
Que l'esgart per meillor prezes,
Se tan con dis d'amor saupes."

"Seigner, vos que l'esgart blasmatz
Dels huoill e lor plazen faisso,
Non sabetz que messatgier so
Del cor, quels hi a enviatz;
C'uoill descobron als amadors
So que reten el cor paors,
Don totz los plazers d'amor fan;
E maintas vetz rizen gaban,
Caucïa·l pe a mainta gen
Dompna, ses autr' entendemen.
E n'Hugo manten faillimen,
Qe·l teners del man non es res,
Ni son cre q'anc d'amor mogues."

"Gaucelm, encontr' amor parlatz
Vos e·l Seigner de Malleo;
E pareis ben a la tenso
Que·il huoill que vos avetz triatz,
E que razonatz pelz meillors,
Ant trahitz mains entendedors.
E de la dompn' ab cor truan,
Si·m caucïava·l pe un an,
No·n auria mon cor gauzen;
E de la man es ses conten
Que l'estreigners val per un cen,
Car ja, si al cor no plagues
L'amors, no·il agra·l man trames."

"Gaucelm, vencutz etz del conten
Vos e n'Hugo certanamen.
E vuoill que fassa·l jutgamen
Mos Garda-Cors, que m'a conques,
E na Maria, on bons pretz es."

"Seigner, vencutz no sui nien,
Et al jutgar er ben parven;
Per qu'eu vuoill i sia eisamen
Na Guillelma de Benauges,
Ab sos digz amoros cortes."

"Gaucelm, tant ai razon valen,
C'amdos vos fortz'e mi defen;
E sai n'una ab gai cors plazen
En qe·l jutgamens fora mes;
Mas pro n'i a ab meins de tres."

PHILIP THE CHANCELLOR

c. 1160–†1236

PHILIP, Chancellor of Notre Dame, frequently came into conflict with the members of the infant University of Paris, both graduate and undergraduate, particularly with those who belonged to the newly founded mendicant orders.

He was a prolific writer of verse, both French and Latin, but his Latin poems alone have survived. Great both as a satirist and as a hymnographer, he is at his greatest as a writer of *cantiones*, and has not been surpassed in this genre. His *cantio*, *Procedenti puero*, with its tripping metre, is a fine example of its class, while his *Dialogus Virginis cum cruce* shows greater lyrical power than any of the numerous poetical debates produced by the vernacular poets of his time. The Debate is frequently met in Medieval Latin verse, in which we find, for instance, arguments between priest and layman, Christian and Jew, body and soul, wine and water.

Christmas

PROCEDENTI puero
(Eja novus annus est)
Virginis ex utero,
Gloria laudis!
Deus homo factus est
Et immortalis.

In valle miseriae
(Eja novus annus est)
Venit nos redimere.
Gloria laudis!
Deus homo factus est
Et immortalis.

Christus nobis natus est,
(Eja novus annus est)
Crucifigi passus est.
Gloria laudis!
Deus homo factus est
Et immortalis.

Cujus crucifixio
(Eja novus annus est)
Nostra sit salvatio.
Gloria laudis!
Deus homo factus est
Et immortalis.

Redemptorem saeculi
(*Eja novus annus est*)
Laudent omnes populi.
   Gloria laudis!
Deus homo factus est
   Et immortalis.

Collaudemus Dominum,
(*Eja novus annus est*)
Salvatorem hominum.
   Gloria laudis!
Deus homo factus est
   Et immortalis.

Argument between the Virgin and the Cross

"CRUX, de te volo conqueri:
   Quid est quod in te reperi
   Fructum tibi non debitum?
Fructus quem virgo peperi
Nil debet Adae veteri
Fructum gustanti vetitum.
Intactus fructus uteri
Tuus non debet fieri,
Culpae non habens meritum.

Cur pendet qui non meruit?
Quid, quod te non abhorruit,
Cum sis reis patibulum?
Cur solvit quod non rapuit?
Cur ei qui non nocuit
Es poenale piaculum?
Ei qui vitam tribuit
Mortique nihil debuit
Mortis propinas poculum?

Te reorum suppliciis,
Te culparum flagitiis
Ordinavit justitia.
Cur ergo justum impiis,
Cur virtutem cum vitiis
Sociavit nequitia?
Redditur poena praemiis,
Offensa beneficiis,
Honori contumelia?

Reis in te pendentibus,
Homicidis, latronibus
Inflicta maledictio,
Justo pleno virtutibus,
Ornato charismatibus,
Debetur benedictio;
Ergo quid ad te pertinet?
Cur vita mortem sustinet?
Habitus fit privatio?"

"Virgo, tibi respondeo,
Tibi cui totum debeo
Meorum decus palmitum.
De tuo flore fulgeo,
De tuo fructu gaudeo
Redditura depositum;
Dulce pondus sustineo,
Dulcem fructum possideo,
Mundo non tibi genitum.

Quod si mortem non meruit,
Quid, si mori disposuit,
Ut morte mortem tolleret?
Lignum ligno opposuit,
Solvit quod nunquam rapuit,
Ut debitores liberet;
In Adam vita corruit
Quam secundus restituit,
Ut vita mortem superet.

Ulmus uvam non peperit;
Quid tamen viti deperit
Quod ulmus uvam sustinet?
Fructum tuum non genui,
Sed oblatum non respui
Ne poena culpam terminet.
A te mortalem habui,
Immortalem restitui,
Ut mors in vitam germinet.

Tu vitis, uva filius;
Quid uvae competentius
Quam torcular quo premitur?
Cur pressura fit durius
Nisi quia jucundius
Vinum sincerum bibitur?
Quid uva pressa dulcius?
Quid Christo passo gratius,
In cujus morte vivitur?

Multi se justos reputant,
Filium a te postulant
Et ad me non respiciunt.
Sed postquam tibi creditus
Est apud me depositus:
Extra me non inveniunt.
Quaerant in meo stipite,
Sugant de meo palmite
Fructum tuum quem sitiunt.

Respondeas hypocritis:
'Filium meum quaeritis
Quem cruci dudum tradidi?
Jam non pendet ad ubera;
Pendet in cruce, verbera
Corporis monstrans lividi.
Eum in cruce quaerite,
Guttas cruentas bibite,
Aemulatores perfidi.'"

ANONYMOUS
Coindeta sui
THIRTEENTH CENTURY

The theme of the following example of the Provençal dance-song is that of the French *chanson de mal-mariée*. It is a graceful poem, very simply constructed: all the lines are decasyllabic with feminine endings, and only three rhymes are used. The chorus part is printed in italics, and it will be seen that soloist and chorus share each stanza equally. It was from poems of this type that the French *rondeau* sprang.

Balada

Coindeta sui, si cum n'ai greu cossire,
Per mon marit, quar ne·l voil ne·l desire.

Qu'eu be·us dirai per que son aissi drusa:
Coindeta sui, si cum n'ai greu cossire,
Quar pauca son, joveneta e tosa,
Coindeta sui, si cum n'ai greu cossire,
E degr'aver marit, dont fos joiosa,
Ab cui toz temps pogues jogar e rire.
Coindeta sui, si cum n'ai greu cossire,
Per mon marit, quar ne·l voil ne·l desire.

Ja Deus no·m sal, si ja'n sui amorosa:
Coindeta sui, si cum n'ai greu cossire,
De lui amar mia sui cobeitosa,
Coindeta sui, si cum n'ai greu cossire,
Anz, quant lo vei, ne son tant vergoignosa
Qu'eu prec la mort que·l venga tost aucire.
Coindeta sui, si cum n'ai greu cossire,
Per mon marit, quar ne·l voil ne·l desire.

Mais d'una ren m'en son ben acordada:
Coindeta sui, si cum n'ai greu cossire,
Si·l meus amics m'a s'amor emendada,
Coindeta sui, si cum n'ai greu cossire,
Ve·l bels espers, a cui me son donada;
Plaing e sospir, quar ne·l vei ne·l remire.
Coindeta sui, si cum n'ai greu cossire,
Per mon marit, quar ne·l voil ne·l desire.

E dirai vos de que·m sui acordada:
Coindeta sui, si cum n'ai greu cossire,
Que·l meus amics m'a longament amada;
Coindeta sui, si cum n'ai greu cossire,
Ar li sera m'amors abandonada
E·l bels espers, qu'eu tant am e desire.
Coindeta sui, si cum n'ai greu cossire,
Per mon marit, quar ne·l voil ne·l desire.

En aquest son faz coindeta balada,
Coindeta sui, si cum n'ai greu cossire,
E prec a toz que sia loing cantada,
Coindeta sui, si cum n'ai greu cossire,
E que la chant tota domna ensegnada
Del meu amic, qu'eu tant am e desire.
Coindeta sui, si cum n'ai greu cossire,
Per mon marit, quar ne·l voil ne·l desire.

GAUTIER DE COINCI

1177 — † 1236

GAUTIER DE COINCI became a monk at Soissons in early life and, contrary to the Monk of Montaudon, spent the rest of his life in the cloister. He was the author of an extensive collection of narrative poems on the miracles of the Virgin, and also of some thirty religious lyrics.

The following example, with its imitation of the secular lyric, will serve to illustrate his style. The stanzas are *singulars* of ten lines each with two feminine rhymes used alternately in the first eight lines and a masculine rhyme for the final couplet, while the refrain has a masculine monorhyme.

Pastourelle pieuse

Hui matin a l'ains jornee
　　Toute m'anbleüre
　　Chevauchai par une pree,
Par bonne aventure;
Une florete ai trovee
　　Gente de faiture:
En la fleur qui tant m'agree
　　Tornai lors ma cure;
Adont fis vers dusqu'a sis
De la fleur de paradis.

Chascun lo qu'il aint et lot,
O! o! n'i a tel dorenlot.
　　Pour voir, tout a un mot:
Sache qui m'ot, mar voit Marot,
Qui lait Marie pour Marot.

Qui que chant de Mariete,
　　Je chant de Marie;
Chascun an li doi de dete
　　Une reverdie.
C'est la fleur, la violete,
　　La rose espanie,

[173]

Qui tele oudeur done et jete
Touz nos rasazie.
Haute oudeur sor toute fleur
A la mere au haut seigneur.

Chascun lo qu'il aint et lot,
O! o! n'i a tel dorenlot.
Pour voir, tout a un mot:
Sache qui m'ot, mar voit Marot,
Qui lait Marie pour Marot.

Chant Robins des robardeles,
Chant li soz des sotes.
Mès tu, clerc, qui chante d'eles,
Certes, tu rasotes.
Lessons ces viez pastoureles
Et ces vielles notes:
Si chantons chançons noveles,
Biaus diz, beles notes,
De la fleur dont sanz sejor
Chantent angles nuit et jor.

Chascun lo qu'il aint et lot,
O! o! n'i a tel dorenlot.
Pour voir, tout a un mot:
Sache qui m'ot, mar voit Marot,
Qui lait Marie pour Marot.

Laissons tuit le fol usage
D'amors qui foloie;
Sovent paie le musage
Qui trop i coloie.
Amons la bele, la sage,
La douce, la coie,
Qui tant est de franc corage,
Nului ne faunoie.
En apert se damne et pert
Qui ne l'aime, heneure et sert.

Chascun lo qu'il aint et lot,
O! o! n'i a tel dorenlot.
  Pour voir, tout a un mot:
Sache qui m'ot, mar voit Marot,
Qui lait Marie pour Marot.

  Amons tuit la fresche rose,
    La fleur espanie,
  En qui sainz espirs repose,
    N'i a tele amie:
  Celui qui l'aime et alose
    N'entroublie mie,
  Ainz li done a la parclose
    Pardurable vie.
  Le porpris del ciel a pris
  Qui de s'amor est espris.

Chascun lo qu'il aint et lot,
O! o! n'i a tel dorenlot.
  Pour voir, tout a un mot:
Sache qui m'ot, mar voit Marot,
Qui lait Marie pour Marot.

  A la fin pri la roïne,
    La dame del monde,
  Qui est la doiz, la pecine
    Qui tout cure et monde,
  Qu'ele lest m'ame orpheline,
    M'ame orde et inmonde,
  Si qu'a la fin soit bien fine,
    Bien pure et bien monde,
  Et nos touz de ça desouz
  Daint mener el païs douz.

Chascun lo qu'il aint et lot,
O! o! n'i a tel dorenlot.
  Pour voir, tout a un mot:
Sache qui m'ot, mar voit Marot,
Qui lait Marie pour Marot.

⟦ 175 ⟧

ANONYMOUS

Huc usque

THIRTEENTH CENTURY

The famous lament of a forsaken girl, *Huc usque, me miseram,* contained in the *Carmina Burana,* provides but one of many examples of the use of liturgical metres in secular Latin verse. It is written in the metre of the *Golden Sequence.* The antiphonal basis of Sequences is, indeed, more apparent here than in *Veni, sancte spiritus,* as the final rhyme changes for each pair of strophes.

Planctus peccatricis

Huc usque, me miseram,
Rem bene celaveram,
Et amavi callide.

Res mea tandem patuit,
Nam venter intumuit,
Partus instat gravidae.

Hinc mater me verberat,
Hinc pater improperat,
Ambo tractant aspere.

Sola domi sedeo,
Egredi non audeo,
Nec in palam ludere.

Cum foris egredior,
A cunctis inspicior
Quasi monstrum fuerim.

Cum vident hunc uterum,
Alter pulsat alterum,
Silent dum transierim.

Semper pulsant cubito,
Me designant digito,
Ac si mirum fecerim.

Nutibus me indicant,
Dignam rogo judicant,
Quod semel peccaverim.

Quid percurram singula?
Ego sum in fabula,
Et in ore omnium.

Hoc dolorem cumulat,
Quod amicus exsulat
Propter illud paululum.

Ob patris saevitiam
Recessit in Franciam
A finibus ultimis.

Ex eo vim patior,
Jam dolore morior,
Semper sum in lacrimis.

Sum in tristitia
De ejus absentia,
In doloris cumulum.

AUDEFROI LE BÂTARD

fl. c. 1220—1245

AUDEFROI was one of the group of poets who flourished at Arras in the
earlier part of the thirteenth century, and wrote a number of imitations of
the *chanson de toile*.

In *Bele Ysabiauz* he uses the decasyllable of the old *chanson de toile* for
the first three lines of each stanza, completing it with two octosyllables.
Instead of the monorhymed *coblas singulars* of the old poems, he uses
coblas unissonans, with one feminine rhyme to the long lines and a masculine
rhyme to the shorter ones. Like many others of his imitations, *Bele
Ysabiauz* has an absurd dénouement.

Chanson de toile

BELE Ysabiauz, pucele bien aprise,
Ama Gerart et il li en tel guise
C'ainc de folour par lui en fu requise,
Ainz l'ama de si bone amour
Que mieuz de li guarda s'onnour.
Et joie atent Gerars.

Quant pluz se fu bone amours entr'eus mise,
Par loiauté afermee et reprise,
En cele amour la damoisele ont prise
Si parent, et douné seignour,
Outre son gre, un vavassour.
Et joie atent Gerars.

Quant sot Gerars, cui fine amours justise,
Que la bele fu a seigneur tramise,
Grains et mariz fist tant par sa maistrise
Que a sa dame en un destour
A fait sa plainte et sa clamour.
Et joie atent Gerars.

"Amis Gerart, n'aiez ja couvoitise
De ce voloir dont ainc ne fui requise.
Puis que je ai seigneur, qui m'aimme et prise,
   Bien doi estre de tel valour,
   Que je ne doi penser folour."
    Et joie atent Gerars.

"Amis Gerart, faites ma commandise:
Ralez vous ent, si feroiz grant franchise.
Morte m'avriez, s'od vous estoie prise.
   Maiz metez vous tost u retour.
   Je vous conmant au creatour."
    Et joie atent Gerars.

"Dame, l'amour qu'ailleurs avez assise
Deüsse avoir par loiauté conquise;
Maiz pluz vous truis dure que pierre bise,
   S'en ai au cuer si grant dolour
   Qu'a biau samblant souspir et plour."
    Et joie atent Gerars.

"Dame, pour Dieu", fait Gerars sanz faintise,
"Aiez de moi pitié par vo franchise.
La vostre amours me destraint et atise,
   Et pour vous sui en tel errour,
   Que nus ne puet estre en greignour."
    Et joie atent Gerars.

Quant voit Gerars, cui fine amours justise,
Que sa dolours de noient n'apetise,
Lors se croisa de duel et d'ire esprise,
   Et pourquiert einsi son atour,
   Que il puist movoir a brief jor.
    Et joie atent Gerars.

Tost muet Gerars, tost a sa voie quise;
Devant tramet son escuïer Denise,
A sa dame parler par sa franchise.
    La dame ert ja pour la verdour
    En un vergier cueillir la flour.
      Et joie atent Gerars.

Vestue fu la dame par cointise:
Mout ert bele, graile et grasse, et alise;
Le vis avoit vermeill come cerise.
    "Dame", dit il, "que tresbon jour
    Vous doint cil cui j'aim et aour."
      Et joie atent Gerars.

"Dame, pour Deu", fait Gerars sanz faintise,
"D'outre mer ai pour vous la voie emprise."
La dame l'ot; mieus vousist estre ocise:
    Si s'entrebaisent par douçour,
    Qu'andui cheïrent en l'erbour.
      Et joie atent Gerars.

Ses maris voit la folour entreprise:
Pour voir cuida, la dame morte gise
Les son ami: tant se het et desprise
    Qu'il pert sa force et sa vigour
    Et muert de duel en tel errour.
      Et joie atent Gerars.

De pasmoison lievent par tel devise
Que il font faire au mort tout son servise.
Li deus remaint; Gerars par sainte eglise
    A fait de sa dame s'oissour:
    Ce tesmoignent li ancissour.
      Or a joie Gerars.

PIERO DELLE VIGNE

c. 1180 — † 1249

PIERO DELLE VIGNE, one of the earliest Italian poets, was educated at the University of Bologna and held high office in Sicily under the Emperor Frederick II. Accused of treason after many years of faithful service, he committed suicide. Dante defends him in a famous passage in the *Inferno*.

The technique of his *Amore, in cui disio ed ò speranʒa* is typical of the early Italian *canʒone*. It is written in short stanzas of eight hendecasyllables, the stanzas being *singulars* and *capfinidas*, with four rhymes each. The last stanza is a *comiato*, of the same length as the other stanzas. It is somewhat curious that the shorter *comiato*, which corresponds to the Provençal *tornada*, did not become usual until about 1260.

In the first line, some editors have substituted *fidanʒa* for *speranʒa*, as the latter word recurs at the end of the third line, but there is no manuscript authority for the change.

Canʒone

AMORE, in cui disio ed ò speranza,
Di voi, bella, m'à dato guiderdone,
Guardomi infin che vengna la speranza,
Pur aspettando buon tempo e stagione,
Com' uom ch' è in mare ed à spene di gire;
E quando vede il tempo, ed ello spanna,
E giamai la speranza non lo 'nganna;
Cos' io faccio, madonna, in voi venire.

Or potess' eo venir a voi, amorosa,
Com lo larone ascoso, e non paresse;
Bello mi teria in gioia aventurosa
Se l' amor tanto bene mi facesse.
Sì bel parlante, donna, con voi fora,
E direi como v' amai lungiamente,
Più ca Piramo Tisbia dolzemente,
Ed ameraggio infin ch' io vivo ancora.

Vostro amor è che mi tiene in disiro
E donami speranza con gran gioia,
Ch' io non curo s'io dolglio od ò martiro
Membrando l'ora ched io vengno a voi;
Ca s' io troppo dimoro, aulente lena,
Par ch' io pera, e voi mi perderete;
Adunque, bella, se ben mi volete,
Guardate che non mora in vostra spena.

In vostra spena vivo, donna mia,
E lo mio core adesso a voi dimando,
E l' ora tardi mi pare che sia
Che fino amore a vostro cor mi mando;
E guardo tempo che sia a piacimento
E spanda le mie vele inver voi, rosa,
E prendo porto là 've si riposa
Lo mio core al vostro insengnamento.

Mia canzonetta, porta esti compianti
A quella c' à 'm ballia lo mio core,
E le mie pene contale davanti,
E dille com' io moro per su' amore;
E mandimi per suo messagio a dire
Com' io comforti l' amor che lei porto,
E se ver lei i' feci alcuno torto,
Donimi penitenza al suo volire.

GONZALO DE BERCEO

c. 1180 — † 1246?

GONZALO DE BERCEO, a Spanish secular priest at San Millán de la Cogolla, is known to have taken major orders by 1221. He was a pious versifier of saints' lives, which he turned into the monorhymed Alexandrine quatrain known as the *cuaderna via*.

His *Duelo que fizo la Virgen María* contains a lyrical watch-song, uttered by Jewish soldiers placed on guard around the tomb of Christ to prevent his body from being stolen by the Apostles. Its versification points to a popular origin, traceable perhaps to the songs sung by pilgrims at the shrine of San Millán. It is in roughly octosyllabic couplets with regular rhyme and a simple, effective refrain. There is a considerable amount of repetition and parallelism in its stanzas, which are here arranged in the order suggested by Sr Rodrigues Lapa.

Cantiga de vela

Eya velar, eya velar, eya velar.

VELAT aliama de los judios
    (*Eya velar*)
  Que non vos furten el fijo de Dios.
    Eya velar.

Ca furtárvoslo querran
    (*Eya velar*)
Andres e Peidro et Johan.
    Eya velar.

Todos son ladronçiellos
    (*Eya velar*)
Que assechan por los pestiellos.
    Eya velar.

Todos son omnes plegadizos,
    (*Eya velar*)
Rioaduchos mescladizos.
    Eya velar.

Vuestra lengua tan palabrera
(*Eya velar*)
Ha vos dado mala carrera.
Eya velar.

Vuestra lengua sin recabdo
(*Eya velar*)
Por mal cabo vos ha echado.
Eya velar.

Non sabedes tanto descanto
(*Eya velar*)
Que salgades de so el canto.
Eya velar.

Non sabedes tanto de enganno
(*Eya velar*)
Que salgades ende este anno.
Eya velar.

Non sabedes tanta razon
(*Eya velar*)
Que salgades de la prision.
Eya velar.

El disçipulo lo vendió;
(*Eya velar*)
El maestro non lo entendió.
Eya velar.

Tomaseio e Matheo,
(*Eya velar*)
De furtarlo han grant deseo.
Eya velar.

Don Fhilipo, Simon, e Judas
(*Eya velar*)
Por furtar buscan ayudas.
Eya velar.

Si lo quieren acometer,
       (Eya velar)
Oy es dia de paresçer.
       Eya velar.

Eya velar, eya velar, eya velar.

PEIRE CARDENAL
fl. 1220—1270

PEIRE CARDENAL who, according to his Provençal biographer, lived to
be almost a hundred, was the greatest troubadour of the period immediately
after the Albigensian Crusade. While protesting his orthodoxy, he was
violently anticlerical, his satires on the corruption of the monastic orders
being particularly biting.

In his graceful hymn to the Virgin, which is partly based on the Litany
of Loretto, he falls into line with the new fashion for religious poetry. It is
written in *coblas unissonans*, with two rhymes, one feminine and one
masculine, used alternately. Its metre is the *versus popularis*.

Hymn to the Virgin

VERA vergena Maria,
Vera vida, vera fes,
Vera vertatz, vera via,
Vera vertutz, vera res,
Vera maire, ver' amia,
Ver' amors, vera merces,
Per ta vera merce sia
Qu'estend' en me tos heres.

De patz, si·t plai, dona, traita
Qu'ab ton filh nos sia faita.

Tu restauriest la follia
Don Adam fon sobrepres;
Tu yest l'estela, que guia
Los passans d'aquest paes;
E tu yest l'alba del dia

Don lo Dieus filhs solelhs es,
Que·l calfa e clarifia,
Verais de dreitura ples.
De patz, si·t plai, dona, traita
Qu'ab ton filh nos sia faita.

Tu fust nada de Suria,
Gentils e paura d'arnes,
Umils e pura e pia
En fatz, en ditz, et en pes.
Faita per tal maestria
Ses totz mals, mas ab totz bes,
Tant fust de doussa paria
Per que Dieus en tu se mes.

De patz, dona, si·t platz, traita
Qu'ab ton filh nos sia faita.

Aquel qui en te se fia
Ja no·l cal autre defes,
Que si tot lo mon peria,
Aquel non penria ges;
Car als tieus precx s'umilia
L'autismes, a cui que pes,
E·l tieus filhs non contraria
Ton voler neguna ves.

De patz, dona, si·t platz, traita
Qu'ab ton filh nos sia faita.

David en sa prophetia
Dis, en un salme que fes,
Qu'al destre de Dieu sezia,
Del rey en la ley promes,
Una reyna qu'avia
Vestirs de var e d'aurfres;
Tu yest elha ses falhia,
Non o pot vedar plaides.

De patz, dona, si·t platz, traita
Qu'ab ton filh nos sia faita.

ANONYMOUS

Omnia sol temperat

THIRTEENTH CENTURY

Spring-songs form one of the most attractive classes of the Goliardic lyric, but there is no need to find an origin for them in the Goliards' habit of migrating from one university to another when spring brought opportunities for freer movement. It would have been remarkable if they had not written spring-songs.

The present example, from the *Carmina Burana*, is delicately written in the Goliardic Metre, with internal rhymes.

Spring-song

OMNIA sol temperat
Purus et subtilis,
Nova mundo reserat
Facies Aprilis,
Ad amorem properat
Animus herilis,
Et jucundis imperat
Deus puerilis.

Rerum tanta novitas
In sollemni vere
Et veris auctoritas
Jubet nos gaudere,
Vias praebet solitas,
Et in tuo vere
Fides est et probitas
Tuum retinere.

[185]

Ama me fideliter,
  Fidem meam nota
De corde totaliter
  Et ex mente tota,
Sum praesentialiter
  Absens in remota;
Quisquis amat taliter,
  Volvitur in rota.

GIACOMO DA LENTINO
fl. 1223 — 1243

GIACOMO DA LENTINO, like Piero delle Vigne, was educated at Bologna
and held high judicial office in Sicily under Frederick II. He is generally
referred to in contemporary documents as "the Notary", and is fond of thus
styling himself in his poems.

One of the earliest poets of the Sicilian school, he was also one of the
first writers of the sonnet. His sonnet, *Io m' agio posto*, though irregular
in its prosody, has those features which have ever since characterized the
Italian sonnet, i.e. it is divided into an octave and a sestet, the former
having two rhymes. The sestet, which may have either two rhymes or
three, has two only in the present example.

In his *canzone, Guiderdone aspetto avire*, Giacomo uses the form of a
Victorine Sequence, the stanzas being dimorphic, of three or five lines each,
in alternate pairs. The final lines of each pair of stanzas rhyme together,
different sets of rhymes being used for the other lines, exactly as in a regular
Sequence. This poem is sometimes attributed to Rinaldo d' Aquino.

Sonnet

Io m' agio posto in core a Dio servire,
  Com' io potesse gire im paradiso:
  Al santo loco c' agio audito dire
Ove si mantiene sollazo, gioco, e riso.
Senza la mia donna non vi vorria gire,
Quella c' à la blondda testa e 'l claro viso,
Chè sanza lei nom porzeria gaudire,
Estando dala mia donna diviso.

Ma non lo dico a tale intendimento
Perch' io peccato ci vollesse fare,
Se non vedere lo suo bello portamento,
E lo bello viso, e 'l morbido sguardare;
Ch' elo mi tería in grande comsolamento,
Vegiendo la mia donna in gloria stare.

Canzone

GUIDERDONE aspetto avire
Di voi, donna, cui servire
   Non m' è noia.

Sì mi sete tanto altera,
Ancor spero avere intera
   D' amor gioia.

Non vivo in disperanza,
Ancor che mi diffidi
La vostra disdengnanza:
Cà spesse volte vidi,
   Ed è provato

C' omo di poco affare
Per venire in gran loco,
S' ello sape avanzare,
Moltiprica lo poco
   Conquistato.

In dispranza non mi gietto,
Ch' io medesmo m' imprometto
   D' aver bene.

Di bon core è la speranza
Ch' i' vi porto, e la leanza
   Mi mantene.

A ciò non mi scoragio
D' amor, che m' à distretto:
Sì com' omo salvagio
Faragio, ch' el' è detto
    Ch' ello facie:

Per lo reo tempo ride,
Sperando che poi pera
La laida ara, che vide;
Di donna troppo fera
    Spero pacie.

S' io pur spero in allegranza,
Fina donna, pïetanza
    In voi si mova.

Fina donna, non sïate
Fera, poi tanta bieltate
    In voi si trova.

Cà donna, c' à belleze
Ed è sanza pietade,
Com' omo è, c' à richeze
Ed usa scarsitade
    Di ciò ch' ave;

Se non è bene apreso,
Nè dritto, nè insengnato,
D' ongn' omo n' è ripreso,
Onuto e dispresgiato
    E presgio à grave.

Donna mia, ch' io nom perisca:
S' io vi prego, non vi incrisca
    Mia preghera:

La belleza, ch' en voi pare,
Mi distringie, e lo sguardare
    Dela ciera.

La figura piagiente
Lo core mi diranca;
Quando vi tengno mente,
Lo spirito mi manca
    E torna in ghiaccio.

Nè mica mi spaventa
L' amoroso volere
Di ciò che m' atalenta,
Ch' io no' lo posso avere:
    Ônd' i' mi sfaccio.

COLIN MUSET
fl. 1225

Of the life of Colin Muset nothing is known, apart from what can be de-
duced from his writings. It is probable that he lived in the east of France.
A jongleur by profession, he hung on to the skirts of feudal society, earning
his living by his songs, which he sang from place to place.

    The polyglot *descort* of Raimbaut de Vaqueiras, which has already been
noticed, is an unusual one, as all its stanzas have the same metrical form.
Colin Muset's *descort*, *Quant voi lo douz tens repairier*, resembles the earlier
type of Sequence, its sections being of different lengths and composed of
lines of different lengths. Most of the sections are divisible into two halves,
identical in metrical form, and generally using the same rhymes.

Descort

QUANT voi lo douz tens repairier,
    Que li rosignols chante en mai,
      Et je cuiz que doie alegier
Li mals et la dolors que j'ai,
Adonc m'ocient li delai
D'amors, qui les font engregnier.
Las! mar vi onques son cor gai,
S'a ma vie ne lo conquier.

Amors de moi ne cuide avoir pechiez
Por ceu que sui ses hom liges sosgiez.
Douce dame, pregne vos en pitiez.
Qui plus s'abaisse, plus est essauciez.

Et qant si grant chose empris ai
Con de vostre amor chalengier,
Toz tens en pardons servirai,
Se tost n'en ai altre loieir.
Ma tres douce dame honoree,
    Je ne vos os nes proier;
Cil est mout fols qui si haut bee
    Ou il nen ose aprochier.

        Mais tote voie
    Tres bien revoudroie
    Vostre amors fust moie
    Por moi ensengnier,
        Car a grant joie
    Vit et s'esbanoie
    Cui amors maistroie;
    Meuz s'en doit proisier.

Qui bien vuet d'amors joïr
        Si doit soffrir
        Et endurer
Qan k'ele li vuet merir;
        Au repentir
        Ne doit panser,
C'om puet bien, tot a loisir,
        Son boen desir
        A point mener.
Endroit de moi criem morir
        Meuz que garir
        Par bien amer.

Se je n'ai la joie grant
Que mes fins cuers va chacent,
Deffenir m'estuet briement.
Douce riens por cui je chant,
En mon descort vos demant
Un ris debonairemant,
S'en vivrai plus longemant;
Moins en avrai de torment.

Bele, j'ai si grant envie
D'embracier vostre cors gent,
S'amors ne m'en fait aïe,
J'en morrai coiteusement.
Amors ne m'en faudrat mie,
Car je l'ai trop bien servie
Et ferai tote ma vie
Senz nule fause pansee.
Preuz de tote gent loee
Plus que nule qui soit nee,
Se vostre amors m'est donee,
Bien iert ma joie doublee.

Mon descort ma dame aport
La bone duchesse, por chanter;
De toz biens a li m'acort,
K'ele aime deport, rire, et juer.

Dame, or vos voil bien mostrer
Que je ne sai vostre per
De bone vie mener,
Et de leialment amer.
Adès vos voi enmender
En vaillance et en doner.
Nel lassiez ja por jangler,
Que ceu ne vos puet grever.

PERO DA PONTE

fl. 1230—1252

PERO DA PONTE, a Galician by birth, spent a considerable part of his life
in Aragon and Castile, where he sang the exploits of James I and Ferdinand III. The author of both satires and love-lyrics, he was reproved by
Alfonso X for writing in the native style rather than in that of Provence.
In his work, indeed, the indigenous poetry of the Peninsula triumphs over
the foreign school.

In the following striking *cantiga de amigo*, he introduces an extremely
simple but haunting refrain. The second and fourth lines of each stanza are
in full rhyme, the other two being unrhymed. This poem and the one
on page 219 were perhaps originally written with two long lines to
each stanza.

Cantiga de amigo

VISTES, madr', o escudeiro
Que m'ouver' a levar sigo?
Menti-lhe, vai-mi sanhudo.
Mia madre, ben vo-lo digo:
Madre, namorada me leixou,
Madre, namorada mi-á leixada,
Madre, namorada me leixou.

Madre, vós que me mandastes
Que mentiss' a meu amigo,
Que conselho mi daredes
Ora, poi-lo non ei migo?
Madre, namorada me leixou,
Madre, namorada mi-á leixada,
Madre, namorada me leixou.

Filha, dou-vos por conselho
Que, tanto que vos el veja,
Que toda ren lhi façades,
Que vosso pagado seja:
Madre, namorada me leixou,
Madre, namorada mi-á leixada,
Madre, namorada me leixou.

Pois escusar non podedes,
Mia filha, seu gasalhado,
Des oi mais eu vos castigo
Que lh'andedes a mandado:
Madre, namorada me leixou,
Madre, namorada mi-á leixada,
Madre, namorada me leixou.

GIACOMO PUGLIESE

FIRST HALF OF THIRTEENTH CENTURY

Nothing is known of Giacomo (Giacomino), except that he was an Apulian and a poet of the Sicilian school. His beautiful elegy on his lady, with its sincerity and pathos, entitles him to rank as one of the greatest of that group. It is in hendeçasyllables, except that each stanza has two pentasyllablic lines.

Canzone

MORTE, perchè m' ài fatta sì gran guerra
Che m' ài tolta madonna, ond' io mi dolglio?
La flor de le bellezze è morta in terra
Perchè lo mondo non amo nè volglio.
Villana morte, che non ài pietanza,
Disparti amore e tolgli la allegranza
E dai cordoglio;
La mia allegranza ài posta in gran tristanza,
Chè m' ài tolto la gioia e l' allegranza
C' avere soglio.

Solea aver sollazzo e gioco e riso
Più che null' altro cavalier che sia;
Or n' è gita madonna im paradiso;
Portonne la dolce speranza mia,

Lasciommi in pene e con sospiri e pianti,
Levommi da lo dolze gioco e canti,
    E compangnia.
Or non la veggio, nè le sto davanti,
E non mi mostra li dolzi sembianti,
    Come solia.

Ov' è madonna e lo suo insegnamento,
La sua bellezza e la gran canoscienza,
Lo dolze riso e lo bel parlamento,
Gli occhi e la bocca e la bella sembianza?
Oimè, sia in nulla parte ciò m' è aviso;
Madonna, chi lo tiene, lo tuo viso,
    In sua ballia?
Lo vostro insengnamento dond' è miso?
E lo tuo franco cor chi mi l' à priso,
    Madonna mia?

Oi Deo, perchè m' ài posto in tale stanza?
Ch' io son smarato e non so ove mi sia,
Chè m' ài levato la dolze speranza,
Partita la più dolze compangnia,
Lo adornamento e la sua cortesia.
Madonna, per cui stava tuttavia
    In allegranza,
Or non la vegio nè notte nè dia,
E non m' abella, sì com far solia,
    La sua sembianza.

Se fosse mio 'l reame d' Ungaria,
Con Grezia e la Mangna infino in Franza,
Lo gran tesoro di Santa Sofia,
Non poria ristorar sì gran perdanza
Come fu in quella dia che si n' andao
Madonna, e d' esta vita trapassao
    Con gran tristanza;
Sospiri e pene e pianti mi lasciao,
E giammai nulla gioia mi mandao
    Per confortanza.

Se fosse al mio voler, donna, di voi,
Diciesse a Dio sovran che tutto facie
Che notte e giorno istessimo ambondoi.
Or sia il voler di Dio, da ch' a lui piace.
Membro e ricordo quand' era con meco
Sovente m' apellava dolze amico,
   Ed or nol facie.
Poi Dio la prese e menolla con seco,
La sua vertute sia, bella, con teco,
   E la sua pacie.

THIBAUT IV OF NAVARRE

1201 — † 1253

THIBAUT IV, Count of Champagne and from 1234 to his death King of
Navarre, fought for Louis VIII against the English, and took part in the
Crusade of 1239. He was one of the most celebrated of the trouvères, and
sixty-one of his poems have survived. A number of them are *jeux-partis*,
in the writing of which he was particularly skilful.

His poem, *Por mau tens*, belongs to an uncommon genre—the *rotrouenge*,
which exists also in Old Provençal as the *retroensa*. The *rotrouenge* differs
hardly at all from the ordinary *chanson*, except that it has a refrain. In the
present example, the refrain consists of one word only. The poem is written
in *coblas doblas*, with two rhymes to each stanza—one feminine and one
masculine. The lines vary in length from seven syllables to four.

Rotrouenge

POR mau tens ne por gelee,
 Ne por froide matinee,
  Ne por nule autre riens nee,
Ne partirai ma pensee
  D'amors que j'ai,
  Que trop l'ai amee
  De cuer verai.
  Valara!

Bele et blonde et coloree,
Moi plest quanq'il vous agree.
He, Deus! car me fust donee
L'amor que vous ai rouvee!
    Quant prierai,
    S'ele m'est veee,
    Je me morrai.
    Valara!

Dame, en la vostre baillie
Ai mis mon cors et ma vie.
Por Deu, ne m'ocïez mie!
La ou fins cuers s'umilie
    Doit on trouver
    Merci et aïe
    Pour conforter.
    Valara!

Dame, faites cortoisie!
Plaise vos que en ma vie
Iceste parole die:
Ma bele, tres douce amie
    Vos os nonmer,
    C'onques n'oi envie
    D'autrui amer.
    Valara!

Onques jor ne me soi plaindre,
Tant seroit ma dolor graindre;
Ne d'amer ne me sai faindre,
Ne mes maus ne puis estaindre,
    Se je ne di
    Que touz vueil remaindre
    En sa merci.
    Valara!

Trop seroit fort a estaindre
Chançons de li;
L'amors est a fraindre,
Dont pens a li.
Valara!

THOMAS OF CELANO

c. 1200 — 1255

THOMAS OF CELANO, an early member of the Franciscan Order and the biographer of its founder, is generally considered the author of the *Dies irae*, the greatest of all Latin hymns.

Although it has long been used as the Sequence at Masses for the departed, the *Dies irae* was not written for that purpose, for Sequences had originated from the *Alleluia*—a word which the Latin Church had long avoided at Requiem services—and consequently Requiem Masses had no Sequence. The *Dies irae*, like the *Rosy Sequence*, forced its way into the missal on its own merits, to a place for which it was perfectly suited. In one respect, it was even more suited to Sequence use than *Dulcis Jesu memoria*, for it is written in the trochaic line which is almost inseparable from the Sequence. This, however, is the only point in which it adheres to the normal Sequence form, for all but its last two lines—added, like the previous stanza, later—are acatalectic, and its stanzas are not grouped into pairs by a common end-rhyme.

Sequence for the Dead

DIES irae, dies illa
Solvet saeclum in favilla,
Teste David cum sibylla.

Quantus tremor est futurus
Quando judex est venturus,
Cuncta stricte discussurus!

Tuba mirum sparget sonum
Per sepulcra regionum,
Coget omnes ante thronum.

Mors stupebit et natura,
Cum resurget creatura
Judicanti responsura.

Liber scriptus proferetur
In quo totum continetur
Unde mundus judicetur.

Judex ergo cum censebit
Quicquid latet apparebit;
Nil inultum remanebit.

Quid sum miser tunc dicturus,
Quem patronum rogaturus,
Dum vix justus sit securus?

Rex tremendae majestatis,
Qui salvandos salvas gratis,
Salva me, fons pietatis.

Recordare, Jesu pie,
Quod sum causa tuae viae:
Ne me perdas illa die.

Quaerens me, sedisti lassus,
Redemisti crucem passus;
Tantus labor non sit cassus.

Juste judex ultionis,
Donum fac remissionis
Ante diem rationis.

Ingemisco tamquam reus,
Culpa rubet vultus meus;
Supplicanti parce, Deus.

Qui Mariam absolvisti
Et latronem exaudisti
Mihi quoque spem dedisti.

Preces meae non sunt dignae,
Sed tu bonus fac benigne
Ne perenni cremer igne.

Inter oves locum praesta
Et ab haedis me sequestra,
Statuens in parte dextra.

Confutatis maledictis,
Flammis acribus addictis,
Voca me cum benedictis.

Oro supplex et acclinis,
Cor contritum quasi cinis.
Gere curam mei finis.

Lacrimosa dies illa,
Qua resurget ex favilla
Judicandus homo reus;
Huic ergo parce, Deus.

Pie Jesu, Domine,
Dona eis requiem.

NUNO FERNANDEZ TORNEOL

THIRTEENTH CENTURY

Of Nuno Fernandez nothing is known except that he was a Portuguese
knight of the thirteenth century, and that he visited Valladolid, Toledo,
and Olmedo. About twenty of his poems have survived, among them being
the beautiful dawn-song, *Levad', amigo*. It has the usual features of the
cossante. The first two stanzas are in assonance, the remainder in full
rhyme.

Alva

LEVAD', amigo, que dormides as manhãas frias;
Toda-las aves do mundo d'amor dizian:
        Leda m' and' eu.

Levad', amigo, que dormide'-las frias manhãas;
Toda-las aves do mundo d'amor cantavan:
Leda m'and' eu.

Toda-las aves do mundo d'amor diziam;
Do meu amor e do voss' en ment' avian:
Leda m'and' eu.

Toda-las aves do mundo d'amor cantavan;
Do meu amor e do voss' i enmentavan:
Leda m'and' eu.

Do meu amor e do voss' en ment' avian;
Vós lhi tolhestes os ramos en que siian:
Leda m'and' eu.

Do meu amor e do voss' i enmentavam;
Vós lhi tolhestes os ramos en que pousavan:
Leda m'and' eu.

Vós lhi tolhestes os ramos en que siian,
E lhis secastes as fontes en que bevian:
Leda m'and' eu.

Vós lhi tolhestes os ramos en que pousavan,
E lhis secastes as fontes u se banhavan:
Leda m'and' eu.

RINALDO D'AQUINO

fl. 1240

RINALDO D'AQUINO was probably the elder brother of Saint Thomas Aquinas, whom he kidnapped in a vain attempt to prevent him from becoming a Dominican. He held office under Frederick II and Manfred, but deserted the latter for Charles of Anjou.

A polished stylist of the Sicilian school, he is at his best in the beautiful poem, *Giammai non mi conforto*, in which a girl laments the departure of her lover for the Crusades. It is very simply constructed in heptasyllabic quatrains with crossed rhymes, its metre and general atmosphere being reminiscent of popular poetry. The metre and rhyme are irregular in a number of places.

Lamento

GIAMMAI non mi conforto
   Nè mi voglio rallegrare;
   Le navi son giunte al porto,
E vogliono collare.

Vassene la più gente
In terra d' oltremare,
Ed io lassa dolente,
Come deg' io fare?

Vassen' in altra contrata,
E nol mi manda a dire;
Ed io rimangno ingannata,
Tanti son li sospire,

Che mi fanno gran guerra
La notte co la dia;
E nè in cielo nè in terra
Non mi par ch' io sia.

Santus, santus Deo
Che 'n la virgen venisti,
Tu salva l' amor meo
Poi da me 'l dipartisti.

Oi alta potestate,
Temuta e dottata,
Il dolce mio amore
Ti sia racomandata.

La croce salva la gente,
E me face disviare;
La croce mi fa dolente:
Non mi val Dio pregare.

Oi me, croce pellegrina,
Perchè m' ài così distrutta?
Oi me lassa tapina,
Ch' i' ardo e 'nciendo tutta.

Lo 'mperador con pace
Tutto 'l mondo mantiene,
Ed a me guerra face,
M' à tolta la mia spene.

Oi alta potestade,
Temuta e ridottata,
Lo mio dolce amore
Vi sia racomandata.

Quando la croce pigliao,
Cierto nol mi pensai—
Quel che tanto m' amao
Ed io lui tanto amai,

Ch' io ne fui battuta
E messa in presgioni,
E in cielata tenuta,
Per la vita mia.

Le navi sono alle colle,
In bonora possano andare,
E 'l mio amor con elle,
E la gente che va andare.

Padre criatore,
A santo porto le conduce,
Che vanno a servidore
De la santa croce.

Però ti prego, Dolcietto,
Che sai la pena mia,
Che men faci un sonetto
E mandilo in Soria.

Ch' io nom posso abentare
Notte nè dia;
In terra d' oltremare
Istà la vita mia.

JOÃO D'ABOIM

fl. 1240—1250

JOÃO D'ABOIM, a Portuguese nobleman, was much favoured by Alfonso III of Portugal, whom he accompanied to France before his accession to the throne. He has left fifteen poems, among which is a *pastorela*. It opens like a French *pastourelle* with its "L'autre jour moi chivachai", but, unlike French and Provençal pastorals, has no male participant. It has been conjectured that the earliest Romance pastorals were of this type. Aboim's poem is regularly rhymed, with three rhymes to each stanza. Its metrical basis is the *versus popularis*.

Pastorela

CAVALGAVA noutro dia
    Per o caminho francês,
    E ũa pastor siia
Cantando con outras tres
Pastores, e non vos pês;
E direi-vos toda via
O que a pastor dizia
Aas outras en castigo:
"Nunca molher crêa per amigo,
Pois s'o meu foi e non falou migo."

    "Pastor, non dizedes nada",
    Diz ũa d'elas enton;
    "Se se foi esta vegada,
Ar verrá-s'outra sazon,
E dirá-vos por que non
Falou vosc', ai ben talhada,
E é cousa mais guisada
De dizerdes, com'eu digo:
'Deus, ora veess'o meu amigo,
E averia gram prazer migo.'"

ANONYMOUS

Exiit diluculo

THIRTEENTH CENTURY

This charming little pastoral is from the *Carmina Burana*. The courtly suitor of the vernacular pastoral is here, as befits Goliardic poetry, replaced by a scholar, and the shepherdess makes the advances. The poem, though a perfect cameo, is so short and, above all, so proper, that, when one compares it with other specimens of the *Carmina Burana*, one cannot help wondering whether it is a fragment.

Pastoral

EXIIT diluculo
   Rustica puella
   Cum grege, cum baculo,
Cum lana novella.

Sunt in grege parvulo
   Ovis et asella,
Vitula cum vitulo,
   Caper et capella.

Conspexit in caespite
   Scholarem sedere:
"Quid tu facis, domine?
   Veni mecum ludere."

JOÃO ZORRO

fl. 1250

The jongleur João Zorro, who probably frequented the court of Alfonso III of Portugal, keeps very near to popular poetry, perhaps nearer than any other early Portuguese poet. He is pre-eminently a poet of sea and river, seven of his eleven surviving poems being *barcarolas*.

His *barcarola*, *Per ribeira do rio*, is at the same time one of the simplest and one of the most effective of its kind. It has the usual construction of a *cossante*.

His fine *bailada*, *Bailemos agora*, is in monorhymed quatrains, in full rhyme, the stressed *i* of the first stanza being followed by *a* in the second, as is the rule in *cossantes*.

Barcarola

Per ribeira do rio
Vi remar o navio,
E sabor ei da ribeira.

Per ribeira do alto
Vi remar o barco,
E sabor ei da ribeira.

Vi remar o navio:
I vai o meu amigo,
E sabor ei da ribeira.

Vi remar o barco:
I vai o meu amado,
E sabor ei da ribeira.

I vai o meu amigo:
Quer-me levar consigo,
E sabor ei da ribeira.

I vai o meu amado:
Quer-me levar de grado,
E sabor ei da ribeira.

Bailada

Bailemos agora, por Deus, ai velidas,
So aquestas avelaneiras frolidas,
E quem fôr velida como nós, velidas,
Se amigo amar,
So aquestas avelaneiras frolidas
Verrá bailar.

Bailemos agora, por Deus, ai loadas,
So aquestas avelaneiras granadas,
E quem fôr loada como nós, loadas,
Se amigo amar,
So aquestas avelaneiras granadas
Verrá bailar.

JACOPONE DA TODI

c. 1220 — † 1306

JACOPONE DA TODI, who practised as a lawyer in his native Umbrian city, was converted to religion by the tragic death of his wife, and entered the Franciscan Order. An outspoken critic of Pope Boniface VIII, he was excommunicated and imprisoned by the latter for five years, and did not emerge from prison until Boniface's death.

Jacopone is generally considered the author of the *Stabat mater*. One of the most beautiful and appealing of all Medieval Latin poems, it is written in very simple language and in the simplest and most favoured of all forms of the late or stanzaic Sequence. It contains a number of striking internal rhymes.

The author of the *Stabat mater*, as befitted one who shared the early Franciscan contempt for learning, preferred Italian to Latin, and was a prolific writer of *laude spirituali*. His *Donna del paradiso*, one of the finest poems of this class, is written in simple heptasyllabic quatrains, each quatrain being monorhymed, except that the last lines rhyme together throughout. It will be noticed that the poem is entirely in dialogue, the names of the speakers being given outside the stanzas, and it is therefore suited to performance as a play. Whether it was actually performed as such is uncertain but probable. We know at least that the earliest Italian plays were of this type and were probably produced in Jacopone's lifetime.

Sequence

STABAT mater dolorosa
Juxta crucem lacrimosa,
 Dum pendebat filius;

Cujus animam gementem,
Contristantem et dolentem
 Pertransivit gladius.

O quam tristis et afflicta
Fuit illa benedicta
 Mater unigeniti!

Quae moerebat et dolebat,
Et tremebat cum videbat
 Nati poenas incliti.

Quis est homo qui non fleret,
Matrem Christi si videret
 In tanto supplicio?

Quis non posset contristari,
Piam matrem contemplari
 Dolentem cum filio?

Pro peccatis suae gentis
Jesum vidit in tormentis
 Et flagellis subditum.

Vidit suum dulcem natum
Morientem desolatum,
 Cum emisit spiritum.

Eja, mater, fons amoris,
Me sentire vim doloris
    Fac, ut tecum lugeam.

Fac, ut ardeat cor meum
In amando Christum Deum,
    Ut sibi complaceam.

Sancta mater, illud agas:
Crucifixi fige plagas
    Cordi meo valide.

Tui nati vulncrati,
Jam dignati pro me pati,
    Poenas mecum divide.

Fac me vere tecum flere,
Crucifixo condolere,
    Donec ego vixero;

Juxta crucem tecum stare,
Te libenter sociare
    In planctu desidero.

Virgo virginum praeclara,
Mihi jam non sis amara:
    Fac me tecum plangere.

Fac, ut portem Christi mortem,
Passionis ejus sortem
    Et plagas recolere.

Fac me plagis vulnerari,
Cruce hac inebriari
    Ob amorem filii.

Inflammatus et accensus,
Per te, virgo, sim defensus
    In die judicii.

Fac me cruce custodiri,
Morte Christi praemuniri,
    Confoveri gratia.

Quando corpus morietur,
Fac ut animae donetur
    Paradisi gloria.

Lauda

Nunzio.   DONNA del paradiso,
            Lo tuo filgliolo è priso,
            Jesu Christo beato.

Accurre, donna, e vide
Che la gente l' allide;
Credo che llo s' occide,
Tanto l' on flagellato.

Vergine. Como essere purria,
            Che non fe mai follia
            Christo la spene mia,
            Hom l' avesse pilgliato?

Nunzio. Madonna, ell' è traduto.
Juda sì l' à venduto,
Trenta dinar n' à 'uto,
Facto n' à gran mercato.

Vergine. Succuri, Magdalena:
Jonta m' è adosso pena.
Christo figlio se mena
Como m' è annuntiato.

Nunzio. Succuri, donna, ajuta;
Ch' al tuo figlio se sputa
Et la gente llo muta,
Onlo dato a Pilato.

Vergine. O Pilato, non fare
L filglio mio tormentare,
Ch' io te posso mostrare
Como a torto è accusato.

Turba. Crucifì, crucifige!
Homo che se fa rege,
Secondo nostra lege
Contradice al senato.

Vergine. Prego che m' entennate;
Nel mio dolor pensate;
Forsa mo ve mutate
De quel ch' ete parlato.

Nunzio. Tragon fuor li ladroni,
Che sian sui conpagnoni.

Turba. De spine se coroni,
Ché rege s' è chiamato!

Vergine. O filglio, filglio, filglio,
Filglio, amoroso gilglio,
Filglio, chi dà consilglio
Al cor mio angustiato?

O filglio, occhi jocundi,
Filglio, co non respundi?
Filglio, perché t' ascundi
Dal pecto ó se' lactato?

Nunȝio. Madonna, ecco la croce
Che la gente l' aduce,
Ove la vera luce
Dej' essere levato.

Vergine. O cruce, che farai?
El filglio me torrai?
Et que ce aponerai
Che non ha en sé peccato?

Nunȝio. Curri, piena de dolglia,
Ché l tuo filglio se spolglia;
La gente par che volglia
Che ssia crucificato.

Vergine. Si tollete el vestire,
Lassatelme vedire,
Com el crudel ferire
Tucto l' à 'nsanguenato.

Nunȝio. Donna, la man ll' è presa,
En ella croce stesa,
Con un bollon ll' è fesa,
Tanto ce l' on ficcato.

L' altra mano se prenne,
Ne la cruce se stenne,
Et lo dolor s' accenne
Che più è multiplicato.

Donna, li piè se prenno
Et chiavellanse al lenno,
Omne juntura aprenno,
Tucto l' on desnodato.

Vergine. Et io comenso el corrotto,
Filglio, mio deporto;
Filglio, chi me t' à morto,
Filglio mio delicato?

Mellio averieno facto
Che l cor m' avesser tracto,
Che nella croce rapto
Starce desciliato.

Cristo. Mamma, ov' èi tu venuta?
Mortal me dài feruta,
Ché l tuo piangner me stuta,
Che l vegio sì afferrato.

Vergine. Piagno, che m' agio anvito,
Filglio, pate et marito;
Filglio, chi t' à ferito?
Filglio, chi t' à spolgliato?

Cristo. Mamma, perché te lagni?
Volglio che tu remangni,
Che serve a li conpangni
Ch' al mondo agio aquistato.

Vergine. Filglio, questo non dire.
Volglio teco morire.
Non me volglio partire
Fin che mo m' esce l fiato.

Ch' una agiam sepultura,
Filglio de mamma scura;
Trovarse en affrantura
Mate et filglio affocato!

Cristo. Mamma, col core aflicto,
Entro a le man te mecto
De Joanne mio electo;
Ssia el tuo filglio appellato.

Joanne, esto mia mate.
Tollela en caritate,
Aggine pietate
Ch' à lo core forato.

Vergine. Filglio, l' alma t' è ossita,
Filglio de la smarrita,
Filglio de la sparita,
Filglio mio attossicato.

Figlio bianco e vermilglio,
Filglio sensa similglio,
Filglio, a chi m' apilglio?
Filglio, pur m' ài lassato.

O filglio bianco e biondo,
Filglio, volto jocondo,
Filglio, perché t' à el mondo,
Filglio, cussì sprezato?

Filglio dolce e piacente,
Filglio de la dolente,
Filglio, àtte la gente
Malamente tractato.

Joanne, filglio novello,
Mort' è lo tuo fratello,
Sentito agio l coltello
Che fo profetizato;

Che morto à filglio et mate,
De dura morte afferrate;
Trovarse abraccecate
Mate e filglio a un cruciato!

ANONYMOUS
Est il paradis?

THIRTEENTH CENTURY

The anonymous *rondel, Est il paradis?* is of the eight-line type which, from the circumstance that its first line is used three times, came to be known later as the *triolet*.

Rondel

EST il paradis, amie,
    Est il paradis qu'amer?
    Nenil voir, ma douce amie.
Est il paradis, amie?
Cil qui dort és braz s'amie
A bien paradis trové.
Est il paradis, amie,
Est il paradis qu'amer?

ALFONSO X OF CASTILE
1221 — † 1284

ALFONSO "THE LEARNED", King of Castile, to whom a late tradition attributes the saying that, if he had been consulted about the creation, he would have made a better world, was a voluminous writer of both prose and verse. His prose works were written in Castilian, but practically all the verse attributed to him is in Galician-Portuguese. He is the reputed author of over 400 *cantigas de Santa Maria*, which are written in a great variety of metres and include a number of very charming poems. Some of them are narratives of the legendary miracles of the Virgin, others are *loores*, or lyrics in her praise.

Rosa das rosas, one of the most striking of the latter, has the technique of a popular dance-song. At the same time, its language is more reminiscent of the troubadours than of popular poetry, and its author expresses a wish to be our Lady's troubadour.

The little lyric, *Senhora, por amor Dios*, provides an example of Alfonso's Castilian poems.

Cantiga de loor

Rosa das rosas et fror das frores,
Dona das donas, sennor das sennores.

ROSA de beldad e de parecer,
    Et fror d'alegria et de prazer,
    Dona en mui pïadosa seer,
Sennor en toller coitas et doores,
Rosa das rosas et fror das frores,
Dona das donas, sennor das sennores.

Atal sennor dev' ome muit' amar,
Que de todo mal o pode guardar,
Et pode-ll' os peccados perdõar
Que faz no mundo per máos sabores.
Rosa das rosas et fror das frores,
Dona das donas, sennor das sennores.

Devémol-a muit' amar et servir,
Ca punna de nos guardar de falir,
Des í dos erros nos faz repentir
Que nós fazemos come pecadores.
Rosa das rosas et fror das frores,
Dona das donas, sennor das sennores.

Esta dona que tenno por sennor
Et de que quero seer trobador,
Se eu per ren poss' aver seu amor
Dou ao demo os outros amores.
Rosa das rosas et fror das frores,
Dona das donas, sennor das sennores.

Cantiga de amor

SENHORA, por amor Dios,
  Aved algun duelo de my,
    Que los mos oios como irios
Coirem del dia que vus vy.
Ermanos e primos e tyos,
Todo-los yo por vos perdy.
Se vos non penssades de my,
                              Fy.

ANONYMOUS

O comes amoris

THIRTEENTH CENTURY

The lover's lament, O comes amoris, *from the* Carmina Burana, *provides
but one of many examples of the use of liturgical metres in secular Latin
verse. It is in the metre of the* Stabat mater.

The lover in exile

O COMES amoris, dolor,
    Cujus mala male solor,
        Nec habent remedium.

Dolor urget me, nec mirum,
Quem a praedilecta dirum
    En vocat exsilium,

Cujus laus est singularis,
Pro qua non curasset Paris
    Helenae consortium.

Gaude, vallis insignita,
Vallis rosis redimita,
    Vallis flos convallium,

Inter valles vallis una,
Quam collaudat sol et luna,
Dulcis cantus avium,

Quam collaudat philomena,
Nam quam dulcis et amoena,
Maestis dans solatium

PEDRO EANES SOLAZ

fl. 1250 ?

It has been conjectured that Pedro Eanes, whose nickname was "Solaz",
was a jongleur from Pontevedra or the neighbourhood, but nothing certain
is known about him. His poems contain a number of Castilian forms,
perhaps indicating a desire to cater for a Spanish audience as well as a
Portuguese one.

 The following poem is a *cossante*, but the parallelism is not complete
throughout. Its curious refrain, the first part of which is intercalated between the two lines of each stanza, is probably an onomatopoeic wail, but
is also reminiscent of a Basque dirge. The last two stanzas are probably
a later addition.

Cantiga de amigo

Eu velida non dormia,
 Lelia doura,
 E meu amigo venia,
Edoi lelia doura.

Non dormia e cuidava,
 Lelia doura,
E meu amigo chegava,
 Edoi lelia doura.

E meu amigo venia,
 Lelia doura,
E d'amor tan ben dizia,
 Edoi lelia doura.

E meu amigo chegava,
 Lelia doura,
E d'amor tan ben cantava,
 Edoi lelia doura.

Muito desejei, amigo,
 Lelia doura,
Que vos tevesse comigo,
 Edoi lelia doura.

Muito desejei, amado,
 Lelia doura,
Que vos tevesse a meu lado,
 Edoi lelia doura.

Leli leli, par Deus, leli,
Lelia doura,
Ben sei eu quen non diz leli,
Edoi lelia doura.

Ben sei eu quen non diz leli,
Lelia doura,
Demo x'é quen non diz lelia,
Edoi lelia doura.

MARTIN CODAX

fl. 1250

MARTIN CODAX, a jongleur who perhaps followed Saint Ferdinand in his wars against the Moors, is the author of several beautiful *cossantes*, nearly all of which refer to Vigo. In the following *barcarola* we have an example of the *cossante* in the simplest and briefest form possible.

Barcarola

ONDAS do mar de Vigo,
Se vistes meu amigo?
E ai Deus, se verrá cedo!

Ondas do mar levado,
Se vistes meu amado?
E ai Deus, se verrá cedo!

Se vistes meu amigo,
O por que eu sospiro?
E ai Deus, se verrá cedo!

Se vistes meu amado,
Por que ei gram cuidado?
E ai Deus, se verrá cedo!

CIACCO DELL' ANGUILLAIA

THIRTEENTH CENTURY

CIACCO DELL' ANGUILLAIA may have been the Ciacco mentioned by Dante in the *Inferno*, but nothing is known of him for certain except that he was a Florentine. He was the author of the *contrasto*, *O giema leẑïosa*, which is notable for the simplicity of its style and the delicacy of its treatment, particularly if it is compared with some of the French *pastourelles*. The poem is written in heptasyllables, eight to the stanza. Each stanza falls into well-marked halves, with two alternating rhymes to each half.

Contrasto

"Ogiema lezïosa,
  Adorna villanella,
  Che se' più vertudiosa
Che non se ne favella;
Per la vertute ch' ài,
Per grazia del Sengnore,
Aiutami, chè sai
Ch' i' son tuo servo, amore."

"Assai son gieme in terra
Ed im fiume ed in mare,
C' ànno vertute in guerra,
E fanno altrui alegrare;
Amico, io nom son essa
Di quelle tre nesuna:
Altrove va per essa
E cierca altra persona."

"Madonna, tropp' è grave
La vostra rispomsione:
Càd io non àgio nave
Nè no son marangone,
Ch' io sappia andar ciercando
Colà ove mi dite;
Per vui perisco amando,
Se no mi socorite."

"Se perir ti dovessi
Per questo ciercamento,
Non crederia ch' avessi
In te 'namoramento;
Ma stu credi morire,
Inanzi ch' esca l' anno
Per te fo messe dire,
Come altre donne fanno."

"Oi, villanella adorna,
Fa sì ch' io nom perisca,
Chè l' om morto non torna,
Per far poi cantar messa.
Di voi mi dà conforto,
Madonna, non tardare;
Quand' odi ch' i' sia morto
Non far messa cantare."

"Se morir non ti credi,
Molt' ài folle credenza,
Se quanto in terra vedi
Trapassi per sentenza;
Ma stu se' Dio terreni,
Non ti posso scampare:
Guarda che legie tieni,
Se non credi al' altare."

"Per l' altar mi richiamo
Ch' adoran li Cristiani:
Però merzè vi chiamo,
Poi sono in vostre mani;
Pregovi in cortesia
Che m' aitate, per Dio,
Perch' io la vita mia
Da voi conosca im fio."

"Sì sai chieder merzede
Con umiltà piagiente,
Giovar de' ti la fede:
Sì ami coralmente.
A 'm tanto predicata
E sì saputo dire,
Ch' io mi sono acordata:
Dimmi, che t' è im piaciere?"

"Madonna, a me nom piacie
Castella nè monete:
Fatemi far la pacie
Com quel che vi sapete.
Questo adimando a vui
E facciovi fenita:
Donna siete di lui,
Ed elgli è la mia vita."

ANONYMOUS
Ver redit
THIRTEENTH CENTURY

The following example of a Goliardic spring-song occurs in the *Carmina Burana*. It is in lines of six and four syllables, the former being trochaic, the latter iambic.

Spring-song

VER redit optatum
   Cum gaudio,
   Flore decoratum
Purpureo;
Aves edunt cantus
   Quam dulciter,
Revirescit nemus,
Cantus est amoenus
   Totaliter.

Juvenes ut flores
   Accipiant
Et se per odores
   Reficiant,
Virgines assumant
   Alacriter,
Et eant in prata
Floribus ornata
   Communiter.

JOÃO SERVANDO

fl. 1250

JOÃO SERVANDO was perhaps a jongleur, but nothing is known of his life. His *Ora van a San Servando* is a good example of the Galician-Portuguese *cantiga de romaria*. The second line rhymes with the fourth in each stanza, the others being unrhymed.

Cantiga de romaria

ORA van a San Servando
Donas fazer romaria,
E non me leixan con elas
Ir, ca log' alá iria,
Por que ven i meu amigo.

Se eu foss' en tal companha
De donas, fora guarida,
Mais non quis oje mia madre
Que fezess' end' eu a ida,
Por que ven i meu amigo.

Tal romaria de donas
Vai alá, que non á par,
E fora oj' eu con elas,
Mais non me queren leixar,
Per que ven i meu amigo.

Nunca me mia madre veja,
Se d'ela non for vingada,
Por que oj' a San Servando
Non vou e me ten guardada,
Por que ven i meu amigo.

ANONYMOUS

Omittamus studia

THIRTEENTH CENTURY

The students' song, *Omittamus studia*, with its swinging rhythm and its admirable rhymes, is one of the finest poems in the *Carmina Burana*. Its metre is trochaic, the stanzas being an expansion of the *versus popularis* and the refrain a Goliardic couplet with internal rhyme. A couplet has perhaps slipped out of the first stanza.

Students' song

OMITTAMUS studia:
Dulce est desipere;
Et carpamus dulcia
Juventutis tenerae.
Res est apta senectuti
Seriis intendere.

Velox aetas praeterit
Studio detenta;
Lascivire suggerit
Tenera juventa.

Ver aetatis labitur,
Hiems nostra properat;
Vita damnum patitur,
Cura carnem macerat;
Sanguis aret, hebet pectus,
Minuuntur gaudia;
Nos deterret jam senectus
Morborum familia.

Velox aetas praeterit
Studio detenta;
Lascivire suggerit
Tenera juventa.

Imitemur superos:
Digna est sententia,
Et amoris teneros
Jam venantur otia.
Voto nostro serviamus,
Mos iste est juvenum;
Ad plateas descendamus
Et choreas virginum.

Velox aetas praeterit
Studio detenta;
Lascivire suggerit
Tenera juventa.

Ibi quae fit facilis
Est videndi copia;
Ibi fulget mobilis
Membrorum lascivia,
Dum puellae se movendo
Gestibus lasciviunt,
Asto videns et videndo
Me mihi surripiunt.

Velox aetas praeterit
Studio detenta;
Lascivire suggerit
Tenera juventa.

JOÃO AIRAS

fl. 1250

JOÃO AIRAS, a native of Santiago de Compostela, was one of the most prolific of the early Galician-Portuguese poets. The following example of his *cantigas de amigo*, though it has a refrain, is otherwise in troubadour style. It is written in *coblas singulars*, with correct metre and perfect rhyme, and ends with a *finda*. As in many a troubadour poem, the speaker is dying for love.

Cantiga de amigo

MEU amigo, vós morredes,
    Por que vos non leixam migo
    Falar, e moir' eu, amigo,
Por vós e, fé que devedes,
Algun conselh' i ajamos,
Ante que assi moiramos.

Ambos morremos, sen falha,
Por quanto nos non podemos
Falar e, pois que morremos,
Amigo, se Deus vos valha,
Algun conselh' i ajamos,
Ante que assi moiramos.

De mia madr' ei gram queixume,
Por que nos anda guardando,
E morremos i cuidando;
Ai meu amigu' e meu lume,
Algun conselh' i ajamos,
Ante que assi moiramos.

E por que o non guisamos,
Pois nós tant' o desejamos?

[[221]]

SAINT THOMAS AQUINAS

1227 — † 1274

SAINT THOMAS AQUINAS, greatest of all Dominicans, wrote few hymns, but all are great, and all are on one theme—the Mass. This is not due to his own choice, but to the accident that, owing to the institution of the new feast of Corpus Christi in 1264, hymns were required on that specific subject, and the task of writing them was committed to him by the Pope. Few writers can have succeeded so admirably in writing on a set theme; for, while Aquinas's hymns are packed with dogmatic teaching, they are also grand and beautiful poems. Full also of Dominican severity and objectivity, they lack the emotional appeal of Franciscan hymnody. They appeal chiefly through their technical perfection, their dignity and majesty of style.

His sequence, *Lauda, Sion*, is closely modelled on the Easter Sequence, *Zyma vetus expurgetur*, of Adam of Saint Victor, and incorporates several phrases from it. The constructional differences between the third and fourth strophes and their antistrophes are reproduced from Adam, but the few such differences which exist elsewhere in the earlier composition are ignored.

Pange, lingua, the Vesper hymn for the new feast, uses the opening words and the metre of Fortunatus's great hymn, but with accent replacing quantity and with double rhymes throughout.

Sequence for Corpus Christi

LAUDA, Sion, salvatorem,
Lauda ducem et pastorem
    In hymnis et canticis.

Quantum potes, tantum aude,
Quia major omni laude,
    Nec laudare sufficis.

Laudis thema specialis
Panis vivus et vitalis
    Hodie proponitur,

Quem in sacrae mensa cenae
Turbae fratrum duodenae
    Datum non ambigitur.

Sit laus plena, sit sonora,
Sit jucunda, sit decora
    Mentis jubilatio;

Dies enim sollemnis agitur
In qua mensae prima recolitur
    Hujus institutio.

In hac mensa novi regis
Novum pascha novae legis
    Phase vetus terminat:

Vetustatem novitas,
Umbram fugat veritas,
    Noctem lux eliminat.

Quod in cena Christus gessit,
Faciendum hoc expressit
　In sui memoriam.

Docti sacris institutis
Panem, vinum in salutis
　Consecramus hostiam.

Dogma datur Christianis
Quod in carnem transit panis
　Et vinum in sanguinem.

Quod non capis, quod non
　　vides,
Animosa firmat fides
　Praeter rerum ordinem.

Sub diversis speciebus,
Signis tantum et non rebus,
　Latent res eximiae:

Caro cibus, sanguis potus,
Manet tamen Christus totus
　Sub utraque specie.

A sumente non concisus,
Non confractus, non divisus,
　Integer accipitur.

Sumit unus, sumunt mille,
Quantum isti, tantum ille:
　Nec sumptus consumitur.

Sumunt boni, sumunt mali,
Sorte tamen inaequali
　Vitae vel interitus.

Mors est malis, vita bonis:
Vide paris sumptionis
　Quam sit dispar exitus.

Fracto demum sacramento
Ne vacilles, sed memento
Tantum esse sub fragmento
　Quantum toto tegitur.

Nulla rei fit scissura,
Signi tantum fit fractura,
Qua nec status nec statura
　Signati minuitur.

Ecce panis angelorum
Factus cibus viatorum,
Vere panis filiorum
　Non mittendus canibus.

In figuris praesignatur
Cum Isaac immolatur,
Agnus paschae deputatur,
　Datur manna patribus.

Bone pastor, panis vere,
Jesu, nostri miserere.
Tu nos pasce, nos tuere,
Tu nos bona fac videre
　In terra viventium.

Tu qui cuncta scis et vales,
Qui nos pascis hic mortales,
Tu nos ibi commensales
Coheredes et sodales
　Fac sanctorum civium.

Corpus Christi

PANGE, lingua, gloriosi
　　Corporis mysterium
　　Sanguinisque pretiosi
　Quem in mundi pretium
Fructus ventris generosi
　Rex effudit gentium.

Nobis datus, nobis natus
　Ex intacta virgine,
Et in mundo conversatus
　Sparso verbi semine,
Sui moras incolatus
　Miro clausit ordine.

In supremae nocte cenae
　Recumbens cum fratribus,
Observata lege plene
　Cibis in legalibus,
Cibum turbae duodenae
　Se dat suis manibus.

Verbum caro panem verum
　Verbo carnem efficit,
Fitque sanguis Christi merum,
　Et, si sensus deficit,
Ad firmandum cor sincerum
　Sola fides sufficit.

Tantum ergo sacramentum
　Veneremur cernui,
Et antiquum documentum
　Novo cedat ritui,
Praestet fides supplementum
　Sensuum defectui.

Genitori genitoque
　Laus et jubilatio,
Salus, honor, virtus quoque
　Sit et benedictio;
Procedenti ab utroque
　Compar sit laudatio.

RUTEBEUF

c. 1230—1285

Much of the life of Rutebeuf, whose birthplace is unknown, was passed at Paris, and a great part of his poetry consists of satires on the religious orders—the friars especially—whose influence predominated in the youthful University of Paris. His verse is full of its author's personality, and is remarkable for vigour and sincerity. These features are as conspicuous in his satires and Crusade-songs as in the religious poetry of his later years.

　　The following poem, a palinode, is written in one of his favourite forms—a stanza of twelve octosyllabic lines with two rhymes, the stanzas being *singulars*.

La repentance Rutebeuf

LESSIER m'estuet le rimoier,
　Quar je me doi molt esmaier
　　Quant tenu l'ai si longuement;
Bien me doit li cuers lermoier,
Qu'onques ne me poi amoier
A Dieu servir parfetement;
Ainz ai mis mon entendement
En jeu et en esbatement,
Qu'ainz ne daignai nes saumoier;
Se por moi n'est au jugement
Cele ou Diex prist aombrement
Mau marchié pris au paumoier.

Tart serai mes au repentir.
Las moi! qu'onques ne sot sentir
Mes fols cuers quels est repentance,
N'a bien fere lui assentir.
Coment oseroie tentir
Quant nes li juste auront dotance?
J'ai toz jors engressié ma pance
D'autrui chatel, d'autrui substance.
Ci a bon clerc au miex mentir:
Se je di: "C'est par ignorance
Que je ne sai qu'est penitance",
Ce ne me puet pas garantir.

Garantir! las! en quel maniere?
Ne me fist Diex bonté entiere,
Qui me dona senz et savoir
Et me fist a sa forme fiere?
Encor me fist bonté plus chiere,
Que por moi vout mort recevoir.
Senz me dona de decevoir
L'anemi qui me vuet avoir

Et metre en sa chartre premiere,
La dont nus ne se puet ravoir:
Por priere ne por avoir
N'en voi nul qui reviengne arriere.

J'ai fet au cors sa volenté,
J'ai fet rimes et s'ai chanté
Sor les uns por aus autres plere,
Dont anemis m'a enchanté
Et m'ame mise en orfenté
Por mener au felon repere.
Se cele en qui toz biens resclere
Ne prent en cure mon afere,
De male rente m'a renté
Mes cuers, ou tant truis de contrere:
Fisicien, n'apoticaire
Ne me pueent doner santé.

Je sai une fisiciene,
Que a Lion ne a Viane,
Ne tant come li siecles dure,
N'a si bone serurgiene,
N'est plaie, tant soit anciene,
Qu'ele ne netoit et escure
Puis qu'ele i vuet metre sa cure.
Ele espurja de vie obscure
La beneoite Egypciene,
A Dieu la rendi nete et pure:
Si com c'est voirs, si praingne en cure
Ma lasse d'ame crestiene.

Puis que morir voi foible et fort,
Coment prendrai en moi confort
Que de mort me puisse desfendre?
N'en voi nul, tant ait grant esfort,
Qui des piez n'ost le contrefort;
Si fet le cors a terre estendre.

Que puis je fors la mort atendre?
La morz ne lest ne dur ne tendre,
Por avoir que l'en li aport,
Et quant li cors est mis en cendre
Si covient a Dieu reson rendre
De quanques fist dusqu'a la mort.

Or ai tant fet que ne puis mes,
Si me covient tenir en pes:
Diex doinst que ce ne soit trop tart!
Toz jors ai acreü mon fes,
Et oi dire a clers et a les:
"Com plus cove li feus, plus art."
Je cuidai engigner Renart;
Or n'i valent engin ne art,
Qu'asseür est en son pales.
Por cest siecle qui se depart
M'en covient partir d'autre part:
Qui que l'envie, je le les.

AIRAS NUNES
fl. 1250

Comparatively few poems by Airas Nunes, a cleric of Santiago, have survived, but they show him to have been a poet of high talent, with a fine
ear for rhythm and a great admiration for popular poetry. Among them
are two *bailadas*, of which the following is one. It is in a lilting amphibrachic metre, in monorhymed quatrains, with a partly intercalated
refrain.

Bailada

"BAILAD' oj', ai filha, que prazer vejades,
Ant' o voss' amigo, que vós muit' amades."
"Bailarei eu, madre, pois mi-o vós mandades,
Mais pero entendo de vós ũa ren:
De viver el pouco muito vos pagades,
Pois me vós mandades que bail' ant' el bem."

"Rogo-vos, ai filha, por Deus, que bailedes
Ant' o voss' amigo, que ben parecedes."
"Bailarei eu, madre, pois mi-o vós dizedes,
Mais pero entendo de vós ũa ren:
De viver el pouco gram sabor avedes,
Pois me vós mandades que bail' ant' el bem."

"Por Deus, ai mia filha, fazed' a bailada
Ant' o voss' amigo de so a milgranada."
"Bailarei eu, madre, d'aquesta vegada,
Mais pero entendo de vós ũa ren:
De viver el pouco sodes mui pagada,
Pois me vós mandades que bail' ant' el bem."

"Bailad' oj', ai filha, por santa Maria
Ant' o voss' amigo que vos ben queria."
"Bailarei eu, madre, por vós todavia,
Mais pero entendo de vós ũa ren:
De viver el pouco tomades perfia,
Pois me vós mandades que bail' ant' el bem."

GUIRAUT RIQUIER
fl. 1254—1294

GUIRAUT RIQUIER, a native of Narbonne and for some years a protégé
of Alfonso X of Castile, is commonly called "the last of the troubadours".

His work is abundant and of great variety. He created a new genre in
the *serena*, in which a lover longs for evening, and revived old ones,
particularly the *pastorela*, of which he wrote a series of six. The same
shepherdess reappears in all of them—as maiden, wife, mother, widow—
but rejects all his advances. In the last poem of the series, his suggestion
that he should transfer his attentions to the shepherdess's daughter is also
ill received.

The chief merit of Riquier's *pastorelas* lies in their technical perfection.
Their metrical acrobatics, says M. Jeanroy, make one wonder whether they
were the outcome of a wager. In the example given here—the first of the
series—the stanzas are *singulars*, of fourteen lines each, with three rhymes,
the alternate stanzas being *capfinidas*. The use of long stanzas and short
lines suggests the influence of the Northern *pastourelle.*

Pastorela

L'AUTRE jorn, m'anava
Per una ribeira,
Soletz delichan;
Qu'amors me menava
Per aital maneira
Que pesses de chan.
Vi gaya bergeira,
Bell'e plazenteira,
Sos anhels gardan;
La tengui carreira,
Trobei la fronteira
A for benestan,
E fe·m belh semblan
Al primier deman.

Qu'ieu li fi demanda:
"Toza, fos amada,
Ni sabetz amar?"
Respos mi ses guanda:
"Senher, autreyada
Mi suy ses duptar."
"Toza, mot m'agrada
Quar vos ai trobada,
Si·us puesc azautar."
"Trop m'avetz sercada,
Senher? Si fos fada,
Pogra m'o pessar."
"Toza, ges no·us par?"
"Senher, ni deu far."

"Toza de bon aire,
Si voletz la mia,
Yeu vuelh vostr' amor."
"Senher, no·s pot faire:
Vos avetz amia
Et ieu amador."

"Toza, quon que sia
Ye·us am, don parria
Que·us fos fazedor."
"Senher, autra via
Prenetz, tal que·us sia
De profieg major."
"Non la vuelh melhor."
"Senher, faitz folhor."

"No folley, na toza;
Tan m'es abellida
Qu'amors m'o cossen."
"Senher, fort cochoza
Son que fos partida
D'aquest parlamen."
"Toza, per ma vida
Trop es afortida,
Qu'ie·us prec humilmen."
"Senher, no m'oblida
Tropa for' aunida,
Si crezes leumen."
"Toza, forsa·m sen."
"Senher, no·us er gen."

"Toza, que que·m diga,
Non ajatz temensa,
Que no·us vuelh aunir."
"Senher, vostr' amiga
Suy, quar conoyssensa
Vo·n fai abstenir."
"Toza, quan falhensa
Cug far, per sufrensa
Belh Deport m'albir."
"Senher, mot m'agensa
Vostra benvolensa,

Qu'ar vos faitz grazir."
"Toza, que·us aug dir?"
"Senher, que·us dezir."

"Digatz, toza gaya,
Que·us a fag dir ara
Dig tan plazentier?"
"Senher, on que·m vaya,
Gays chans se perpara
D'en Guiraut Riquier."
"Toza, ges encara
Le ditz no·s despara
De qu'ieu vos enquier."

"Senher, no·us empara
Belhs Deportz que·us gara
De laus esquerrier?"
"Toza, no·m profier."
"Senher, a·us entier."

"Toza, tot m'afara
May 'n Bertrans m'ampara
D'Opian l'entier."
"Senher, mal si gara;
Et iretz vo·n ara,
Don ai cossirier."
"Toza, sovendier
Aurai est semdier."

GUITTONE D' AREZZO

c. 1230 — † 1294

GUITTONE D' AREZZO, one of the earliest poets of the Tuscan school, was the son of a citizen of Arezzo. In 1269, after leading a worldly life, he experienced a religious conversion and entered the ranks of the *frati gaudenti*. Shortly before his death, he helped to found the church of Santa Maria degli Angeli at Florence, in which city he probably died. Before his conversion, he wrote love-lyrics. After it, he turned to more serious matters, and his poetry was confined to religious and political themes.

His religious poetry is illustrated by the sonnet, *Donna del cielo*, his political poetry by his *Ai lasso, or è stagion*, addressed to the Florentines after the battle of Montaperti in 1260. In this battle, the exiled Ghibellines of Florence, aided by the Ghibelline city of Siena and the German cavalry of King Manfred, routed the Florentine Guelfs. Guittone, though he was a citizen of Ghibeline Arezzo, was a great admirer of Florence,

"Fiorenza, fior che sempre rinovella",

and deplores the battle, condemning those Florentines who had gained their ends by allying themselves with a rival city and with foreigners. The poem has six stanzas of fifteen lines each, together with a *comiato*. The lines, except for two heptasyllables in each stanza, are hendecasyllabic. Each stanza has seven rhymes and is *capfinida*, beginning with the last word of the previous stanza.

Sonnet

DONNA del cielo, glorïosa madre
    Del buon Gesù, la cui sacrata morte,
    Per liberarci dalle infernal porte,
Tolse l' error del primo nostro padre,
Risguarda Amor con saette aspre e quadre,
A che strazio n' adduce ed a qual sorte.
Madre pietosa, a noi cara consorte,
Ritra'ne dal seguir sue turbe e squadre.
Infondi in me di quel divino amore
Che tira l' alma nostra al primo loco,
Sì ch' io disciolga l' amoroso nodo.
Cotal rimedio ha questo aspro furore,
Tal' acqua suole spegner questo foco,
Come d' asse si trae chiodo con chiodo.

Canzone

AI lasso, or è stagion di doler tanto
    A ciascun om che ben ama rasgione;
    Ch' io meraviglio chi trova guerigione,
Che morto nol agia corotto e pianto,
Vegiendo l' alta fior, sempre granata,
E l' onorato antico uso romano,
Che cierto per crudel sorte è villano
Se d' avaccio non è ricoverato;
Che l' onorata sua rica grandeza
E 'l presgio quasi è già tutto perito
E lo valor e 'l poder si disvia.
    Ai lasso, or quale dia
Fu mai tanto crudel danagio audito?
    Deo, com' ài lo sofrito?
Diritto pena, e torto entra in alteza.

Alteza tanta, e la fiorita fiore,
Fu, mentre ver sè stessa era leale,
Che riteneva mondo imperiale,
Aquistando per suo alto valore
Provincie e terre presso e lungi mante;
E sembrava che far volesse impero
Sicomo Roma già fece, e legiero
Gli era, ciascuno non contrastante,
E ciò gli stava ben cierto a rasgione,
Chè non s' indi penava a suo pro tanto
Como per ritener giustizia e poso;
     E poi fu li amoroso
Di fare ciò, si trasse avanti tanto
       C' al mondo non fu canto
Che non sonasse il presgio del leone.

Leone, lasso, or non è, ch' i' lo veo
Tratto l' unghie e le denti e lo valore,
E 'l gran lingnagio suo mortal dolore,
E di suo bel presgio messo a gran reo.
E ciò li a fatto chi? Quegli che sono
De la gientil sua schiatta stratti e nati,
Che fur per lui cresciuti ed avanzati
Sovra tutti altri, e collogati im bono;
E per la grande alteza ove li mise
E' mostran sì che 'l piagan quasi a morte,
Ma Dio di guerisgion feceli dono,
     Ed ei fe lor perdono;
Ed anche refedir, poi mal fu forte,
      E perdonò lor morte,
Or ànno lui e sue membra conquise.

Conquiso è l' alto comun fiorentino,
E col sanese in tal modo à cangiato
Che tutta l' onta e lo danno che dato
Li à sempre, como sa ciascun latino,
Li rende, e tolle il pro e l' onor tutto;

Chè Montalcino à combattuto a forza
E Montepulcian miso a sua rinforza,
E di Maremma a la Cervia lo frutto,
San Gimignan, Poggibonize e Colle,
E Volterra ed il paese a suo tene,
E la campana, le insegne, e gli arnesi,
  E li onor tutti presi
Ave, con ciò che seco avea di bene;
  E tutto ciò gli avene
Per quella schiatta ch' è più c' altra folle.

Folle è chi fugie il suo pro e cria danno
E l' onor suo fa che 'n vergongna torna,
Di bona libertà, ove sogiorna
A gram piacier, s' addice a suo malanno
Sotto una sengnoria fella e malvasgia,
E suo sengnor fa suo grande nemico.
A voi, che siete or in Firenze, dico:
Che ciò ch' è divenuto par v' adagia;
E poi che gli Alamanni in casa avete,
Servite bene e fatevi mostrare
Le spade lor con che v' àn fesso i visi
  E padri e filgli aucisi;
E piacemi che lor degiate dare—
  Perch' ebero in ciò fare
Fatica assai—di vostre gran monete.

Monete mante e gran gioie presentate
Ai Conti ed a gli Uberti, e a gli altri tutti
Ch' a tanto grand' onor v' ànno condutti,
Che miso v' ànno Sena in potestate,
Pistoia e Colle e Volterra fann' ora
Vostre castelle guardar a lor spese;
E 'l Conte Rosso à Maremma e 'l paese;
Montalcin stà sicuro sanza mura;
Di Ripafratte teme or il Pisano,
E 'l Perugin, che 'l lago nolgli tolliate;

E Roma vuol con voi far compangnia,
  Onore e sengnoria.
Or dunque pare ben che tutto abiate
  Ciò che disiavate,
Potete far cioè rè del Toscano.

Baron lombardi e romani e pulgliesi
E toschi e romangnuoli e marchisgiani,
Fiorenza, fior che sempre rinovella,
  A sua corte v' apella,
Chè fare vuol di sè rè de' Toscani,
  Poi tutti gli Alamanni
E conquisi per forza ave i Senesi.

ADAM DE LA HALLE
c. 1235 — † 1288 ?

ADAM DE LA HALLE, otherwise known as the Hunchback of Arras, is chiefly famous for his plays, which are remarkable for their originality. His songs, which show him to have been a skilful and talented lyrist, include a number of charming *rondels*. If the following example be compared with the anonymous *Est il paradis ?* [212] it will be noticed that it has the same structure, though in an expanded form.

Rondel

A*DIEU commant amouretes,*
    Car je m'en vois
    Souspirant en terre estrainge.
Dolans lairai les douchetes
    Et mout destrois.
A Dieu commant amouretes,
    Car je m'en vois.
J'en feroie roïnetes,
    S'estoie roys.
Comment que la chose empraigne,
A Dieu commant amouretes,
    Car je m'en vois
Souspirant en terre estrainge.

GUIDO GUINICELLI

c. 1240 -- † 1276 ?

Little is known of Guido Guinicelli, except that he was of noble birth and was expelled from Bologna, with the rest of his family, for his adherence to the Ghibelline cause.

His philosophical conception of love is stated, in beautiful language, in his *canzone*, *Al cor gentil ripara sempre amore*, which influenced Dante greatly. In its thought, as also in its style, it stands among the finest gems of the Italian lyric. Each stanza has ten lines and five rhymes. Seven lines in each stanza have eleven syllables, the others seven. Most of the stanzas are *capfinidas*.

Canzone

AL cor gentil ripara sempre amore
    Com alla selva augello in la verdura;
      Nè fè amor anzi che gentil core,
Nè gentil core anzi d' amor natura,
    C' adesso che fu il sole
Sì tosto lo splendore fu lucente,
      Nè fu davanti al sole;
E prende amor in gentilezza loco
    Così propiamente
Come chiarore in clarità di foco.

Foco d' amor in gentil cor aprende,
Come vertute in pietra preziosa,
Chè alla stella valor non discende
Anzi che 'l sol la faccia gentil cosa;
    Poichè n' à tratto fore
Per forza il sole ciò che 'n ell' è vile,
    Stella li dà valore;
Così al cor ch' è fatto da natura
    Schietto, puro e gentile
Donna a guisa di stella lo 'namora.

Amor per tal ragion sta in cor gentile
Per qual lo foco in cima del doppiero,
Splendeli al suo diletto, claro, sottile,
Non li sta in altra guisa, tant' è fero;
    Però prava natura
Rincontra amor come fa l' aigua il foco,
    Caldo per la fredura;
Amor in cor gentil prende rivera
    Per suo consimil loco
Come damas del ferro in la minera.

Fere lo sole il fango tutto 'l giorno,
Vile riman, nè 'l sol perde calore;
Disse omo altier: "Gentil per schiatta torno";
Lui sembro al fango, al sol gentil valore;
    Chè non de' dar om fè
Che gientilezza sia fuor di coragio
    In dengnità di re,
Se da vertute non à gentil core;
    Com' aigua porta ragio,
E 'l ciel retien le stelle e lo splendore.

Splende in la intelligenzia del cielo
Deo creator più ch' in nostri occhi 'l sole
Quella intende 'l suo fattor oltre cielo,
Lo ciel volgendo a lui obedir tole,
    E eom segue al primero
Dal giusto Deo beato compimento,
    Così dar dovria il vero
La bella donna che negli occhi splende
    Del suo gentil talento
Chi mai da lei ubidir non disaprende.

Donna, Deo mi dirà: "Che presumisti?"
(Istando l' alma mia a lui davanti),
"Il ciel passasti e fino a me venisti,
E desti in vano amor me per sembianti;

C' a me convien la laude,
E alla reina del reame dengno,
Per cui cessa ogni fraude."
Dirli poria: "Tenne d' angiel sembianza
Che fosse del tuo rengno;
Non mi fu fallo s' io le posi amanza."

ANONYMOUS

Gregis pastor Tityrus

THIRTEENTH CENTURY

The song, *Gregis pastor Tityrus*, was written for the sub-deacons' festival held at the feast of the Circumcision or at the Epiphany, and which, from the unedifying and even blasphemous ritual which accompanied it, was known as *festum stultorum*. The song is in monorhymed tercets, in the metre of the *Golden Sequence* with a refrain. The declension of the word "Tityrus" will be noticed.

The Feast of Fools

GREGIS pastor Tityrus,
Asinorum dominus,
Noster est episcopus.
Eja, eja, eja,
Vocant nos ad gaudia
Tityri cibaria.

Ad honorem Tityri
Festum colant baculi
Satrapae et asini.
Eja, eja, eja,
Vocant nos ad gaudia
Tityri cibaria.

Applaudamus Tityro
Cum melodis organo,
Cum chordis et tympano.
Eja, eja, eja,
Vocant nos ad gaudia
Tityri cibaria.

Veneremur Tityrum,
Qui nos propter baculum
Invitat ad epulum.
Eja, eja, eja,
Vocant nos ad gaudia
Tityri cibaria.

ONESTO DA BOLOGNA

LATE THIRTEENTH CENTURY

Practically nothing is known of Onesto, who is said to have been a lawyer of Bologna and to have been still alive in 1301. He was the author of a number of sonnets, some of which are merely scholastic philosophy versified. His best poem is his one *ballata*, *La partenza che fo dolorosa*. In it, he uses the decasyllabic line—a metre which had not been used before in Italian. The poem, which has a catching dactylic movement, has a *ripresa* of three lines and four stanzas of seven lines. Each stanza has five rhymes, the second, fifth, sixth, and seventh lines also rhyming internally with the end of the previous line.

Ballata

LA partenza che fo dolorosa
E gravosa più d' altra m' aucide
Per mia fede di voi, bel diporto.

Sì m' aucide 'l partir doloroso
Ch' eo non oso pur a pensare
Al dolor che convienmi portare
Nel mio core di vita pauroso:
Per lo gravoso stato e dolente
Lo qual sente: com dunque faraggio
M' aucideraggio per men disconforto.

S' eo mi dico di dar morte fera,
Gioia stranera non vi paia audire;
Ahi, null' omo ode il mio languire,
Mea pena dogliosa e crudera
Che dispera lo coraggio e l' alma;
Tanta salma à di pena e abbondanza,
Poi pietanza a merzè fece torto.

Torto fece, e fallì ver me lasso,
Ch' eo trapasso ogni amante leale;
Ciascun giorno più cresce più sale
L' amor fino ch' eo porto nel casso,

[238]

E non lasso per null' increscenza,
Chè 'n sofrenza conviene che sia
Chi disia l' amoroso conforto.

Poi pietanza in altrui non si sciovra,
E s' adovra in altrui fuor che meve,
Pianto mio, vanne a quella che deve
Rimembrarsi di mia vita povra;
Dì che scovra ver me suo volere;
Se 'n piacer l' è ch' eo senta la morte,
A me forte gradisce esser morto.

PAE GOMES CHARINHO
† 1295

PAE GOMES CHARINHO, a Galician, entered the service of Alfonso the Learned, and became Admiral of Castile. He died by the hand of an assassin. His *cantigas de amor*, contrary to so many of their class, are conspicuous for their sincerity. In the following example, he attacks the *morrer de amor* theme, which has already been noticed in João Airas. The poem is written in *coblas singulars*, all its lines being decasyllabic. Each stanza has two rhymes, excluding the refrain, which rhymes with the *finda*.

Cantiga de amor

MUYTOS dizem con gram coyta d'amor
Que querriam morrer, e que assy
Perderiam coytas; mays eu de mi
Quero dizer verdad' a mha senhor:
Queria-me lh'eu mui gram ben querer,
Mays non queria por ela morrer.

Com' outros morreron, e que prol ten?
Ca, des que morrer, non a veerey,
Nen bõo serviço nunca lhi farey;
Por end' a senhor que eu quero ben:
Queria-me lh'eu mui gram ben querer,
Mays non queria por ela morrer.

Com' outros morreron no mundo já,
Que depoys nunca poderon servir
As por que morreron, nen lhis pedir
Ren, por end' esta que m'estas coitas dá:
Queria-me lh'eu mui gram ben querer,
Mays non queria por ela morrer.

Ca nunca lhi tan ben posso fazer
Serviço morto, como sse viver.

CECCO ANGIOLIERI

c. 1250 — 1312

The poetry of Cecco Angiolieri of Siena is a faithful record of his dissolute life—his quarrels with his ugly wife, his love for a shoemaker's daughter who ultimately married another, his gambling, his drinking, his hatred of a father who kept him on a small allowance.

The sonnets in which his sensual outlook on life is expressed are extraordinarily well written, and are as remarkable for their freshness and frankness as for their style. In the first example given here, he satirizes a frenchified snob who has returned to Italy, and prophesies that he will soon be reduced to his lowest terms. In the second example, which is his best known poem, the unnatural feeling which he shows towards his parents is probably uttered out of sheer bravado. At least, we find quite contrary feelings expressed in some of his other sonnets.

Sonnet

QUANDO Ner Picciolin tornò di Francia,
Era sì chaldo de' molti fiorini
Che li huomin li parean topolini
E di ciascun si facea beff' e ciancia.
Ed usava di dir: "Mala mesciança
Possa venir a tutt' i mie' vicini,
Quand' e' son apo mme sì picciolini,
Che mmi fuora disnor la loro usança!"

Or è per lo su sen a ttal chondotto,
Che non à neun sì picciol vicino
Che non si disdengnasse farli motto.
Ond' io mettere'l chuor per un fiorino
Che, ançi che passati sien mesi otto,
S' egli avrà pur del pan, dirà: "Bonino."

Sonnet

S' io fossi fuoco, arderei lo mondo;
S' io fossi vento, io 'l tempesterei;
S' io fossi acqua, io l'allagherei;
S' io fossi Iddio, lo mandere' in profondo.
S' io fossi papa, allor sare' giocondo,
Chè tutti i Cristïan tribolerei.
S' io fossi imperador, sai che farei?
A tutti mozzerei lo capo a tondo.
S' io fossi morte, io n' andre' da mio padre;
S' io fossi vita, non stare' con lui,
E similmente farei a mia madre.
S' io fossi Cecco, com' io sono e fui,
Torrei per me le giovane leggiadre,
E brutt' e vecchie lascerei altrui.

FOLGORE DA SAN GEMIGNANO

c. 1250 — 1315

Nothing is known of the life of Folgore da San Gemignano except that he was a native of Siena and was pensioned for military services. He was the author of two sonnet-cycles, one for the days of the week, the other for the months of the year, in which he describes the pleasures appropriate to each day or month. The cycle for the months, of which the sonnet for April is given here, was written for a band of Sienese who were at one time identified with the *brigata spendereccia* condemned by Dante in the *Inferno*. This identification has been disputed for various reasons, not the least cogent of which is that the pleasures offered by Folgore could hardly have satisfied the *brigata*.

Sonnet

D' APRIL vi dono la gentil campagna
    Tutta fiorita di bell' erba fresca,
    Fontane d' acqua che non vi rincresca,
Donne e donzelle per vostra compagna,
Ambianti palafren, distrier di Spagna,
E gente costumata a la francesca,
Cantar, danzar a la provenzalesca
Con istormenti novi della Magna.
E dintorno vi sian molti giardini,
E giachita vi sia ogni persona:
Ciascun con reverenza adori e 'nchini
A quel gentil, ch' ho dato la corona
Di pietre prezïose, le più fini
C' ha 'l Presto Gianni o 'l re di Babilonia.

A MONK OF TOURS

? LATE THIRTEENTH CENTURY

A number of fine *cantiones*, probably written by a monk of Tours, are to be found in a French manuscript dating from the thirteenth or fourteenth century. The first example of them given here has an interesting metrical form. Its stanzas are in the favourite form of the thirteenth-century Sequence, but, like so many troubadour poems, are *unissonans*. Its rhyme-system, with the final line providing a transition to the refrain, is that of popular poetry. The whole *cantio* has a delightful lilt, and the mind sings and dances to it, without knowing its melody. The second example, with its dance-rhythm and its *eja, eja,* also reminds one strongly of popular poetry.

The Assumption

CANTET omnis creatura :
    (*Sua refert nobis jura*)
    Sua refert nobis jura
Virginis assumptio.
    O, O
    Domino
    Concinat haec contio.

Cantet omnis creatura :
    (*Sua refert nobis jura*)
    Cibi potusque mensura
Sit in hoc sollemnio.
    O, O
    Domino
    Concinat haec contio.

Christo regi demus tura :
(*Sua refert nobis jura*)
Pio corde, mente pura,
  Puro desiderio.
    O, O
    Domino
Concinat haec contio.

Dedit suum jus natura :
(*Sua refert nobis jura*)
Rerum factor fit factura
  Virginis in gremio.
    O, O
    Domino
Concinat haec contio.

New Year's Day

Tuta canit Michael
    Gaudia.
  Natus est rex Israel.
  Eja, eja,
  Anni novi
  Nova novi
    Gaudia.

Nostra nobis redditur
    Patria,
In qua bene vivitur.
  Eja, eja,
  Anni novi
  Nova novi
    Gaudia.

In excelsis canitur
    Gloria.
Terris pax indicitur.
  Eja, eja,
  Anni novi
  Nova novi
    Gaudia.

Devitemus igitur
    Vitia
Per quae virtus moritur.
  Eja, eja,
  Anni novi
  Nova novi
    Gaudia.

Sua spargat castitas
    Lilia:
Peperit virginitas.
  Eja, eja,
  Anni novi
  Nova novi
    Gaudia.

GUIDO CAVALCANTI

c. 1255 — † 1300

GUIDO CAVALCANTI, a native of Florence, was about ten years older than Dante, and was his most intimate friend. In June 1300 the Signoria of Florence, in order to free the city from the violent disputes which were raging between White and Black Guelfs, banished the leaders of both factions. Dante, as Prior, consented to this, though it entailed the exile of his friend, who was a prominent White. As the climate of Sarzana, to which Guido had been banished, proved unhealthy, he was soon allowed to return. An illness which he had contracted during his exile proved fatal, however, and he died at Florence before the end of August.

His *ballata, In un boschetto,* borrows its theme from the French *pastourelles,* but presents the greatest possible contrast to the latter in every other respect, its treatment, both of style and of subject, being remarkably delicate. It is written in the usual *ballata* form, with hendecasyllabic lines throughout, and an internal rhyme in the last line of each stanza.

The *ballata, Perch' io non spero di tornar già mai,* was no doubt written at Sarzana, when Guido had already contracted his last illness and did not expect to see Florence again. The first half of each stanza is in hendecasyllables, the second half in heptasyllables.

Ballata

IN un boschetto trovai pasturella
Più che la stella bella al mi' parere.

Cavelli avea biondetti e ricciutelli
E li occhi pien d' amor, cera rosata.
Con sua verghetta pasturav' agnelli,
E, scalza, di rugiada era bagnata.
Cantava come fosse 'nnamorata;
Er' adornata di tutto piacere.

D' amor la salutai inmantenente,
E domandai s' avesse compagnia;
Ed ella mi rispose dolcemente
Che sola sola per lo bosco gia,
E disse: "Sacci, quando l' augel pia,
Allor disia 'l mio cor drudo avere."

Po' che mi disse di sua condizione,
E per lo bosco augelli audio cantare,
Fra me stesso dicea: "Or è stagione
Di questa pasturella gio' pigliare."
Merzè le chiesi sol che di baciare
E d' abracciare, se fosse 'n volere.

Per man mi prese d' amorosa voglia,
E disse che donato m' avea 'l core.
Menommi sott' una freschetta foglia.
Là dov' io vidi fior d'ogni colore;
E tanto vi sentio gioia e dolzore
Che dio d' amore parvemi vedere.

Ballata

PERCH' io non spero di tornar già mai,
        Ballatetta, in Toscana,
        Va tu leggera e piana
        Dritt' a la donna mia,
        Che per sua cortesia
        Ti farà molto onore.

Tu porterai novelle di sospiri,
Piene di doglia e di molta paura;
Ma guarda che persona non ti miri
Che sia nemica di gentil natura.
Chè certo, per la mia disaventura,
        Tu saresti contesa,
        Tanto da lei ripresa,
        Che mi sarebbe angoscia;
        Dopo la morte poscia,
        Pianto e novel dolore.

Tu senti, ballatetta, che la morte
Mi stringe sì, che vita m' abandona,
E senti come 'l cor si sbatte forte
Per quel che ciascun spirito ragiona.
Tant' è distrutta già la mia persona,
    Ch' io non posso soffrire.
    Se tu mi voi servire,
    Mena l' anima teco,
    Molto di ciò ti preco,
    Quando uscirà del core.

De ! ballatetta mia, a la tu' amistate
Quest' anima che trema raccomando.
Menala teco, nella sua pietate,
A quella bella donna a cui ti mando.
De ! ballatetta, dilli sospirando,
    Quando li se' presente:
    "Questa vostra servente
    Ven per istar con voi,
    Partita da colui
    Che fu servo d' amore."

Tu, voce sbigottita e deboletta,
Ch' esci piangendo de lo cor dolente,
Co' l' anima e con questa ballatetta
Va ragionando de la strutta mente.
Voi troverete una donna piacente,
    Di sì dolce intelletto,
    Che vi sarà diletto
    Starle davanti ognora.
    Anim', e tu l' adora
    Sempre nel suo valore.

KING DENIS OF PORTUGAL

1261 — † 1325

If the tradition which ascribes about 140 poems to King Denis is authentic, he was the most prolific poet in the early history of his country. It is probable, however, that he was merely the collector of many of the poems attributed to him. They are of very varied types, and embrace poems in the conventional Provençal style and others in the more popular native style.

Of the three examples given here, the first is a self-confessed imitation of the troubadours. It is in decasyllabic *coblas unissonans*, with three masculine rhymes. Its theme is one of the commonest in troubadour poetry—the perfection of his lady. The second poem, also based on Provençal models, is a *pastorela*. It is written in *coblas singulars*, with three masculine rhymes to each stanza, seven syllables to the line, and two *findas*. The third example—perhaps the best known of all early Galician-Portuguese poems—is a *cossante* constructed on characteristic lines, except that the repetitions make a fresh start after the fourth stanza, owing to a change of speakers.

Cantiga de amor

QUER' eu en maneyra de proençal
    Fazer agora hun cantar d'amor;
      E querrey muyt' i loar mha senhor,
A que prez nen fremusura non fal,
Nen bondade; e mays vos direy en:
Tanto a fez Deus comprida de ben
Que mays que todas las do mundo val.

Ca mha senhor quiso Deus fazer tal
Quando a fez, que a fez sabedor
De todo ben e de mui gran valor;
E con todo est' é mui comunal,
Aly hu deve; er deu-lhi bon sen
E des y non lhi fez pouco de ben,
Quando non quis que lh' outra foss' igual.

Ca en mha senhor nunca Deus pôs mal,
Mays pôs hi prez e beldad' e loor
E falar mui ben e riir melhor

[[247]]

Que outra molher; des y é leal
Muyt', e por esto non sey oj' eu quen
Possa compridamente no seu ben
Falar, ca non á, tra-lo seu ben, al.

Pastorela

VI oj' eu cantar d'amor
En un fremoso virgeu
Ũa fremosa pastor,
Que ao parecer seu
Jamais nunca lhi par vi;
E por en dixi-lh' assi:
"Senhor, por vosso vou eu."

Tornou sañhuda enton,
Quando m'est' oíu dizer,
E diss': "Ide-vos, varon!
Quem vos foi aqui trager,
Pera m'irdes destorvar,
Du dig' aqueste cantar
Que fez quen sei ben querer?"

"Pois que me mandades ir",
Dixi-lh' eu, "Senhor, ir-m'ei;
Mais já vos ei de servir
Sempr' e por voss' andarei,
Ca voss' amor me forçou
Assi que por vosso vou,
Cujo sempr' eu já serei."

Dix' ela: "Non vos ten prol
Esso que dizedes, nen
Mi praz de o oír sol,
Ant' ei noj' e pesar en,
Ca meu coraçon non é
Nen será, per bõa fé,
Se non do que quero ben."

"Nen o meu", dixi-lh' eu, "Já,
Senhor, non se partirá
De vós, por cujo s'el ten."

"O meu", diss' ela, "Será
U foi sempr' e u está,
E de vós non curo ren."

Cantiga de amigo

"   A I flores, ai flores do verde pĩo,
        Se sabedes novas do meu amigo?
           Ai Deus, e u é?
Ai flores, ai flores do verde ramo,
Se sabedes novas do meu amado?
           Ai Deus, e u é?

Se sabedes novas do meu amigo,
Aquel que mentiu do que pôs comigo?
           Ai Deus, e u é?

Se sabedes novas do meu amado,
Aquel que mentiu do que mi á jurado?
           Ai Deus, e u é?"

"Vós me preguntades polo voss' amigo?
E eu ben vos digo que é sã' e vivo.
           Ai Deus, e u é?

Vós me preguntades polo voss' amado?
E eu ben vos digo que é viv' e são.
           Ai Deus, e u é?

E eu ben vos digo que é sã' e vivo,
E seerá vosc' ant' o prazo saido.
           Ai Deus, e u é?

E eu ben vos digo que é viv' e são,
E seerá vosc' ant' o prazo passado.
           Ai Deus, e u é?"

DANTE ALIGHIERI

1265 — † 1321

The sonnet and *canzone* here given are from Dante's first work, the *Vita nuova*, which was probably written in 1292, two years after the death of Beatrice. The sonnet, *Tanto gentile e tanto onesta*, is a beautiful expression of Dante's spiritual love. In the *canzone*, *Donna pietosa*, he receives a vision of the death of Beatrice. It is a wonderful poem, simple and beautiful from the first line to the last.

Al poco giorno is a *sestina*, a form which he was the first Italian poet to use. Vastly superior to Arnaut Daniel's *sestina* aesthetically, it copies its form exactly, except that all its lines are of equal length, whereas in Arnaut Daniel's poem the first line of each stanza is a foot shorter than the others.

Sonnet

TANTO gentile e tanto onesta pare
La donna mia, quand' ella altrui saluta,
Ch' ogne lingua deven tremando muta,
E gli occhi no l' ardiscon di guardare.
Ella si va, sentendosi laudare,
Benignamente d' umiltà vestuta;
E par che sia una cosa venuta
Dal cielo in terra a miracol mostrare.
Mostrasi sì piacente a chi la mira,
Che dà per li occhi una dolcezza al core,
Che 'ntender nolla può chi nolla prova.
E par che de la sua labbia si mova
Un spirito soave pien d' amore,
Che va dicendo a l' anima: "Sospira!"

Canzone

DONNA pietosa e di novella etate,
Adorna assai di gentilezze umane,
Ch' era là ov' io chiamava spesso morte,
Veggendo li occhi miei pien di pietate
E ascoltando le parole vane,
Si mosse con paura a pianger forte;

E altre donne che si fuoro accorte
Di me per quella che meco piangea,
    Fecer lei partir via,
E approssimârsi per farmi sentire.
    Qual dicea: "Non dormire",
E qual dicea: "Perchè sì ti sconforte?"
Allor lassai la nova fantasia,
Chiamando il nome de la donna mia.

Era la voce mia sì dolorosa
E rotta sì da l' angoscia del pianto
Ch' io solo intesi il nome nel mio core;
E con tutta la vista vergognosa,
Ch' era nel viso mio giunta cotanto,
Mi fece verso lor volgere amore.
Elli era tale a veder mio colore,
Che facea ragionar di morte altrui:
    "Deh, consoliam costui!"
Pregava l' una l' altra umilemente;
    E dicean sovente:
"Che vedestu, che tu non hai valore?"
E quando un poco confortato fui,
Io dissi: "Donne, dicerollo a vui."

Mentr' io pensava la mia frale vita,
E vedea 'l suo durar com' è leggero,
Piansemi amor nel core, ove dimora;
Per che l' anima mia fu sì smarrita,
Che sospirando dicea nel pensero:
"Ben converrà che la mia donna mora."
Io presi tanto smarrimento allora,
Ch' io chiusi li occhi vilmente gravati;
    E fuoron sì smagati
Li spirti miei, che ciascun giva errando:
    E poscia imaginando,
Di conoscenza e di verità fora,
Visi di donne m' apparver crucciati,
Che mi dicean: "Pur morràti, morràti."

Poi vidi cose dubitose molto
Nel vano imaginar, dov' io entrai,
Ed esser mi parea non so in qual loco,
E veder donne andar per via disciolte,
Qual lagrimando, e qual traendo guai,
Che di tristizia saettavan foco.
Poi mi parve vedere a poco a poco
Turbar lo sole ed apparir la stella,
E pianger elli ed ella;
Cader li augelli volando per l' âre,
E la terra tremare
Ed omo apparve scolorito e fioco,
Dicendomi: "Che fai? non sai novella?
Morta è la donna tua, ch' era sì bella."

Levava li occhi miei bagnati in pianti,
E vedea (che parean pioggia di manna),
Li angeli che tornavan suso in cielo,
Ed una nuvoletta avean davanti,
Dopo la qual gridavan tutti: "Osanna";
E se altro avesser detto, a voi dirèlo.
Allor diceva amor: "Più nol ti celo;
Vieni a veder nostra donna che giace."
Lo imaginar fallace
Mi condusse a veder madonna morta;
E quand' io l' aveva scorta,
Vedea che donne la covrian d' un velo;
Ed avea seco umiltà verace,
Che parea che dicesse: "Io sono in pace."

Io divenia nel dolor sì umile,
Veggendo in lei tanta umiltà formata,
Ch' io dicea: "Morte, assai dolce ti tegno:
Tu dèi omai esser cosa gentilé,
Poi che tu se' ne la mia donna stata,
E dèi aver pietate, e non disdegno.

Vedi che sì desideroso vegno
D' esser de' tuoi, ch' io ti somiglio in fede.
   Vieni, chè 'l cor te chiede."
Poi mi partia, consumato ogni duolo;
   E quand' io era solo,
Dicea, guardando verso l' alto regno:
"Beato, anima bella, chi ti vede!"
Voi mi chiamaste allor, vostra mercede.

Sestina

A L poco giorno, ed al gran cerchio d' ombra
  Son giunto, lasso! ed al bianchir de' colli,
  Quando si perde lo color nell' erba;
E 'l mio disio però non cangia il verde,
Sì è barbato nella dura pietra,
Che parla e sente come fosse donna.

Similemente questa nuova donna
Si sta gelata, come neve all' ombra;
Che non la muove, se non come pietra,
Il dolce tempo, che riscalda i colli,
E che gli fa tornar di bianco in verde,
Perchè gli copre di fioretti e d' erba.

Quand' ella ha in testa una ghirlanda d' erba
Trae della mente nostra ogni altra donna;
Perchè si mischia il crespo giallo e 'l verde
Sì bel, ch' amor lì viene a stare all' ombra,
Che m' ha serrato intra piccoli colli
Più forte assai che la calcina pietra.

La sua bellezza ha più virtù che pietra,
E 'l colpo suo non può sanar per erba;
Ch' io son fuggito per piani e per colli,
Per potere scampar da cotal donna;
E dal suo lume non mi può far ombra
Poggio, nè muro mai, nè fronda verde.

Io l' ho veduta già vestita a verde
Sì fatta, ch' ella avrebbe messo in pietra
L' amor, ch' io porto pure alla sua ombra:
Ond' io l' ho chiesta in un bel prato d' erba
Innamorata, com' anco fu donna,
E chiuso intorno d' altissimi colli.

Ma ben ritorneranno i fiumi a' colli
Prima che questo legno molle e verde
S' infiammi (come suol far bella donna)
Di me, che mi torrei dormire in pietra
Tutto il mio tempo, e gir pascendo l' erba,
Sol per veder do' suoi panni fanno ombra.

Quandunque i colli fanno più nera ombra,
Sotto un bel verde la giovane donna
La fa sparer, com' uom pietra sott' erba.

BIBLIOGRAPHY

ABBOTT, C. C., *Early Mediaeval French Lyrics*. London, 1932.

ALFONSO EL SABIO, *Cantigas de Santa Maria*, 2 vols. Madrid, 1889.

ALLEN, P. S., *The Romanesque Lyric*. University of North Carolina, 1928.

—— *Medieval Latin Lyrics*. Chicago, 1931.

ANGLADE, J., *Histoire sommaire de la littérature méridionale*. Paris, 1921.

—— *Les troubadours, leurs vies, leurs œuvres, leur influence*. Paris, 1919.

—— *Anthologie des troubadours*. Paris, 1927.

—— *Les poésies de Peire Vidal*. (Classiques français du moyen âge.) Paris, 1913.

APPEL, C., *Provenzalische Chrestomathie*, 6th edition. Leipzig, 1930.

—— *Die Lieder Bertrans von Born*. (Sammlung romanischer Übungstexte.) Halle, 1932.

AUBRY, P., *Trouvères et troubadours*. (Maîtres de la musique.) Paris, 1909.

AUDIAU, J., *La pastourelle dans la poésie occitane*. Paris, 1923.

AUDIAU, J. and LAVAUD, R., *Nouvelle anthologie des troubadours*. Paris, 1928.

BARTOLI, A., *I primi due secoli della letteratura italiana*. Milan, 1880.

BARTSCH, K., *Chrestomathie de l'ancien français*, 12th edition (ed. Wiese, L.). Leipzig, 1927.

—— *Altfranzösische Romanzen und Pastourellen*. Leipzig, 1870.

—— *Chrestomathie provençale*, 6th edition (ed. Koschwitz, E.). Marburg, 1904.

BECK, F., *Dantes Vita Nova*. Munich, 1896.

BÉDIER, J., *Les chansons de Colin Muset*. (Classiques français du moyen âge.) Paris, 1912.

BELL, A. F. G., *Studies in Portuguese Literature*. Oxford, 1914.

—— *Portuguese Literature*. Oxford, 1922.

BERRY, A., *Florilège des troubadours*. Paris, 1930.

BERTONI, G., *I trovatori d' Italia*. Modena, 1915.

—— *Il duecento*. (Storia letteraria d' Italia.) Milan, 1930.

BLAKENEY, E. H., *Twenty-four Hymns of the Western Church*. London, 1930.

BRAGA, T., *Cancioneiro portuguez da Vaticana*. Lisbon, 1878.

BREUL, K., *The Cambridge Songs*. Cambridge, 1915.

BRITT, M., *The Hymns of the Breviary and Missal*. London, 1922.

BURN, A. E., *The Hymn Te Deum and its Author*. London, 1926.

BUTLER, A. J., *The Forerunners of Dante*. Oxford, 1910.

CABROL, F. and LECLERCQ, H., *Dictionnaire d'archéologie chrétienne et de liturgie*. Paris, 1901– , in progress.

CHAYTOR, H. J., *The Troubadours*. Cambridge, 1912.

CHEVALIER, U., *Poésie liturgique du moyen âge*. Paris, 1893.

CLÉDAT, L., *Rutebeuf*. (Les grands écrivains français.) Paris, 1909.

CRESCINI, V., *Manuale per l' avviamento agli studi provenzali*, 3rd edition. Milan, 1926.

CRUMP, C. G. and JACOB, E. F. (ed.), *The Legacy of the Middle Ages*. Oxford, 1926.

D'ANCONA, A. and COMPARETTI, D., *Le antiche rime volgari secondo la lezione del Codice Vaticano* 3793, 5 vols. Bologna, 1875–88.

DI BENEDETTO, L., *Rimatori del dolce stil novo*. Turin, 1925.

DOBIACHE-ROJDESVENSKY, O., *Les poésies des Goliards*. Paris, 1931.

DREVES, G. M., BLUME, C. and BANNISTER, H. M., *Analecta hymnica medii aevi*, 55 vols. Leipzig, 1886–1922.

FIGURELLI, F., *Il dolce stil novo*. Naples, 1933.

FRERE, W. H., *The Winchester Troper*. (Henry Bradshaw Society.) London, 1894.

GASELEE, S., *The Oxford Book of Medieval Latin Verse*. Oxford, 1928.

—— *The Transition from the Late Latin Lyric to the Medieval Love Poem*. Cambridge, 1931.

GASPARY, A., *History of Early Italian Literature*, trans. and ed. Oelsner, H. London, 1901.

GENNRICH, F., *Formenlehre des mittelalterlichen Liedes*. Halle, 1932.

—— *Rondeaux, Virelais, und Balladen*, 2 vols. Dresden and Göttingen, 1921–7.

GREENE, R. L., *The Early English Carols*. Oxford, 1935.

GRILLO, E., *Early Italian Literature*, vol. 1, Pre-Dante Poetical Schools. London, 1920.

HILKA, A. and SCHUMANN, O., *Carmina Burana*, vol. I, 1 and vol. II, 1. Heidelberg, 1930.

HUET, G., *Chansons de Gace Brulé*. (Société des anciens textes français.) Paris, 1902.

HUGHES, H. V., *Latin Hymnody*. (Church Music Monographs.) London, 1922.

JEANROY, A., *Origines de la poésie lyrique en France*, 3rd edition. Paris, 1925.

—— *La poésie lyrique des troubadours*, 2 vols. Paris and Toulouse, 1934.

—— *Les chansons de Guillaume IX*. (Classiques français du moyen âge.) Paris, 1913.

JEANROY, A., *Les chansons de Jaufré Rudel.* (Classiques français du moyen âge.) Paris, 1915.

JEANROY, A. and LÅNGFORS, A. *Chansons satiriques et bachiques du treizième siècle.* (Classiques français du moyen âge.) Paris, 1920.

JONES, W. P., *The Pastourelle, a Study of a Lyric Type.* Cambridge (Mass.), 1931.

JULIAN, J., *Dictionary of Hymnology*, 2nd edition. London, 1907.

KAWCZYNSKI, M., *Essai comparatif sur l'origine et l'histoire des rythmes.* Paris, 1889.

KER, W. P., *The Dark Ages.* London, 1904.

KRESSNER, A., *Rustebuef's Gedichte.* Wolfenbüttel, 1885.

KUHNMUENCH, O. J., *Early Christian Latin Poets.* Chicago, 1929.

LABRIOLLE, P. DE, *Histoire de la littérature latine chrétienne*, 2nd edition. Paris, 1924.

LAISTNER, M. L. W., *Thought and Letters in Western Europe* A.D. 500–900. London, 1931.

LANG, H. H., *Das Liederbuch des Königs Denis von Portugal.* Halle, 1894.

LAVAUD, R., *Les poésies d'Arnaut Daniel*, réédition critique d'après Canello. Toulouse, 1910.

—— *see also* AUDIAU.

LEHMANN, P., *Die Parodie im Mittelalter.* Munich, 1922.

—— *Parodistische Texte.* Munich, 1923.

LINDSAY, J., *Medieval Latin Poets.* London, 1934.

LOEWE, H., *Some Mediaeval Hebrew Poesy.* London, 1927.

LOMMATZSCH, E., *Provenzalisches Liederbuch.* Berlin, 1917.

MANITIUS, M., *Die Gedichte des Archipoeta.* Munich, 1929.

—— *Geschichte der lateinischen Literatur des Mittelalters*, 3 vols. Munich, 1911–31.

MARTIN, E. J., *Twenty-one Medieval Latin Poems.* London, 1931.

MASSÓ TORRENTS, J., "Riambau de Vaqueres en els cançoners catalans" in *Anuari de l'Institut d'Estudis Catalans.* Barcelona, 1907, pp. 414–62.

MENÉNDEZ PIDAL, R., *Poesía juglaresca y juglares.* Madrid, 1924.

MENÉNDEZ Y PELAYO, M., *Antología de poetas líricos castellanos*, vol. I. Madrid, 1924.

MEYER, P., *Recueil d'anciens textes bas-latins, provençaux, et français.* Paris, 1877.

MEYER, W., *Gesammelte Abhandlungen zur mittellateinischen Rythmik*, 3 vols. Berlin, 1905–36.

MICHAËLIS DE VASCONCELLOS, C., *Cancioneiro da Ajuda*, 2 vols. Halle, 1904.

MILÁ Y FONTANALS, M., *Los trovadores en España*. Barcelona, 1889.

MOLTENI, E., *Il canzoniere portoghese Colocci-Brancuti*. Halle, 1880.

MONACI, E., *Crestomazia italiana dei primi secoli*. Città di Castello, 1912.

—— *Il canzoniere portoghese della biblioteca Vaticana*. Halle, 1875.

MOORE, E., and TOYNBEE, P. *Le opere di Dante Alighieri*, 4th edition. Oxford, 1924.

MULLER, H. F. and TAYLOR, P., *A Chrestomathy of Vulgar Latin*. Boston, 1932.

NANNUCCI, V., *Manuale della letteratura italiana del primo secolo*, vol. I, poesia, 2nd edition. Florence, 1856.

NICOLAU, M. G., *Origines du "Cursus" rythmique et les débuts de l'accent d'intensité en latin*. Paris, 1930.

—— *Les deux sources de la versification latine accentuelle*. Paris, 1934.

NOVATI, F. and MONTEVERDI, A., *Le origini*. (Storia letteraria d' Italia.) Milan, 1920.

NUNES, J. J., *Cantigas d'amigo dos trovadores galego-portugueses*, 3 vols. Coimbra, 1926–8.

—— *Cantigas d'amor dos trovadores galego-portugueses*. Coimbra, 1932.

OZANAM, F., *Franciscan Poets*. London, 1914.

PARIS, G., *La littérature française au moyen âge*. Paris, 1888.

—— *Esquisse historique de la littérature française au moyen âge*. Paris, 1907.

PHILLIMORE, J. S., *The Hundred Best Latin Hymns*. London, 1926.

Poetae Latini Aevi Carolini, ed. Dümmler, etc., 4 vols. (Monumenta Germaniae Historica.) Hanover, 1881–1923.

RABY, F. J. E., *History of Christian-Latin Poetry from the Beginnings to the Close of the Middle Ages*. Oxford, 1927.

—— *History of Secular Latin Poetry in the Middle Ages*, 2 vols. Oxford, 1934.

RAYNAUD, G., *Recueil de motets français des douzième et treizième siècles*, 2 vols. Paris, 1881–3.

RAYNOUARD, F., *Choix des poésies originales des troubadours*, 6 vols. Paris, 1816–21.

RIVALTA, E., *Le rime di Guido Cavalcanti*. Bologna, 1902.

RODRIGUES LAPA, M., *Das origens da poesia lírica em Portugal na Idade-Média*. Lisbon, 1929.

ROSSETTI, D. G., *The Works of*, ed. Rossetti, W. M., revised and enlarged edition (pp. 281–498, "Dante and his Circle"). London, 1911.

SAVJ-LOPEZ, P. and BARTOLI, M., *Altitalienische Chrestomathie*. Strasburg, 1903.

SCHMELLER, J. A., *Carmina Burana*. Stuttgart, 1847.

SCHUMANN, O., "Über einige Carmina Burana", in *Zeitschrift für deutsches Altertum*, LXIII (1926), 81–99.

—— see also HILKA.

SMYTHE, B., *Trobador Poets*. London, 1911.

SPANKE, H., *Beziehungen zwischen romanischer und mittellateinischer Lyrik*. Berlin, 1936.

STRECKER, K., *Die Cambridger Lieder*. (Monumenta Germaniae Historica.) Berlin, 1926.

—— *Die Gedichte Walters von Chatillon*. Berlin, 1925.

SYMONDS, J. A., *Wine, Women, and Song—Mediaeval Latin Students' Songs*. London, 1925.

TAYLOR, H. O., *The Mediaeval Mind*, 3rd edition, 2 vols. London, 1919.

TOZZETTI, O. T., *Antologia della poesia italiana*, 21st edition (ed. Pellegrini, F. C.). Leghorn, 1927.

TRENCH, R. C., *Sacred Latin Poetry*. London, 1849.

VORETZSCH, K., *Introduction to the Study of Old French Literature*. Halle, 1931

WADDELL, H., *The Wandering Scholars*. London, 1927.

—— *Mediaeval Latin Lyrics*. London, 1929.

WALLENSKÖLD, A., *Les chansons de Conon de Béthune*. (Classiques français du moyen âge.) Paris, 1921.

—— *Les chansons de Thibaut de Champagne*. (Société des anciens textes français.) Paris, 1925.

WALPOLE, A. S. and MASON, A. J., *Early Latin Hymns*. Cambridge, 1922.

WRANGHAM, D. S., *The Liturgical Poetry of Adam of St Victor*, 3 vols. London, 1881.

WRIGHT, F. A. and SINCLAIR, T. A., *History of Later Latin Literature*. London, 1931.

SOURCES OF TEXTS
WITH REFERENCES TO TRANSLATIONS

References are to pages, unless it is otherwise stated.

References enclosed in square brackets are to English translations.

E.H. = The *English Hymnal*, the reference being to the number of the hymn.

INDEX OF FIRST LINES

GENERAL INDEX